SUSTAINABLE AND RESILIENT SUPPLY CHAIN

ADVANCES IN ENVIRONMENTAL ACCOUNTING & MANAGEMENT

Series Editor: Venancio Tauringana

Recent volumes:

Volume 11:	Green House Gas Emissions Reporting and Management in Global Top Emitting Countries and Companies, 2023
Volume 10:	Environmental Sustainability and Agenda 2030, 2022
Volume 9:	Environmentalism and NGO Accountability, 2020
Volume 8:	Environmental Reporting and Management in Africa, 2019
Volume 7:	Sustainability Accounting: Education, Regulation, Reporting Stakeholders, 2018
Volume 6:	Social and Environmental Accounting in Brazil, 2017
Volume 5:	Accounting for the Environment: More Talk and Little Progress, 2014
Volume 4:	Sustainability, Environmental Performance and Disclosures, 2010
Volume 3:	Environmental Accounting: Commitment or Propaganda, 2006
Volume 2:	Advances in Environmental and Management, 2003
Volume 1:	Advances in Environmental Accounting and Management, 2000

ADVANCES IN ENVIRONMENTAL ACCOUNTING & MANAGEMENT VOLUME 12

SUSTAINABLE AND RESILIENT SUPPLY CHAIN: ENVIRONMENTAL ACCOUNTING AND MANAGEMENT FOCUS

EDITED BY

ARUN A. ELIAS
Rajagiri Business School, Kochi, India;
Victoria University of Wellington, New Zealand

MATTHEW PEPPER
University of Wollongong, Australia;
Rajagiri Business School, Kochi, India

ANAND GURUMURTHY
Indian Institute of Management, Kozhikode, India

And

AVANISH K. SHUKLA
Fiji National University, Fiji

emerald PUBLISHING

United Kingdom – North America – Japan
India – Malaysia – China

Emerald Publishing Limited
Emerald Publishing, Floor 5, Northspring, 21-23 Wellington Street, Leeds LS1 4DL

First edition 2024

British Library Cataloguing in Publication Data
A catalogue record for this book is available from the British Library

ISBN: 978-1-83608-033-6 (Print)
ISBN: 978-1-83608-032-9 (Online)
ISBN: 978-1-83608-034-3 (Epub)

ISSN: 1479-3598 (Series)

Printed and bound by CPI Group (UK) Ltd, Croydon, CR0 4YY

Arun A. Elias dedicates this book to his wife Preetha and his children Ananya and Alaap.

Matt Pepper dedicates this book to Alison, Camilla, Abigail and Buffy.

Anand Gurumurthy dedicates this book to his gurus, parents (Gurumurthy and Lalitha) and family (Sowmiya, Raghav, Nandhana and Soundarya).

Avanish K. Shukla dedicates this book to Professor Arun Elias, Abha and Kushagra.

CONTENTS

ABOUT THE EDITORS

Arun A. Elias is currently the Dean and Director of Rajagiri Business School, Kochi, India. He is also a Professor in Management with Rajagiri Business School, Kochi, and an Adjunct Professor in Management with School of Management, Victoria University of Wellington, New Zealand. Previously, he was the Dean of Business, Hospitality and Tourism Studies at Fiji National University and the Associate Dean (International and Accreditation) and Director of MBA and post experience programmes with the Business School of Victoria University of Wellington. In addition to his PhD in Management from Victoria University of Wellington, Arun has two Master's degrees, one in Industrial Engineering and Management from the Indian Institute of Technology, Kharagpur, and the other in Agricultural Engineering from Allahabad University, India. He also serves as an AASCB mentor and an AMBA panel member for business schools seeking international accreditations. His main research interests include systems thinking, stakeholder analysis and sustainable and resilient supply chains. He publishes in journals such as *Supply Chain Management: An International Journal*, *Energy Policy*, *R&D Management*, *International Journal of Logistics Management* and *Journal of Strategic Marketing*. He is one of the editors for this edition of Advances in Environmental and Management Accounting focusing on Sustainable and Resilient Supply Chain: Environmental Accounting and Management Focus.

Matthew Pepper is an Associate Professor of Management in the Faculty of Business and Law, University of Wollongong. He holds a PhD in Supply Chain Management from UOW in addition to BEng (Hons) and MSc from University of Greenwich, UK. His research interests include supply chain management and strategy, performance management and continuous improvement. He sits on the editorial boards of the Journal for Manufacturing Technology Management, International Journal of Lean Six Sigma and the International Journal of Information and Operations Management Education. In addition to publishing journal articles, Matt has recently co-authored two books on performance management and measurement in the public sector.

Anand Gurumurthy is a Professor in the area of Quantitative Methods and Operations Management (QM and OM) at the Indian Institute of Management Kozhikode (IIMK), Kerala, India. He has over 20 years of teaching experience, with almost 13 years at IIMK. He teaches courses related to Operations, Supply Chain and Quality Management. He recently designed new courses such as Humanitarian Supply Chain Management, Readings in Operations Excellence, etc. He was recently awarded the 'Outstanding Professor in Lean Six Sigma' by the Industrial Engineering and Operations Management (IEOM) Society, USA. His research interests include Operational Excellence (through Lean thinking, Six Sigma, Total Quality Management, Total Productive Maintenance, Industry 4.0, etc.) and Humanitarian Supply Chain Management (HSCM). Prof Anand has published more than 70 papers in high-impact peer-reviewed journals. His articles are widely cited. He is also on the editorial board of the International Journal of Lean Six Sigma and the Journal of Manufacturing Technology Management. He has trained over 1000 executives from different corporations in India, such as Reliance India Limited, Nokia, SBI Life Insurance, etc., to name a few. Similarly, he was the coordinator for a collaboration platform between IIM Kozhikode and HELP Logistics, Switzerland. Through this collaboration, he has provided training on HSCM to international participants and executives from international non-governmental organisations (INGOs) such as the World Food Programme (WFP) Bhutan, World Vision Bangladesh, etc. Before joining academia, he worked as an industrial engineer with the TVS Group of companies. He played a crucial role in establishing the production line for a new product – an integrated point-of-sale terminal. Prof. Anand is a Mechanical Engineer who completed his Master's in Manufacturing Systems Engineering and his PhD in Lean Manufacturing from the prestigious Birla Institute of Technology and Science (BITS), Pilani, Pilani Campus, Rajasthan, India.

Avanish K. Shukla is the Associate Dean of Research at the College of Business, Hospitality and Tourism Studies, Fiji National University, Fiji. He is also an Assistant Professor in Accounting with the School of Accounting and Law in the same college. He holds a PhD in Budgetary Control Practices in Steel Industry from Banaras Hindu University, India. Dr Shukla is also a qualified Chartered Accountant and a professional member of Certified Practising Accountant (CPA) Australia. He is well connected and active with various business leaders and industry stakeholders in Fiji and is a member of the Professional Development Committee of Fiji Institute of Chartered Accountants. He also serves as a tutor for CPA Australia's professional courses in Fiji. He has done consultancy for many organisations in Fiji like the Office of the Auditor General and Indian High Commission in Fiji. He has successfully supervised one PhD candidate and is currently supervising four PhD candidates. His main research includes management accounting, business ethics, sustainability development goals and also in the area of system thinking. He has published in high-ranked journals like the *Economic Resources* and *Global Journal of Flexible Systems Management*. He is also a reviewer for many reputed peer-reviewed journals and an examiner for PhD thesis for different universities.

LIST OF REVIEWERS

Arun A. Elias	*Rajagiri Business School, Kochi, India;* *Victoria University of Wellington, New Zealand*
Anand Gurumurthy	*Indian Institute of Management, Kozhikode, India*
Olayinka Moses	*Victoria University of Wellington, New Zealand*
Matthew Pepper	*University of Wollongong, Australia;* *Rajagiri Business School, Kochi, India*
Gajanand M S	*Indian Institute of Management, Tiruchirappalli, India*
Erin Snape	*University of Wollongong, Australia*
Venancio Tauringana	*University of Southampton, UK*

RESEARCH ASSOCIATE

Lakshmy Venugopal — *Rajagiri Business School, Kochi*

ABOUT THE CONTRIBUTORS

Sheetal Deo has obtained her PhD (Accounting) from the University of Wollongong and holds a Bachelor of Honours (Accounting) and Bachelor of Commerce (Accounting and Business Law) from the University of Wollongong. Sheetal has been head hunted and held various senior-level positions in tax accounting roles which has given her an insight of accounting from a practical viewpoint. During her PhD work, she has worked closely with the industry for her dissertation maintaining the links to accounting professional bodies Chartered Accountants Australia and New Zealand (CAANZ) and Certified Public Accountant (CPA). Currently, Sheetal's research outputs have centred on curriculum development in tertiary in the light of Sustainable Development Goals (SDGs), carbon accounting, environmental accounting and continual work in accounting education and the accounting professional worlds.

Rohit G is a PhD scholar specialising in network design and its application to last-mile delivery optimisation. His research focuses on developing innovative algorithms and methodologies to improve efficiency, sustainability and customer satisfaction in last-mile delivery systems. Before obtaining a PhD, Rohit gained industry experience as a Senior Engineer in the Production department of Larsen and Toubro Ltd.

Lijo John did his postdoctoral research at HUMLOG Institute at Hanken School of Economics, Helsinki. His research focuses on various aspects of humanitarian and disaster supply chain management including coordination between various humanitarian agencies, vaccine pricing, aid material procurement and their pricing, etc. He holds a Bachelor's and Master's in engineering with a specialisation in Mechanical (Production) Engineering and Industrial Engineering and Management, respectively, and a doctoral degree from the Indian Institute of Management Kozhikode in Operations and supply chain management with a special focus on mathematical modelling in designing contracts on humanitarian supply chain management. He was also a Visiting researcher at Sauder School of Business, University of British Columbia (UBC, Vancouver), and a lifetime Fellow of Shastri Indo-Canadian Institute. In his previous research, he explored the vaccine pricing models in the wake of epidemics motivated by the Yellow Fever outbreak in the Democratic Republic of Congo, Kenya and Angola. He has developed vaccine pricing models that can help address the supply chain issues between humanitarian agencies such as UNICEF and vaccine manufacturers.

George Joseph, an Assistant Professor specialising in entrepreneurship, operations management, sustainability and strategy, brings a wealth of experience from both academic and industrial sectors. Renowned for innovative pedagogy and curriculum design, Dr Joseph has made significant research contributions and demonstrates a strong commitment to community service. Poised for a senior academic role, he aims to leverage his capabilities to significantly contribute to organisational development and enhance student learning. His notable achievements include leading the Institutional Innovation Council and Incubation Centre at Rajagiri Business School, being a member of the AACSB and NBA core teams, and volunteering with Alison with several others to create a widely translated, free certifiable course on COVID-19. This team effort led to Alison receiving the EESC Civil Solidarity Prize 2020 from the European Union. Additionally, as a Round 1 online judge in the 2021 Milken-Penn GSE Education Business Plan Competition, Dr Joseph supported emerging EdTech ventures. He has also won a start-up grant under the RUSA Scheme by CUSAT TBI, played a crucial role in securing a significant grant for the DDUKK Centre for Vocational Education at CUSAT and received the Young Researcher Award in 2013 from the Service Research Institute, USA, along with the Best Technical Paper Award from PMI, Kerala Chapter in 2013 and 2015. In 2016, he was certified as an Online Faculty and Master Research Supervisor at the University of Roehampton online, UK.

Ramesh Krishnan is an Assistant Professor in the Quantitative Methods and Operations Management area at the Indian Institute of Management Kozhikode. He has completed Joint PhD in Operations Management from the Department of Management Studies of the Indian Institute of Technology Madras, India, and Business School of the University of Technology Sydney, Australia. His broad research interest includes Supply Chain Network Optimisation, Supply Chain Analytics, Sustainability, Industry 4.0 and Digital Transformation. He has published several research articles in journals like *Computers & Industrial Engineering*, *International Journal of Production Research*, *Journal of Cleaner Production*, *Journal of Manufacturing Technology Management*, etc. He has also presented his work in several international conferences and symposiums.

P N Ram Kumar is a Professor in the operations area at the Indian Institute of Management Kozhikode, India. His research interests are developing mixed integer linear programming (MILP) models and heuristics/meta-heuristics-based solution methodologies for solving combinatorial optimisation problems arising in supply chain network optimisation, drone-based logistics and other routing and scheduling problems. His work has been published in reputed A* and A category journals such as *Transportation Research Part E*, *Annals of Operations Research*, *Journal of Scheduling*, *Journal of the Operational Research Society*, *Computers and Industrial Engineering* and *International Journal of Production Research*, to name a few.

Shalendra Satish Kumar serves as an Assistant Professor in the Department of Management at Fiji National University, having earned his PhD and Master of

Arts in Human Resource Management and Organisational Behaviour from Chungnam National University in South Korea through the prestigious Korean Government Scholarship. His professional journey commenced as a primary school teacher and evolved through roles including secondary school teacher, manager of human resources for the Ministry of Education in Fiji and lecturer, culminating in his current position as an assistant professor at FNU. His expertise lies in Human Resource Management, organisational behaviour, corporate venture capital, stock market, SME and MME. He is actively engaged in teaching postgraduate and Master's students. As a trained supervisor, he play a pivotal role for Master's and PhD candidates who are doing higher degrees by research. Beyond the confines of academia, He is a founder of the Nasinu Junior Chamber, an NGO reflecting my dedication to community service. Furthermore, his commitment extends beyond his professional responsibilities and his involvement in community development during my spare time. His well-rounded profile as an academician and community leader, coupled with diverse research interests, underscores his dedication to advancing knowledge and effecting positive change both within and beyond the academic realm.

Avisekh Asish Lal serves as an Assistant Lecturer in Industrial Arts Education in the Department of Secondary Education at Fiji National University. He obtained his Master of Education from the University of the South Pacific, Fiji, and Bachelor's from the Fiji National University. His professional journey commenced as a Secondary School Teacher and evolved as an Assistant Lecturer at FNU. His research interest lies in sustainable education practices in Fiji relating industrial practices. His work involves liaising with industries, relevant stakeholders and improving courses to meet the industry's needs, providing training and reviewing courses to meet industry needs and standards. I am a co-founder of the Nasinu Junior Chamber, an NGO reflecting his dedication to community service and leading many projects for the community. Community service has allowed him to reach to the people from a different background and ethnicity, which aspired me to understand their needs better and provide necessary trainings for lifelong skills.

Shiu Lingam is currently working as a Lecturer at the Department of Accounting, Fiji National University, Fiji. He obtained a Master of Commerce in Accounting and a Master of Commerce in Forensic Accounting from Fiji National University. He is a Chartered Accountant in Fiji registered with Fiji Institute of Chartered Accountants. His professional career began as a Secondary School Teacher teaching in Western, Central and Maritime Zones of Fiji. While being a Teacher in secondary school, He was actively involved in authoring accounting textbooks for years 11, 12 and 13. His proficiency lies in Public Sector Accounting, Taxation, Business Ethics, SME, Corporate Accounting and Forensic Accounting teaching undergraduate students at my current employment and supervising them writing their graduation projects. Further to this, He was involved in reviewing courses to meet local industry needs and having the Fiji National University accounting programs get accreditation from Fiji Institute of

Chartered Accountants (FICA), CPA Australia and CAANZ. With my experience in accounting, He had been appointed as the treasurer of community serving organisations in Fiji. Moreover, in my spare time, he is actively involved in community outreach programs improving the lives of people with special abilities.

Jonathon Mackay is an interdisciplinary academic interested in exploring the interconnections between organisations, supply chains and risk.

Dr Mackay's research areas specifically look at the areas of supply chain risk and resilience, modern slavery and sustainability, individual decision-making and ethics. His current projects explore labour exploitation within supply chains (including modern slavery) and worker attitudes towards sustainability initiatives. Dr Mackay has published works across a wide range of fields within the area of supply chain management, including supply chain risk, humanitarian relief supply chain and food supply chains. He was awarded his PhD in 2019 which explored how individual agents perceive and react to disruptions in workplace settings.

In terms of teaching, Dr Mackay has a wealth of experience teaching across undergraduate and postgraduate courses within supply chain management, management and systems thinking. He is a passionate educator, with current interests exploring the role of ethics within business education from a Deweyan lens and incorporating systems thinking into course and curriculum design.

He is currently employed as a Senior Lecturer (Supply Chain Management) at the University of Wollongong's School of Business.

Wojciech D Piotrowicz (PhD Brunel, UK, MA Gdańsk, PL, PGDipLATHE Oxon, UK) is an Associate Professor in Supply Chain Management and Social Responsibility, at Hanken School of Economics, Finland, and former Director of the Humanitarian Logistics and Supply Chain Research Institute (HUMLOG Institute). His PhD was focused on e-procurement evaluation. While his current research is related to risk and resilience especially in supply chain management, as well as humanitarian logistics, disaster preparedness and security. Wojciech has considerable experience as a member of large international research projects within both the public and private sectors. He is a recipient of Outstanding and Highly Commended paper awards from Emerald Literati Network. Since 2019, Wojciech leads an Academy of Finland research project focused on humanitarian logistics in conflict areas and serves as PI in the EU CORE project.

Rajneel Ravinesh Prasad is currently working as a Lecturer in Accounting at Department of Accounting, Fiji National University. He obtained a Master of Commerce in Accounting from Fiji National University. Currently, he is pursuing doctorate degree in Accounting at Dongbei University of Finance and Economics under Chinese Government Scholarship. His professional experience began from Finance Officer and Secondary School Teacher for more than 10 years. His research interest lies in risk assessment, internal control and sustainable development. His teaching field lies in business sustainability, risk management, internal control and financial reporting. He is an active member of Fiji Institute of Accountants. His professional engagements in non-profit organisation include as a vice president for local youth club named as Coboi Youth Club for 6 years, and volunteer member for Fiji Red Cross Society. Detailed roles in NGOs includes planning and delivering a youth work programme for children between Year 3 and Year 13. Working with young people in accordance with the core values of youth work is his passion. Taking responsibilities and initiatives in terms of organising, general operational issues, building a rapport with young people, listening to their concerns and assisting in rebuilding the communities are always my core priorities in times of crisis. Hence, as an academician, he is dedicated to bringing positive change beyond academic expertise.

Aino Ruggiero serves as a Postdoctoral Researcher at Hanken School of Economics, Humanitarian Logistics and Supply Chain Research Institute, in Helsinki, Finland. She received her PhD from the University of Jyväskylä focusing on crisis communication in the context of terrorism. She is currently engaged with the EU-funded H2020 project CORE (sCience & human factOr for Resilient sociEty). Her ongoing research delves into various aspects of crisis management, including governmental crisis communication, disaster risk governance, security of supply and societal preparedness and resilience. Ruggiero's contributions to the field have been published, among others, in the *Journal of Contingencies and Crisis Management*. She is committed to societal problem-solving by aiming to advance our understanding of crisis management and resilience in the face of complex crises.

Ciorstan Smark is a Senior Lecturer in Accounting and Finance with over 20 years' experience at both undergraduate and postgraduate levels. Her publications cover a wide range of accounting, finance and business ethics issues. Ciorstan currently has three major areas of research interest: the role of accounting in government policy and decision-making, the social and ethical impact of accounting analysis and the role of government and private sector financial reporting in society. Ciorstan is affiliated with two professional accounting bodies: Chartered Accountants Australia and New Zealand (CAANZ) and the Institute of Certified Management Accountants, Australia (ICMA). Ciorstan is also on the Founder and Managing Editor of Australasian Accounting Business and Finance Journal (AABFJ).

Karalaini Tubuna is a Principal Lecturer in Office Administration, Business Process Outsourcing and Management at the Fiji National University. She obtained a Master of Commerce in Management and Public Administration at the University of the South Pacific, Fiji, in 2005. Her research interests are TVET, how Fiji can fill the gaps created by labour migration, how training institutions can understand the needs of the industries and how collaborations between these two parties can better assist in meeting the needs of the industries. Skills anticipation and green technology are new areas of interest. My involvement with Outsource Fiji has enabled her to better understand the Outsourcing landscape.

This has also enabled a positive working relationship with Outsourcing providers in Fiji to allow for guest speakers, student visitations, review of lecture notes and provision of other relevant information which are important to students. Her work involves liaising with industries and developing courses to meet industry's needs, providing training and reviewing courses to meet industry needs and standards. She has also worked with the Ministry of Education and Fiji Higher Education Commission to review curriculum for Office Technology taught in Secondary schools. Her community involvement allows her to better understand the village and informal settlements needs for training.

Anura De Zoysa holds the position of Associate Professor and serves as the Deputy Discipline Leader in the Accounting discipline at the University of Wollongong in Australia. He earned his PhD (Accounting) from the University of Wollongong, and he also holds an MEc (Hons) from Wakayama University in Japan, as well as a BCom (Hons) degree from the University of Sri Jayewardenepura in Sri Lanka. Anura's scholarly achievements include publishing his work in top-tier international journals, such as the *International Journal of Accounting, American Business Review, Meditari Accountancy Research, Industrial Management & Data Systems* and the *Journal of Small Business Management.* Also, Anura is affiliated with three professional accounting bodies: the Certified Public Accountant (CPA), the Fellow Chartered Accountant (FCA) and the Certified Management Accountant (CMA). His ongoing research pursuits are centred on several areas, including cost management, carbon accounting, considerations of Corporate Social Responsibility (CSR) and Environmental, Social and Governance (ESG) factors, performance management and sustainability.

SUSTAINABLE AND RESILIENT SUPPLY CHAINS: OPPORTUNITIES FOR RESEARCH

Arun A. Elias[a,b], Matthew Pepper[a,c], Anand Gurumurthy[d] and Avanish K. Shukla[e]

[a]*Rajagiri Business School, Kochi, India*
[b]*Victoria University of Wellington, New Zealand*
[c]*University of Wollongong, Australia*
[d]*Indian Institute of Management, Kozhikode, India*
[e]*Fiji National University, Fiji*

ABSTRACT

Resilient and sustainable supply chain management is emerging as a focused area of research in the field of supply chain management. This article aims to introduce this edition of Advances in Environmental Accounting and Management and explore opportunities for research related to resilient and sustainable supply chain management. A critical analysis of literature found the need for developing the theory underpinning resilient and sustainable supply chains and the need for rich empirical studies. The six articles included in this edition present a variety of contexts including food supply chain, environmental accounting models, energy sector, human resources, modern slavery, horticultural worker exploitation and sustainable transport in jurisdictions like Australia, European Union, Fiji and India. Overall, this edition contributes to both theoretical and empirical literature on resilient and sustainable supply chain management and presents a repository of research that explores this area using an accounting and environmental management perspective.

Keywords: Resilience; sustainability; supply chain; resilient and sustainable supply chains; environmental accounting

Sustainable and Resilient Supply Chain
Advances in Environmental Accounting & Management, Volume 12, 1–11

ISSN: 1479-3598/doi:10.1108/S1479-359820240000012001

INTRODUCTION

The global economy is passing through a period of major disruptions (Meyer & Li, 2022). The pandemic, environmental impacts linked to climate change and numerous geopolitical issues are disrupting the world at an unprecedented level (Singh et al., 2021). Consequently, supply chains across the globe continue to be affected by these disruptions (Katsaliaki et al., 2021; Olivares-Aguila & ElMaraghy, 2021). Disruptions affect the ability of supply chains to be sustainable. A sustainable approach to supply chain operations incorporates considerations of environmental impacts and natural resources, social implications and public policies beyond the conventional economic focus (Ahmed et al., 2022; Linton et al., 2007; Sarkar et al., 2021). During major disruptions, when core activities face unprecedented uncertainties, and even survival itself is challenged, maintaining supply chain sustainability intensely becomes difficult.

Notwithstanding the daunting circumstances, several sustainable supply chains and supply networks manage to find creative ways to be resilient and survive the times (Elias et al., 2021). Issues around supply chains, especially during disruptions such as the COVID-19 pandemic, have gained research and policy traction in recent times (Ahmed et al., 2022; Salama & McGarvey, 2023). However, specific insights into the resilience of sustainable supply chains and their interconnectedness to accounting and environmental management, especially during disruptions, are sparse in the literature. Thus, worthy of further research to develop our understanding of the issues and their workable solutions.

Accounting for and the management of sustainable supply chains are distinct yet related complex processes. The reasoning perhaps is a contradiction of the traditional value creation perspective and a more inclusive accounting incorporating social and environmental values (Ahmed et al., 2022; Burritt & Schaltegger, 2014). Accounting for resilience and sustainable supply chains is complex, especially under periods of uncertainty. Further, the implications of supply chain activities on the environment, given the interconnectedness of global economies, are by no means an easy task to unravel. Hence, the need for additional insights that can help us understand these impacts, particularly the role of accounting and management in highlighting the implications of supply chain strategies on the environment is timely in addressing global concerns linked to the Sustainable Development Goals (SDGs) (Ahmed et al., 2022; Moses et al., 2022; Moses & Tauringana, 2022).

In this context, the purpose of this chapter is to introduce this edition and to explore opportunities for research related to resilient and sustainable supply chains during and after the times of disruption. After this introduction, the chapter reviews the existing literature on resilient and sustainable supply chains. This is followed by an analysis of the six articles presented in this issue before providing a set of conclusions.

REVIEW OF LITERATURE

This section provides a brief review of the existing literature. As the concept of sustainability continues to gain prominence, organisations endeavour to make their operations and supply chains sustainable. Sustainability is considered as an organisation's responsibility to balance social, economic and environmental issues involved in human development (Kaptein & Wempe, 2001). However, this is not easy to achieve. A core element of social responsibility is community involvement and development. According to Zhalechian et al. (2016), increasing employment opportunities and ensuring a balanced economic development for local communities remain the main goals of social responsibility. However, if an organisation invests in community development, it has to make additional investments. This, in turn, would reduce the profitability of the organisation. Hence, organisations shy away from social commitment despite its importance. Zahiri et al. (2017) reports that the social aspects have rarely been addressed in the literature as well as in practice.

Zahiri et al. (2017) also mentions that the stakeholders acknowledge that if environmental impacts are left uncontrolled, it may result in major changes to the climate and the environmental systems. Hence, governments worldwide are under immense pressure to enact legislation to curb these impacts. Naturally, organisations are forced to bring changes that minimise the environmental impacts caused by their operations and supply chains to demonstrate compliance with such legislation (Ding et al., 2016). Moreover, enacting changes in their operations and supply chains requires companies to increase their investment in the same. They have to redesign their products by opting for environmentally friendly practices such as repair (set the damaged product right and use again), reduce (say, energy consumption), recycle (using recyclable materials), reuse (findings alternate use for the product), refurbish (making the existing product look new) or redesign and revamp of processes such that they consume less energy, and shift to renewable sources (Gharfalkar et al., 2016). They can also find alternative eco-friendly delivery modes or redesign packing materials to reduce environmental impact within their supply chains. These changes also require the organisations to invest, thereby significantly impacting their economic capabilities (Bui et al., 2020).

It is evident from these discussions that 'for-profit' organisations would find it challenging to balance the three aspects of sustainability. In addition, these organisations and their supply chain members have to protect themselves from global financial and other crises and increasing natural and anthropogenetic disasters (Fahimnia & Jabbarzadeh, 2016). Therefore, to quickly adjust to disorders and disruptions, today's organisations and their supply chain networks must be more resilient (Tipi & Elgazzar, 2021). In particular, there is a need for management approaches and optimisation strategies to establish resilient and sustainable supply chains (Elias et al., 2021; Fahimnia & Jabbarzadeh, 2016). Adding these resilient aspects to the supply chain would also make the organisations invest in redundant capabilities, thereby disturbing the balance among the three pillars of sustainability. Nevertheless, considering the ever-increasing disruptions through economic recessions, wars and pandemics, it is inevitable for practitioners and researchers to consider resilience as a crucial dimension of sustainability along with its three pillars (Nüchter et al., 2021).

In this context, researchers have attempted to integrate, balance and establish trade-offs between sustainability and resilience (e.g. Roostaie et al., 2019). Following is a brief review of recent papers that dealt with various issues in designing and developing resilient and sustainable supply chains.

Modelling Resilient and Sustainable Supply Chains

Lotfi et al. (2021) noted that energy supply is essential for supply chain (SC) to function. Hence, they attempted to design a resilient and sustainable supply chain by considering renewable energy sources. They found that organisations having their own renewable energy source in addition to the government-supplied energy can improve resilience and contribute to sustainability. They created a new two-stage robust stochastic optimisation model for a resilient sustainable supply chain network design based on renewable energy (RSSCNDRE). The first stage of their model identifies the facility location and the source of renewable energy, while the second stage defines flow quantity between supply chain components. Their research suggested that equipping supply chain and renewable energy ensures that supply chains become resilient against demand fluctuation, and the use of renewable energy helps in having a sustainable energy resource.

Sazvar et al. (2021) designed a resilient, sustainable supply chain (RSSC) using a case study of the influenza vaccine manufacturer. They used a multi-objective mathematical model to proactively plan for an optimal configuration of supply chain to satisfy customer demands when the firm is highly vulnerable to operational and disruption risks. They included capacity planning in their models to account for redundancy, which contributed to resilience. A robust fuzzy optimisation approach is employed to cope with uncertainties, which was followed by a multi-choice goal programming with a utility function approach to solve a multi-objective model. They found that having redundancies in the supply chain does not always increase the total costs.

Modelling resilient and sustainable supply chains is now a significant literature stream in this area. While there are some interesting works in the area, as shown in the examples above, this literature stream needs further research, covering a broader set of aspects relating to resilient and sustainable supply chain management.

Building Conceptual Foundations

Negri et al. (2021) commented that confusion about concepts, implementation methods and measurements for resilient and sustainable supply chain remains. Hence, they carried out a systematic literature review of this domain. They found that the concept of sustainable supply chains is well established and possesses necessary theoretical foundations. However, supply chain resilience is relatively less mature. They pointed to the need for more clarity on what practices could jointly advance both areas, as sustainability generally focuses on efficiency, while resilience seeks effectiveness. They identified some research gaps apart from recommending that a performance measurement system need to be developed to assess supply chain sustainability and resilience performance, taking explicit considerations of time horizons considered in these measures.

Negri et al. (2022) collected data from six firms through semi-structured interviews to understand how to develop resilient and sustainable supply chain practices. They also explored how to advance knowledge on synergies and trade-offs between sustainability and resilience. They concluded that firms more explicitly implement sustainability practices, while resilience practices are sometimes neglected. They also highlighted that the most widely implemented practices, such as green logistics, certifications, and eco-design practices, can be considered both sustainable and resilient.

Ruiz-Benitez et al. (2019) studied the impact of lean and resilient supply chain practices on the three dimensions of sustainability. They utilised the aerospace sector and its supply chain as the context. They attempted to develop relationships between lean and resilient supply chain practices with the three dimensions of sustainability through Interpretive Structural Modelling (ISM). They found synergetic effects between lean and resilient practices, with lean practices acting as the driver of resilient practices.

Performance Measurement

Hervani et al. (2022) employed the resource-based view to theorise a performance measurement framework for organisations to measure their supply chain resilience capabilities and social sustainability. This performance measurement framework is based on (i) digitalisation using blockchain technology to improve supply chain process sustainability and resilience and (ii) the valuation of environmental goods to assess social sustainability. They encouraged future researchers to further evaluate the effectiveness of the proposed performance measurement framework and advance it theoretically.

Vergara et al. (2023) found that there is no agreement regarding the measures for performance evaluation of sustainable and resilient supply chains. So, they used a hybrid approach, comprising of a literature review and 'Fuzzy Delphi Technique (FDT)', to identify a total of 15 criteria, and categorised them into four major dimensions of resiliency, economic, environmental and social. Among these dimensions, they found that the most important criteria as visibility, flexibility, supply chain risk management, culture, work conditions and communication.

Research Gap

Although the literature review presented above is brief, a critical analysis found some significant gaps in the literature. For example, it was seen that the theoretical underpinnings of resilient and sustainable supply chains are not fully developed. As resilience and sustainability have already been studied by researchers from different bodies of knowledge, resilient and sustainable supply chain management can benefit from using theories from other fields, developing it into a multidisciplinary area (Moses & Tauringana, 2022). Additionally, researchers are finding the problems related to resilience and sustainability to be complex and 'wicked' (e.g. Braga Marsola et al., 2021). This situation calls for research that takes a holistic approach, based on theories that capture the interconnections between different aspects and dimensions of resilient and sustainable supply chain. Here, systems thinking is proposed as a possibility (Elias, 2022).

Secondly, some of the literature streams discussed in this section will benefit from further research. For example, supply chain modelling researchers who attempted to optimise between sustainability and resilience practices used a number of assumptions and are limited to very narrow aspects such as capacity planning and renewable energy. They also ignored other crucial aspects to reduce modelling complexity. Naturally, the optimal solutions they provided using their models may not deliver realistic results in practice. Another literature stream that calls for further attention is performance and impact measurement. While some researchers have identified a few criteria for measuring the performance of resilience and sustainability in a supply chain, other issues, such as the impact of integrated resilience and sustainable supply chain practices on the firms' performance, understanding the effect of resilience and sustainability on environmental impact, and short-term and long-term effects of resilience and sustainability on competitive advantage, are yet to be explored.

Thirdly, the field of resilient and sustainable supply chains will benefit from more empirical studies, including quantitative, qualitative, and mixed methods, covering different aspects and problems facing it. For example, researchers can further explore the cost-benefit aspects of incorporating resilient and sustainable practices in operations and supply chains. Implementing sustainability and resilience in the operations and supply chain of an organisation may require significant investment, which tends to pull back the managers of for-profit organisations in effectively achieving sustainability and resilience. Empirical studies exploring the implementation of sustainability and resilience practices from an accounting perspective is another space where this field can grow. For example, the effectiveness of accounting approaches like triple bottom line and carbon tax may differ in different countries and contexts (Moses & Hopper, 2022). Finally, this field would also benefit from in depth case studies highlighting the benefits and challenges of resilient and sustainable supply chains in different parts of the world.

MULTIPLE APPROACHES TO RESILIENT AND SUSTAINABLE SUPPLY CHAINS

This section summarises the contributions to this special issue through six articles. These articles provide multiple approaches to resilient and sustainable supply chains. Each article is briefly summarised here, and its unique features highlighted.

In the first article, Krishnan et al. (2024) presents a multi-objective optimisation model for an integrated sustainable and resilient food supply chain. They propose four objective functions, considering the three dimensions of sustainability and one for resilience. They solve this model using an augmented ϵ-constraint method. Compared to the previous models available in the literature, they show the trade-off between the sustainability dimensions and resilience. For example, they show that an exclusive focus on economic dimension may negatively impact the environmental, and social sustainability, as well as resilience of a food supply chain. Similarly, when the focus is purely on a single dimension of sustainability or resilience, other dimensions are negatively impacted. Overall, this study aims at helping the decision maker to develop a balanced solution considering both sustainability and resilience. In doing so, it helps in addressing the research gap related to the need for an integrated model in the literature stream pertaining to modelling resilient and sustainable supply chains.

The second article, by Deo et al. (2024), considers the practical implementation of two environmental accounting models, the Triple Bottom Line (TBL) and Carbon Tax. The benefits and drawbacks for each are examined within the context of two Australian case studies. Using discourse and content analysis, this article seeks to provide further understanding of the practical implementation of such disclosure frameworks. In order to achieve transparent disclosures from supply chain actors, the authors advocate for a comprehensive approach that leverages the strengths of both models within an integrated framework. This is considered the most appropriate way forward to foster resilience and sustainability for organisations seeking a more systemic approach to environmental disclosures and offsetting environmental and social impacts in their supply chain network. Overall, this paper helps in addressing the research gap for more empirical studies, by providing an Australian study on the effectiveness of accounting approaches like triple bottom line and carbon tax.

The third article, by John et al. (2024), analyses the cascading impacts of supply chain disruptions on energy sector and in turn on the security of supply of energy from a European Union standpoint. As this is a complex issue, they point to the need for an analysis at a much broader level, using a systems thinking approach to study the effects of supply chain disruptions on energy services. More specifically, they develop a qualitative systems model in the form of a causal loop model to gain further insights into how supply chain disruptions caused by COVID-19 affects the coping capabilities of society, focusing on its effect on critical and essential services. Overall, this study contributes to the literature on sustainable and resilient energy systems, by explaining how the pandemic has prompted discussions about the future of the energy industry and the need for a more sustainable and resilient energy system. It also addresses the research need for additional empirical research, by presenting a European Union perspective on the resilience and sustainability of energy services.

The fourth article, by Kumar et al. (2024), investigates employee learning agility as an antecedent of knowledge sharing in supply chains. They base this study on conservation resource theory, which postulates that resources of employees like knowledge, ability, and skills act as motivational factors that they strive to protect, retain, and at the same time invest in favour of obtaining more resources. They collected data from participants based in public sector organisations in Fiji, and analysed it using structural equation modelling. The results confirm that employee learning agility is a significant aspect for knowledge-sharing behaviour in supply chains. Overall, this paper adds to the discussion on the importance of human resource management on sustainable and resilient supply chains. It also addresses the research gap for theory development, showing how a theory from another field, namely conservation resource theory from human resource management, can contribute to the theory development on resilient and sustainable supply chain management.

The fifth article, by Mackay (2024), explores supply chain sustainability and its links to resilience through the lens of ethics. Taking sustainability as a wicked problem, this paper proposes the need for systems thinking approaches to acknowledge and navigate the inherent links between ethics, sustainability and supply chain resilience. Two examples within the Australian context, modern slavery legislation and horticultural worker exploitation, are used to illustrate the utility of systems thinking approaches to capture the underlying complexity of these issues. The paper concludes by advocating for a holistic lens to analyse how morality of actions influence supply chain sustainability practices. This paper also contributes to theory development, by using the principles of systems theory, to understand the complexities in resilient and sustainable supply chain management.

The final article, by Joseph and Elias (2024), presents the Kochi Water Metro as a pioneering project in sustainable urban transit, integrating cutting-edge technologies and innovative management practices. This study underscores the project's success in addressing complex urban challenges, like traffic congestion and pollution, through a sustainable transport solution. It highlights the importance of stakeholder collaboration, particularly in government and community engagement, in achieving such transformative initiatives. The Kochi Water Metro emerges not only as a model for sustainable transportation but also as a catalyst for broader urban development and environmental stewardship, but in doing so, acts as a key driver for the development of a more sustainable and resilient supply chain in the region by presenting the benefits of sustainable transportation. Overall, this paper also aids in addressing the research gap for further empirical research in the field, by providing a South Indian case of sustainable transportation.

These six articles highlight different contexts and aspects of resilient and sustainable supply chains. These contexts include food supply chain, environmental accounting models, disruptions in the energy sector, employee learning agility, modern slavery legislation, horticultural worker exploitation, and the case of a water metro. These studies also present the contexts of different geographies like India, Australia, European Union, and Fiji. Overall, they provide a variety of empirical and theoretical approaches to understand the complex nature of resilient and sustainable supply chains.

CONCLUSION

Resilient and Sustainable Supply Chains is emerging as a focused area of research in the field of supply chain management (Jabbarzadeh et al., 2018). During these times of disruptions, caused by the pandemic, climate change, geopolitical issues and other events, this area has become extremely relevant. This edition of the 'Advances in Environmental Accounting and Management' attempts to develop a repository of research that explores resilient and sustainable supply chains with an accounting and environmental management perspective.

This edition includes six articles covering different aspects and approaches to resilient and sustainable supply chain management. The first article presents a model, showing the trade-off between the economic, social and environmental dimensions of sustainability and resilience. The second article uses discourse analysis to examine the benefits and drawbacks of two environmental accounting models, the TBL and Carbon Tax, within the context of resilient and sustainable supply chains. The third article uses a qualitative systems model to capture the cascading impacts of supply chain disruptions in the energy sector and to develop policy recommendations that can make the system more resilient and sustainable. The fourth article approaches resilient and sustainable supply chain management from a human resources perspective and explores employee learning agility as an antecedent of knowledge-sharing behaviour in supply chains. The fifth article approaches resilient and sustainable supply chain management through the lens of ethics and proposes systems thinking methodologies to acknowledge and navigate the inherent links between ethics, sustainability and supply chain resilience. The final article presents the case of Kochi Water Metro as a success story in sustainable transport, explaining how it contributes to the development of a more resilient and sustainable supply chain.

Overall, this edition contributes to both theoretical and empirical literature on resilient and sustainable supply chain management. For theory building, some of the papers in this edition illustrate how theoretical approaches from other fields, like the conservation resource theory and systems theory can contribute to the development of theory related to resilient and sustainable supply chains. For empirical research on resilient and sustainable supply chains, this edition presents a variety of contexts including food supply chain, environmental accounting models, energy sector, human resources, modern slavery, horticultural worker exploitation and sustainable transport in geographies like Australia, European Union, Fiji and India. However, it is acknowledged that these six articles are confined to a limited number of aspects, contexts, applications and theories related to this emerging field. Finally, this edition aims at encouraging further empirical research, which will help build theory related to resilient and sustainable supply chain management.

REFERENCES

Ahmed, S., Chapple, L., Christ, K., & Osborne, S. (2022). Modern slavery risk disclosures in business operations and supply chains. In *Environmental sustainability and agenda 2030: Efforts, progress and prospects* (pp. 67–104). Emerald Publishing Limited.

Braga Marsola, K., Leda Ramos de Oliveira, A., Filassi, M., Elias, A. A., & Andrade Rodrigues, F. (2021). Reverse logistics of empty pesticide containers: Solution or a problem? *International Journal of Sustainable Engineering*, *14*(6), 1451–1462.

Bui, B., Moses, O., & Houqe, M. N. (2020). Carbon disclosure, emission intensity and cost of equity capital: Multi-country evidence. *Accounting and Finance*, *60*(1), 47–71.

Burritt, R., & Schaltegger, S. (2014). Accounting towards sustainability in production and supply chains. *The British Accounting Review*, *46*(4), 327–343.

Deo, S., Pepper, M., De Zoysa, A., & Smark, C. (2024). Disclosures: Driving supply chain sustainability through accounting. In A. A. Elias, M. Pepper, A. Gurumurthy & A. K. Shukla (Eds.), *Sustainable and resilient supply chain* (pp. 49–64). Emerald Publishing Limited.

Ding, H., Liu, Q., & Zheng, L. (2016). Assessing the economic performance of an environmental sustainable supply chain in reducing environmental externalities. *European Journal of Operational Research*, *255*(2), 463–480.

Elias, A. A. (2022). Multi-stakeholder participation for achieving sustainable development goals: A systems thinking approach. In V. Tauringana & O. Moses (Eds.), *Environmental sustainability and agenda 2030 (Advances in environmental accounting & management)* (Vol. 10, pp. 45–65). Emerald Publishing Limited.

Elias, A. A., Donadelli, F., Paiva, E. L., & Bacic Araujo, P. P. (2021). Analysing the complexities of sustainable wood supply chain in the Amazon: A systems thinking approach. *International Journal of Logistics Management*, *32*(4), 1481–1505.

Fahimnia, B., & Jabbarzadeh, A. (2016). Marrying supply chain sustainability and resilience: A match made in heaven. *Transportation Research Part E: Logistics and Transportation Review*, *91*, 306–324.

Gharfalkar, M., Ali, Z., & Hillier, G. (2016). Clarifying the disagreements on various reuse options: Repair, recondition, refurbish and remanufacture. *Waste Management & Research*, *34*(10), 995–1005.

Hervani, A. A., Nandi, S., Helms, M. M., & Sarkis, J. (2022). A performance measurement framework for socially sustainable and resilient supply chains using environmental goods valuation methods. *Sustainable Production and Consumption*, *30*, 31–52.

Jabbarzadeh, A., Fahimnia, B., & Sabouhi, F. (2018). Resilient and sustainable supply chain design: Sustainability analysis under disruption risks. *International Journal of Production Research*, *56*(17), 5945–5968.

John, L., Piotrowicz, W. D., & Ruggiero, A. (2024). Supply chain disruptions and their impact on energy sector during COVID-19. In A. A. Elias, M. Pepper, A. Gurumurthy & A. K. Shukla (Eds.), *Sustainable and resilient supply chain* (pp. 65–92). Emerald Publishing Limited.

Joseph, G., & Elias, A. A. (2024). Assessing the sustainability and resilience of urban transit: The case of Kochi water metro. In A. A. Elias, M. Pepper, A. Gurumurthy & A. K. Shukla (Eds.), *Sustainable and resilient supply chain* (pp. 141–157). Emerald Publishing Limited.

Kaptein, M., & Wempe, J. (2001). Sustainability management: Balancing conflicting economic, environmental and social corporate responsibilities. *The Journal of Corporate Citizenship*, *2*, 91–106.

Katsaliaki, K., Galetsi, P., & Kumar, S. (2022). Supply chain disruptions and resilience: A major review and future research agenda. *Annals of Operations Research*, *319*, 965–1002. https://doi.org/10.1007/s10479-020-03912-1

Krishnan, R., Rohit, G., & Ram Kumar, P. N. (2024). An integrated sustainable and resilient closed-loop supply chain network design: A case study of the Indian mango pulp industry. In A. A. Elias, M. Pepper, A. Gurumurthy & A. K. Shukla (Eds.), *Sustainable and resilient supply chain* (pp. 13–47). Emerald Publishing Limited.

Kumar, S. S., Tubuna, K., Lal, A. A., Prasad, R. R., & Lingam, S. (2024). Employee learning agility as an antecedent of knowledge sharing in the supply chain: An examination through the lens of conservation of resource theory. In A. A. Elias, M. Pepper, A. Gurumurthy & A. K. Shukla (Eds.), *Sustainable and resilient supply chain* (pp. 93–114). Emerald Publishing Limited.

Linton, J. D., Klassen, R., & Jayaraman, V. (2007). Sustainable supply chains: An introduction. *Journal of Operations Management*, *25*(6), 1075–1082.

Lotfi, R., Kargar, B., Hoseini, S. H., Nazari, S., Safavi, S., & Weber, G. W. (2021). Resilience and sustainable supply chain network design by considering renewable energy. *International Journal of Energy Research*, *45*(12), 17749–17766.

Mackay, J. (2024). Avenues for systems thinking towards exploring the ethics of sustainability within supply chains. In A. A. Elias, M. Pepper, A. Gurumurthy & A. K. Shukla (Eds.), *Sustainable and resilient supply chain* (pp. 115–139). Emerald Publishing Limited.

Meyer, K. E., & Li, C. (2022). The MNE and its subsidiaries at times of global disruptions: An international relations perspective. *Global Strategy Journal*, *12*(3), 555–577.

Moses, O., & Hopper, T. (2022). Accounting articles on developing countries in ranked English language journals: A meta-review. *Accounting, Auditing & Accountability Journal*, *35*(4), 1035–1060.

Moses, O., Nnam, I. J., Olaniyan, J. D., & Tariquzzaman, A. T. M. (2022). Sustainable Development Goals (SDGS): Assessment of implementation progress in BRICS and MINT. In *Environmental sustainability and agenda 2030: Efforts, progress and prospects* (pp. 11–44). Emerald Publishing Limited.

Moses, O., & Tauringana, V. (2022). Environmental sustainability and the progress towards agenda 2030. In *Environmental sustainability and agenda 2030: Efforts, progress and prospects* (pp. 1–9). Emerald Publishing Limited.

Negri, M., Cagno, E., & Colicchia, C. (2022). Building sustainable and resilient supply chains: A framework and empirical evidence on trade-offs and synergies in implementation of practices. *Production Planning & Control*, 1–24.

Negri, M., Cagno, E., Colicchia, C., & Sarkis, J. (2021). Integrating sustainability and resilience in the supply chain: A systematic literature review and a research agenda. *Business Strategy and the Environment*, *30*(7), 2858–2886.

Nüchter, V., Abson, D. J., Von Wehrden, H., & Engler, J. O. (2021). The concept of resilience in recent sustainability research. *Sustainability*, *13*(5), 2735.

Olivares-Aguila, J., & ElMaraghy, W. (2021). System dynamics modelling for supply chain disruptions. *International Journal of Production Research*, *59*(6), 1757–1775.

Roostaie, S., Nawari, N., & Kibert, C. J. (2019). Sustainability and resilience: A review of definitions, relationships, and their integration into a combined building assessment framework. *Building and Environment*, *154*, 132–144.

Ruiz-Benitez, R., López, C., & Real, J. C. (2019). Achieving sustainability through the lean and resilient management of the supply chain. *International Journal of Physical Distribution & Logistics Management*, *49*(2), 122–155.

Salama, M. R., & McGarvey, R. G. (2023). Resilient supply chain to a global pandemic. *International Journal of Production Research*, *61*(8), 2563–2593.

Sarkar, B., Sarkar, M., Ganguly, B., & Cárdenas-Barrón, L. E. (2021). Combined effects of carbon emission and production quality improvement for fixed lifetime products in a sustainable supply chain management. *International Journal of Production Economics*, *231*, 107867.

Sazvar, Z., Tafakkori, K., Oladzad, N., & Nayeri, S. (2021). A capacity planning approach for sustainable-resilient supply chain network design under uncertainty: A case study of vaccine supply chain. *Computers & Industrial Engineering*, *159*, 107406.

Singh, S., Kumar, R., Panchal, R., & Tiwari, M. K. (2021). Impact of COVID-19 on logistics systems and disruptions in food supply chain. *International Journal of Production Research*, *59*(7), 1993–2008.

Tipi, N., & Elgazzar, S. (2021). Considerations towards a sustainable and resilient supply chain: A modelling perspective. *International Business Logistics Journal (IBL)*, *1*(1), 6–13.

Vergara, J. I. T., Martínez, J. A. S., & Salais-Fierro, T. E. (2023). Performance measurement of a resilient-sustainable supply chain through fuzzy multi-criteria techniques. *Computers & Industrial Engineering*, *177*, 109059.

Zahiri, B., Zhuang, J., & Mohammadi, M. (2017). Toward an integrated sustainable-resilient supply chain: A pharmaceutical case study. *Transportation Research Part E: Logistics and Transportation Review*, *103*, 109–142.

Zhalechian, M., Tavakkoli-Moghaddam, R., Zahiri, B., & Mohammadi, M. (2016). Sustainable design of a closed-loop location-routing-inventory supply chain network under mixed uncertainty. *Transportation Research Part E: Logistics and Transportation Review*, *89*, 182–214.

AN INTEGRATED SUSTAINABLE AND RESILIENT CLOSED-LOOP SUPPLY CHAIN NETWORK DESIGN: A CASE STUDY OF THE INDIAN MANGO PULP INDUSTRY

Ramesh Krishnan, Rohit G and P N Ram Kumar

Indian Institute of Management, Kozhikode, India

ABSTRACT

Considering sustainability and resilience together is crucial in food supply chain (FSC) management, as it ensures a balanced approach that meets environmental, economic and social needs while maintaining the system's capacity to withstand disruptions. Towards this, a multi-objective optimisation model is proposed in this study to create an integrated sustainable and resilient FSC. The proposed model employs four objective functions – each representing a dimension of sustainability and one for resilience and utilises an augmented ϵ-constraint method for solving. The findings highlight the interplay between sustainability aspects and resilience, illustrating that overemphasis on any single dimension can adversely affect others. Further, the proposed model is applied to the case of Indian mango pulp supply chain and several inferences are derived. The proposed model would assist decision-makers in making a well-balanced choice based on sustainability and resilience considerations.

Keywords: Sustainability; resilience; food supply chain; network design; closed-loop supply chain

Sustainable and Resilient Supply Chain
Advances in Environmental Accounting & Management, Volume 12, 13–47

ISSN: 1479-3598/doi:10.1108/S1479-359820240000012005

INTRODUCTION

An intricate supply chain (SC) network plays a crucial role in the production, processing and distribution of the food we consume. Within this network, various entities, including farmers, processors and retailers, collaborate to form the food supply chain (FSC), which transforms raw materials into the wide array of food products available to us. The FSCs not only contribute significantly to a country's economic development but also generate employment opportunities. One specific segment of the food sector that showcases the importance of FSCs is the global fresh fruits market. In 2023, the market value of fresh fruits reached an impressive USD 665.3 billion and is projected to grow substantially in the coming years (Fresh Fruits – Worldwide, 2023). This growth can be attributed to increased production, changing dietary preferences and the availability of fruits throughout the year (Reynolds et al., 2014).

India, in particular, holds a prominent position in fruit production, cultivating a staggering 20 million tonnes of mangoes, making it the largest producer worldwide (S&P Global, 2020). Across the country, popular mango varieties like Alphonso, Kesar and Totapuri are grown specifically for mango pulp production. However, despite India's status as the leading mango producer, more than half of the harvested mangoes end up as waste in landfills after the extraction of mango pulp. This wastage not only discards a potentially valuable resource but also contributes to soil pollution (Kummu et al., 2012). The existing literature acknowledges the potential for utilising mango waste to create valuable products (C. Ajila et al., 2007; Banerjee et al., 2018). However, it is worth noting that the literature lacks comprehensive studies focused on mango pulp FSC design and waste management.

In addition, the FSC consumes a large volume of natural resources and releases a significant amount of greenhouse gas (GHG) emissions. For instance, the agriculture sector globally releases 9.3 billion tons of GHG emissions (FAO, 2020). In addition, 17% of global food production goes to waste (UN, 2022). Such wastage poses a severe risk to a country's food security and the sustainability of the FSC (Krishnan et al., 2022). For instance, processing mangoes to produce mango pulp results in waste equivalent to 50% of the processed mangoes' weight (C. M. Ajila et al., 2010; Krishnan et al., 2020). The waste generated is seeds and peels of mango. The disposal of this substantial waste volume in landfills leads to soil pollution due to the excessive accumulation of a specific nutrient. While these wastes are inevitable, the literature demonstrates the potential for valorisation, which involves processing them to create value-added components such as pectin and seed oil (C. M. Ajila et al., 2010; Banerjee et al., 2018). Hence, researchers and policymakers are increasingly focusing on addressing the FSC issues and improving the sustainability of the FSC operation. León-Bravo et al. (2021) rightly concluded that improving the FSC's sustainability is crucial for 'high-quality, safe, secure, nutritious and responsible food' for society.

Besides sustainability, in light of recent disruptive events, such as the pandemic caused by severe acute respiratory syndrome coronavirus 2

(SARS-CoV-2) – also called COVID-19, the jamming of the Suez Canal and the Russia–Ukraine war, it is equally important to focus on assessing and improving the 'resilience' of the FSCs. In FSC, resilience is the ability to resist disruption and ensure the supply of raw materials to SC entities to provide continuous food supply to end consumers (Stone & Rahimifard, 2018). For example, in the initial phase of the COVID-19 pandemic in India, the government instituted stringent lockdowns that disrupted FSC operations. Similarly, the obstruction of the Suez Canal resulted in knock-on effects such as congestion at ports and ships not being in the correct location for their next scheduled journey. These events exacerbated SCs' container shortage woes during the COVID-19 buying boom (Stevens, 2021). Global household food spending increased 34% over the previous year due to the Russia–Ukraine war (Ghosh & Bhowmick, 2022). To address a crisis of this magnitude, it is critical to measure and improve the resilience of the FSCs by focusing on the 'availability, accessibility, suitability and stability of food supply' in changing environmental conditions (Stone & Rahimifard, 2018).

Such major disruptions challenge SC's survival, making maintaining sustainable SC even more difficult. These incidents highlight the necessity for a detailed understanding of sustainable SCs' resilience and how they relate to sustainability, especially in times of disruption (Elias et al., 2021, 2022; Fahimnia & Jabbarzadeh, 2016). Exploring such trade-offs is even more critical in the context of FSCs characterised by perishable products with a short lifespan (Behzadi et al., 2020). Previous studies have developed models to enhance the sustainability of the FSC by reducing GHG emissions (Babbar & Amin, 2018; Bortolini et al., 2016), creating more job opportunities (Krishnan et al., 2022) and even enhancing equity in food distribution (Martins et al., 2019). Studies on the resilience aspects addressed FSC by modelling with demand uncertainty or epidemic conditions (Gholami-Zanjani, Klibi, et al., 2021) or studying their resilience under the pandemic (Burgos & Ivanov, 2021). However, these studies only focus either on the resilience or the sustainability aspects of the FSC and have ignored the integration effects. Das (2019) was the only study in the FSC context that focused on such integration but did not study the trade-offs of resilience and sustainability. Studies that integrate sustainability and resilience in the FSC context remain underexplored (Negri et al., 2021). Such integration of resilience and sustainability must begin at the strategic level for better coordination between multiple echelons (Gupta et al., 2021). We have addressed this gap in this study by proposing an optimisation model.

In addition, the proposed model is applied to the case of mango pulp FSC. Mangoes are a seasonal product, and India holds a prominent position as a leading producer and exporter of mango pulp. It is of utmost importance for the mango processing industry to ensure a consistent and uninterrupted supply to both local and international markets to retain their customer base. Any disruption in the SC could lead buyers to explore alternative suppliers, resulting in the potential loss of valuable customers. However, if a company chooses to stockpile more inventory as a means of enhancing resilience, this decision can have a negative impact on both the economic and environmental aspects of sustainability. It can lead to increased costs associated with inventory holding and contribute to environmental emissions arising from the resources consumed in maintaining that inventory. Therefore, it is important to understand the trade-off between sustainability and resilience and make a well-informed decision.

The following are the key contributions of this work:

- A multi-objective optimisation model is developed considering all sustainability dimensions and resilience.
- The model is implemented in the case of the Indian mango pulp FSC, and the study's results showed a trade-off between the dimensions of sustainability and resilience.
- The effects of FSC operations on social sustainability are captured.
- Towards addressing the waste generated from producing mango pulp, the waste recovery plant (WRP) is captured as an additional entity of the FSC, making it a closed-loop SC.

Following this introduction, Section 'Literature Review' presents the review of existing literature and research gaps. Section 'Details of the Model' details the problem description and the proposed optimisation model. Section 'Description of the Case of Indian Mango Pulp FSC' presents the proposed model's results for the Indian mango pulp FSC. Section 'Results and Discussions' explains this study's theoretical and managerial contributions. This study closes in Section 'Theoretical Contributions and Managerial Implications' with a summary of its findings and a discussion of potential future research directions.

LITERATURE REVIEW

Sustainability and FSC Management

Sustainable supply chain management (SSCM) aims to enhance performance along economic, environmental and social aspects drawn from various stakeholder requirements while regulating the flow of material, information and capital and cooperation among businesses throughout the SC (Seuring & Müller, 2008). In SSCM literature, researchers have recognised the importance of working on FSCs since they are highly resource-intensive and food products are perishable, requiring FSC-specific decisions (Banasik et al., 2019; Bortolini et al., 2016; Krishnan et al., 2020; Validi et al., 2014). Since agri-food, by nature, is perishable, its wastage amounts to a global financial loss of 2.6 trillion USD (FAO, 2014). Such wastage poses a severe risk to the food security of a country. The high environmental impact of FSCs has subjected them to increased public scrutiny, threatening their legitimacy (Askham, 2019). Further, the FSC also contributes to social benefits by creating employment in rural and urban areas and contributing to the development of the surrounding community. Improving the condition of workers in such FSCs can help eradicate poverty and achieve sustainable development goals as a consequence (Ahmed et al., 2022).

To improve the sustainability of FSC, extensive studies have paid significant attention to sustainability in supply chain network (SCN) modelling. They frequently employed a multi-objective optimisation model where the primary objective has been cost minimisation or profit maximisation over the SC. The other objective functions typically capture environmental and social performance. The carbon or GHG emitted while setting up facilities, during operational activities in these facilities and during the transportation of goods are considered measures of environmental sustainability (Babbar & Amin, 2018; Bortolini et al., 2016; Mogale et al., 2020). Existing literature also used water footprint (Rajakal et al., 2021), energy wastage (Banasik et al., 2019; Rajakal et al., 2021) and waste generation (Manteghi et al., 2021; Tsai & Hung, 2009) as a measure of the environmental impact of FSC.

Similarly, the social sustainability in literature aimed at improving the number of job opportunities (Krishnan et al., 2020), enhancing equity in food distribution (Martins et al., 2019) and ensuring safe and healthy food (Manteghi et al., 2021) in the FSC. More measures of the social performance of the SC have been discussed in Hutchins and Sutherland (2008). Among these measures, employment creation has been more popular in literature (Allaoui et al., 2018; Krishnan et al., 2020, 2022), and we have used the same in this study. The summary of environmental and social sustainability measures is provided in Table 1.

Table 1. Environmental and Social Sustainability Metrics Found in the Reviewed Literature.

Environmental			Social		
References	Performance Metrics	Definition	References	Performance Metrics	Definition
Bortolini et al. (2016)	Carbon footprint	Carbon dioxide equivalent (CO_2EQ.) emissions released as a direct or indirect consequence of an activity.	Ramos et al. (2014)	Equity among human resources	Maximum working hours for all drivers in the planning horizon
Babbar and Amin (2018)	CO_2 emission	Carbon emissions are released by a particular supplier to produce a product in a given time period.	Fahimnia et al. (2018)	Aggregated weighted social score	Score based on guidelines and standards of SA8000, GRI and GSLCAP
Banasik et al. (2019)	Exergy loses	Thermodynamic measure for measuring how inefficiently energy is used in a process because of system irreversibility.	Martins et al. (2019)	Equitable access to donated food	Given by highest level of unsatisfied demand

(Continued)

Table 1. *(Continued)*

Environmental			Social		
References	Performance Metrics	Definition	References	Performance Metrics	Definition
Martins et al. (2019)	The total value of food waste generated	Cost of disposing of food waste.	Manteghi et al. (2021)	Endangerment of consumer health	Linear function based on a percentage of additives used
Rajakal et al. (2021)	Water footprint	The total amount of freshwater used in production activities.	Krishnan et al. (2022)	Number of job opportunities created	Jobs created by the FSC
Sabouhi et al. (2021)	An aggregate weighted environmental score	*k*-means clustering on environmental effect evaluation methods based on CML2001, IMPACT 2002+ and Eco-indicator 99	Mogale et al. (2023)	Social benefits	Weighted average of employment creation, balanced economic development, economic welfare, farmer growth and public health level.

Past studies have used the above measures to improve the sustainability of various parts of the FSC, from sourcing to distribution and reverse logistics. For example, Babbar and Amin (2018) studied supplier selection and order quantity determination with a two-phase model, keeping environmental performance in mind for the beverage industry. Multiple studies have worked to keep the costs and emissions related to distribution to a minimum (Amorim et al., 2013; Bortolini et al., 2016; Govindan et al., 2019; Krishnan et al., 2022). Krishnan et al. (2022) considered the emissions in reprocessing the wastes of a mango pulp FSC using valorisation to close the loop. Similarly, Banasik et al. (2019) compared economic and environmental performance trade-offs for a closed-loop mushroom SC. Readers are directed to Zhu et al. (2018) for further reading on sustainable FSCs.

Existing literature has focused more on the economic and environmental dimensions. But working on the sustainable development of the FSC would mean balancing the triple bottom line (Ghadge et al., 2017), including the social dimension (Jacob-John et al., 2022).

Resilience and FSC Management

Resilience in the FSC is the ability of the SC to resist disruption and continue food supply to end consumers to ensure food security (Stone & Rahimifard, 2018). For example, lockdowns during the COVID-19 pandemic disrupted the entire FSCs. One in five homes in West Bengal was reported to have experienced 'some food crisis' due to these interruptions (Pratichi, 2022). To prevent such crises, it is essential to measure and improve the resilience of the FSCs by focusing on the 'availability, accessibility, suitability and stability of food supply' in changing environmental conditions (Stone & Rahimifard, 2018). Since FSC are characterised by perishable products with short lifespans, resilience becomes highly critical to improve the survival of products and their quality as well (Behzadi et al., 2020).

To improve the resilience of their SC, managers require performance metrics to formulate mitigative and contingent initiatives (Munoz et al., 2015). The four categories of SC resilience metrics: Recovery time (e.g. out-of-service time, lead-time ratio), recovery level (e.g. service level, stock out rate, unfulfilled demand rate), loss of performance while recovery (inventory backorder cost during recovery) or a modification of these performances developed by Behzadi et al. (2020) serve this purpose. Studies in the FSC literature have primarily ensured resilience by optimising SC performance under various disruption scenarios. Gholami-Zanjani, Jabalameli, et al. (2021) studied the effects of the FSC's readiness, responsiveness and flexibility on the expected profits over a discrete multi-period time horizon. Similarly, Gholami-Zanjani, Klibi, et al. (2021) modelled an FSC under demand uncertainty and epidemic disruptions. They aimed to maximise expected profit under various scenarios and analysed the effects of different resilience strategies. Burgos and Ivanov (2021) used 'time to recovery' to measure the German retail FSC's resilience in the pandemic. They conduct simulations and study the impacts of lockdowns, customer behaviour and supplier disruption on the SC performance due to the pandemic.

Apart from the ones listed above, studies focusing on the resilience of the FSC are scarce in the literature. Existing models are severely limited because they require information about disruptions for probability estimation. However, certain disruptions have limited or no historical data, limiting the applicability of such models. For instance, the COVID-19 pandemic (Lowe et al., 2021) and the Russia–Ukraine conflict (Ghosh & Bhowmick, 2022) have caused two significant disruptions to FSCs in India. However, it is difficult to estimate the likelihood of such low-probability, high-impact disruptions (Taleb, 2007), and managers have a tendency to misallocate resources to counteract such uncommon events. To address this gap, this study has captured the resilience of FSC using 'time to recover' and 'time to survive', which does not suffer from such limitations (Simchi-Levi et al., 2014). Accordingly, for this present study on FSC which also gets affected due to disruptions such as floods, pandemics, etc. 'time to recover' and 'time to survive' have been used as a measure of the resilience of the FSC. The summary of resilience metrics used in the SC literature is listed in Table 2.

Sustainability and Resilience in SC Network Design

The three levels of SC management decisions are strategic, tactical and operational. Among these decision levels, strategic level decisions are long term and focus on selecting the location for facilities, the capacity of the facility, the choice of suppliers and the distribution network (Chopra et al., 2016). To meet consumer requests, the SCN design process entails making the aforementioned choices while considering

Table 2. Resilience Metrics for SC in the Reviewed Literature.

References	Performance Metrics	Definition
Zobel (2011)	Adjusted resilience measure	A function of projected loss, recovery time and decision-maker preferences.
Carvalho et al. (2012)	Lead time ratio	The ratio between actual and promised lead time.
Zahiri et al. (2017)	Non-resiliency	The sum of node criticality, flow complexity, node complexity, demand dissatisfaction level and production with old technology.
Fang and Zio (2019)	Resilience to natural hazards	Ratio of cumulative real to cumulative target performance over the period.
Gholami-Zanjani, Klibi, et al. (2021)	Expected profits	Profits under different disruption scenarios.
Burgos and Ivanov (2021)	Time to recovery	Time to return an SC network node to the needed functionality after a disruption.
Sazvar et al. (2021)	Capacity redundancy	Capacity to replace disruption-related losses or shortages.

the network as a whole (Mohammadi Bidhandi et al., 2009). The SCN design is costly, and frequent changes will significantly impact the return on investment (Simchi-Levi et al., 2004). Tactical-level decisions are medium term and focus on production, inventory and distribution decisions. Similarly, operational-level decisions are short term and focus on inventory allocation and replenishment planning based on demand (Chopra et al., 2016). All these three levels of decisions impact the sustainability and resilience of the SC (Ivanov, 2018). For example, holding more inventories might improve resilience, but it will increase the inventory cost and emissions arising from the resources consumed in maintaining that inventory. Accordingly, the model proposed in this study considers all three levels of SC decisions. For modern SCs, SCN decisions must integrate sustainability and resilience along with the economic objectives, as discussed in Sections 'Sustainability and FSC Management' and 'Resilience and FSC Management'. When integrating sustainability and resilience into SCN models, it is essential to note that they may influence each other (Fahimnia & Jabbarzadeh, 2016). For instance, reducing the firms' stocks or sourcing from a single sustainable supplier might improve efficiency and sustainability, but it would also reduce its capability to respond to disruptions (Ivanov, 2018). On the other hand, under some circumstances, sustainability practices may help improve resilience. For instance, a firm can maintain ecosystem services despite disruptions by building trust within a community through sustainable 'buy local' strategies (Sarkis, 2020). In FSC, improving resilience has mixed results on food waste and sustainability. While resilience through improved flexibility, communication, innovation and collaboration may reduce food waste, redundancy and financial health impact food waste negatively (Costa et al., 2022). Hence, understanding the trade-offs between resilience and sustainability in the SCN models is crucial.

Table 3. Characteristics of Published Integrated Resilience and Sustainable SC Network Designs.

References	Economic Pillar Measure	Environmental Pillar Measure	Social Pillar Measure	Resilience Measure Captured in the Objective Function	Industry	Country	Vulnerable Elements
Jabbarzadeh et al. (2018)	Cost	SS	SS	NC	Plastic pipe	Iran	SU, FA
Zahiri et al. (2017)	Cost	EI	JC	NR	Pharmaceutical	France	FA, DC
Taleizadeh et al. (2022)	Profit	PE	Tax spent on public services	NC	Electronics	Iran	SU
Salehi et al. (2022)	Cost	EI	JC, H&S	NR	Biomass	Iran	FA
Vali-Siar and Roghanian (2022)	Cost	EI	JC	NC	Tyre	Iran	SU, FA
Sabouhi et al. (2021)	SC costs	SS	SS	NC	Petrochemical	Iran	FA
Mehrjerdi and Shafiee (2021)	Cost	PE	JC	NC	Tyre	Iraq	SU
Govindan and Gholizadeh (2021)	Cost	EC	JC	NC	End of Life vehicles	Iran	SU, DC, FA, TR
Sazvar et al. (2021)	Cost	PE	JC	RL	Pharmaceutical	Iran	SU, DC, FA
Nayeri et al. (2021)	Cost	EI	H&S	NR	Water Heater	Iran	SU, DC, FA
Fahimnia and Jabbarzadeh (2016)	Cost	SS	SS	NC	Sportswear	Australia	SU
Fahimnia et al. (2018)	Cost	SS	NC	NC	Apparel	Australia	FA, DC
Jabbarzadeh et al. (2019)	Cost	PE	NC	FP	Power	Iran	FA, TR
Das (2019)	Profit	Waste reduction	Supplier performance	NC	Food	USA	SU

Notes: SS: Sustainability score, EI: Environmental impact, JC: Jobs created, PE: Pollutants emitted, EC: Environmental costs, H&S: Health and Safety, NC: Not captured in objective function, NR: Non-resiliency, RL: Resilience level, FP: Failure probability, SU: Suppliers, FA: Factory, DC: Distribution centres, TR: Transportation routes.

Multiple studies have integrated sustainability and resilience into their SCN design models, as shown in Table 3. But, some of these studies have not captured resilience in the objective function. For instance, Jabbarzadeh et al. (2018) studied the supplier selection problem, where a choice of an appropriate resilience strategy reduced the SC cost and improved sustainability during disruptions using trade-off analysis. Fahimnia et al. (2018) modelled an apparel SC to understand the relationship between greening and building robustness to improve resilience. This study performed greenness and robustness analysis using environmental performance scoring and elastic-p robustness measure. The results showed that greening and building robustness incur a cost; however, the cost of recovery from disruption is much more than the investment required for building greenness and robustness. Further, the results highlighted that green SCs are more sensitive to disruptions, so improving the resilience of green SCs is essential. Taleizadeh et al. (2022) used a Stackelberg model to study remanufacturing under emission regulations. Their studies highlight the importance of keeping extra reserved stock to tide over disruptions sustainably.

The studies that captured resilience in their objective function and showed the trade-off with sustainability-based objectives are discussed below. Zahiri et al. (2017) designed a multi-objective, resilient-sustainable SCN for a multi-period planning horizon for the pharmaceutical SC. They showed that adding more distribution centres or manufacturing facilities can be useful when the variable costs are high to improve sustainability and minimise 'non-resiliency' in their model. The 'non-resiliency' comprised network-level resilience factors like node criticality and complexity. Nayeri et al. (2021) employed similar resilience measures in their model. Jabbarzadeh et al. (2019) used a multi-objective robust optimisation model to optimise the electricity SC considering economic, environmental and resilience aspects. Here, resilience is captured as the probability of not meeting the demand of critical customers. The authors observed that tighter economic constraints forced trade-offs between environmental and resilience goals. Sazvar et al. (2021) investigated the trade-off between sustainability and resilience by looking at a real-world SC for influenza vaccines. They employed the 'resilience level' metric, which took into account the lead-time ratio, redundancy and customer de-service level effects of fully operational factories and warehouses.

The above-mentioned studies have focussed on pharmaceutical, manufacturing, apparel and electricity SCs. For the food SCN, Das (2019) developed a model integrating sustainability and resilience. He showed that lean and green grid-based SC development processes combined with resilience criteria improved the sustainable performance of the SC. However, their model has not studied the trade-offs of resilience and sustainability. In literature, studies integrating sustainability and resilience into food SCN and comparing their trade-off are lacking (refer to Table 3) despite their importance highlighted in previous sections. This study addresses this significant gap.

Research Gaps

FSCs are crucial to the economy and well-being of a country, and it's essential to make them sustainable. While there are extensive studies on the economic and environmental dimensions, there is a dearth of studies focusing on the social pillar, especially in developing economies (Jacob-John et al., 2022). Along with sustainability, the resilience of an FSC is crucial for it to operate during times of disruptions. The lack of resilient FSCs can adversely affect food security and the population's health, as observed in the recent COVID-19 pandemic (Bhargava & Bhargava, 2021). However, only a few studies have worked on the resilience of the FSCs. Even the existing models require some data to estimate the probability of disruptions. For instance, Gholami-Zanjani, Jabalameli, et al. (2021) required data on various parameters under different disruption scenarios to maximise the expected profit. However, such data might be non-existent or even unavailable in the case of rare disruptions. Since resilience and sustainability influence each other, it is important to understand their trade-offs in a FSC. Such trade-offs between resilience and sustainability in FSCs have only been studied by Das (2019), as seen in Table 3. However, even that study failed to explore the trade-off between resilience and sustainability in the context of food SCN design. Thus, there is a need for studies that improve the resilience and sustainability of FSCs in a balanced manner and study their trade-offs.

DETAILS OF THE MODEL

Problem Description

We address the research gaps mentioned above by considering the Indian mango pulp FSC case study since India produces and exports large volumes of mango pulp. Further, the processing of mango pulp generates a large volume of waste (around 50% of the weight of the mango), which could be valorised to produce value-added products. For example, the pectin and mango seed oil could be extracted from mango peels and mango seeds, respectively. The extracted

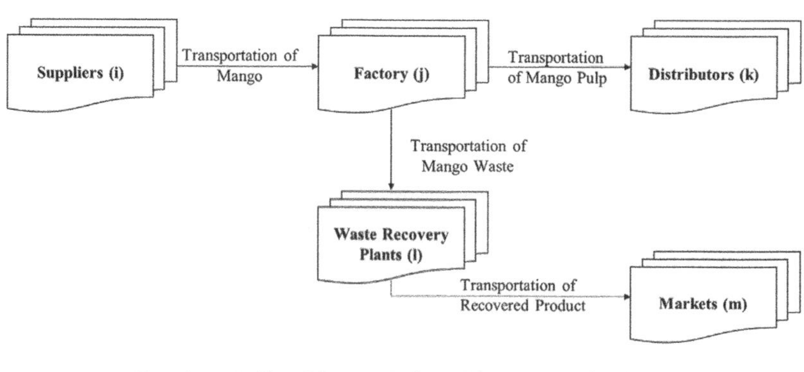

Fig. 1. Indian Mango Pulp FSC. *Source:* Authors.

products have applications in the food, medicine and beauty products industry (Arora et al., 2018; Banerjee et al., 2018). Considering such a waste recovery option, we have proposed an integrated FSC configuration by adding a WRP to traditional food SCN, as shown in Fig. 1.

According to the model, the mangoes from suppliers are transported to processing plants. Mangoes are procured directly from farmers if they have a large volume; otherwise, the procurement happens from the agents. Hence, here, suppliers indicate both farmers and agents. The processing plant maintains some inventory of mangoes and produces the pulp following the make-to-stock inventory policy with its limited production capacity. Although mango is a perishable product, mango pulp has a shelf life of up to 24 months (Indian Fruits Pulp, 2023). Also, due to seasonality, mango pulp is produced and stored as an inventory. Hence, a make-to-stock policy is followed for mango pulp. Pulp is transported in accordance with the order obtained from the distributor.

Pulp production in processing plants leaves behind a certain volume of waste. The waste is transported to the WRPs, where a value-added product ('Pectin' in this study) is recovered. The inventories are maintained following a make-to-stock policy to address demand variations.

The notations used in this section are specific to this case study. For the economic dimension of sustainability, the cost involved for all the FSC operations, such as fixed cost for the establishment of facilities, the variable cost for the operation of facilities and transportation costs, are considered. The variable costs are calculated based on the cost of all the resources used in operation, including raw materials, labour, water and energy consumed. Transportation cost is calculated considering the cost it will incur for a fully loaded vehicle to transport the product between the nodes in the network. For the environmental dimension, GHG emission is widely used in the literature (Maiyar & Thakkar, 2019; Sazvar et al., 2014; Yavari & Geraeli, 2019) as an indicator of the environmental impact of FSC operations, and hence, the environmental impact corresponding to transportation, processing of mango and mango waste and mango cultivation is calculated in terms of its GHG emission. Consideration of the social dimension of sustainability ensures that FSC operations improve the quality of life, encouraging diversity and providing an equitable opportunity to the community (Pullman et al., 2009). The creation of job opportunities has been considered an important social indicator of sustainability in the literature (Devika et al., 2014). The European Commission highlighted that recycling, remanufacturing and recovery-related activities are creating more job opportunities (Samadi et al., 2018). Accordingly, the WRP considered in this study creates more number of fixed and variable job opportunities, which are non-existent when food wastes are landfilled. Hence, in this study, the number of fixed and variable job opportunities created across the stages has been considered as an indicator of the social dimension of sustainability. The fixed-job opportunities indicate the manager-level roles, which are constant irrespective of the variability in quantity processed every day. In contrast, the variable job opportunities depend on the quantity of mangoes processed every day. The resilience of FSC is captured in terms of the time taken for recovery from a particular disruption and the time until the SC can survive with existing resources during the time of disruption (Simchi-Levi et al., 2015). The details of assumptions, various notations used, decision variables and parameters are described below.

Assumptions

The proposed optimisation model considers the following assumptions:

- All the model parameters are considered to be known, deterministic and depend on the FSC operation under consideration.
- The quality of mangoes is the same within the same variety – yielding the same quantity of pulp.
- The model is discrete, and there is a definite number of farmers, processing plants, WRPs, distributors and market for selling recovered products.
- An unlimited number of vehicles are assumed to be available.
- The distributor demand is considered as the market (retailers) demand for mango pulp produced.
- The environmental impact associated with opening a facility is not considered.

Sets and Indices

I	Set of raw material suppliers, ($i = 1,..., I$)
J	Set of factories ($j = 1,..., J$)
K	Set of distributors ($k = 1,..., K$)
l	Set of WRPs ($l = 1,..., L$)
m	Set of recycled product market ($m = 1,..., M$)
t_1	Set of type of vehicle for mango transport ($t_1 = 1,..., T$)
t_2	Set of type of vehicle for pulp transport ($t_2 = 1,..., T$)
t_3	Set of type of vehicle for waste and pectin transport ($t_3 = 1,..., T$)
p	Set of Periods (days), ($p = 1,..., P$)
a	Set of mango age (days) ($a = 1,..., SL_m$)
b	Set of mango waste age (days) ($b = 1,..., SL_{mw}$)

Decision Variables

x_i	A binary variable whose value is 1 if the supplier is selected and 0 otherwise.
y_j	A binary variable whose value is 1 if the factory is open and 0 otherwise.
z_l	A binary variable whose value is 1 if the WRP is open and 0 otherwise.
m_{pt_1ij}	Number of kg of mangoes procured from supplier i and transported (t_1) to factory j at time period p.
q_{pja}	Number of kg of mango pulp extracted from mango of age 'a' in the factory j at time period p.
tp_{pt_2jk}	Number of kg of pulp shipped from factory j to distributor k using vehicle t_2 at time period p.
w_{pj}	Number of kg of waste created in factory j at time period p.
tw_{pt_3jl}	Number of kg of waste shipped from factory j to WRP l using vehicle t_3 at time period p.

r_{plb}	Number of kg of pectin extracted from waste of age 'b' in the WRP l at time period p.
tr_{pt_3lm}	Number of kg of pectin shipped from WRP l to market using vehicle t_3 at time period p.
$\mathrm{Winvm}_{\mathrm{pja}}$	Inventory quantity of mango of age 'a' in factory j at time period p.
$\mathrm{invp}_{\mathrm{pj}}$	Inventory quantity of mango pulp in factory j at time period p.
$\mathrm{wastem}_{\mathrm{pja}}$	Number of kg of mango exceeds its maximum shelf life $a = \mathrm{SL}_M$ in factory j in time period p.
$\mathrm{invmw}_{\mathrm{plb}}$	Inventory quantity of mango waste of age 'b' in WRP l at time period p.
$\mathrm{invrp}_{\mathrm{pl}}$	Inventory quantity of pectin in WRP l at time period p.
$\mathrm{wastemw}_{\mathrm{plb}}$	Number of kg of mango waste exceeds its shelf-life $b = \mathrm{SL_{MW}}$ in WRP l in time period p.
$\mathrm{m}_{\mathrm{pja}}$	Number of kg of mango with age 'a' available in factory j in time period p.
$\mathrm{mw}_{\mathrm{plb}}$	Number of kg of mango waste of age 'b' is there in WRP l in time period p.
$\mathrm{stktp}_{\mathrm{pk}}$	Quantity of stock-out of pulp to distributor k in period p.
$\mathrm{stktr}_{\mathrm{pm}}$	Quantity(kg) of stock-out of recycled product in market m period p.

Parameters

Economic-Related Parameters

FCP_j	Fixed cost of establishing the factory j
VCP_j	Variable cost of operating the factory j
PV_j	Maximum capacity of factory j
MQ	Mango to pulp conversion ratio
CM_{pi}	Cost of mango from supplier i in time period p
HCW_j	Cost of waste management in factory j
ICM_j	Cost of holding mango in factory j
ICP_j	Cost of holding mango pulp in factory j
QoP	Ratio of peel to mango waste
FCR_l	Fixed cost of establishing the WRP l
VCR_l	Variable cost of operating the WRP l
PV_l	Maximum capacity of WRP l
WQ	Mango waste to pectin conversion ratio
ICMW_l	Cost of holding mango waste in WRP l
ICRP_l	Cost of holding pectin in WRP l
HCW_l	Cost of waste management in WRP l
TCM_{t_1ij}	Cost of transport of mango from supplier i to factory j using vehicle type t_1
TCP_{t_2jk}	Cost of transport of pulp from factory j to distributor k using vehicle type t_2
TCW_{t_3jl}	Cost of transport of waste from factory j to WRP l using vehicle type t_3
TCR_{t_3lm}	Cost of transport of pectin from WRP l to market m using vehicle type t_3

Environmental-Related Parameters

EIP_j	GHG emitted from factory j
EIM_i	GHG emitted from mango cultivation at the supplier i location

$EIIM_j$	GHG emitted from holding mango inventory in factory j
$EIIP_j$	GHG emitted from holding mango pulp in factory j
$EIMW_j$	GHG emitted from mango waste in factory j
EIR_l	GHG emitted from WRP l
$EIIMW_l$	GHG emitted from holding mango waste inventory in WRP l
$EIIRP_l$	GHG emitted from holding pectin inventory in WRP l
$EIMW_l$	GHG emitted from mango waste in WRP l
$EITM_{t_1ij}$	GHG emitted from shipping mango from supplier i to factory j using vehicle type t_1
$EITP_{t_2jk}$	GHG emitted from shipping pulp from factory j to distributor k using vehicle type t_2
$EITW_{t_3jl}$	GHG emitted from shipping mango waste from factory j to WRP l using vehicle type t_3
$EITR_{t_3lm}$	GHG emitted from shipping pectin from WRP l to market m using vehicle type t_3

Social-Related Parameters

$JOPP_j$	Number of fixed jobs created out of opening factory j
JO_{pj}	Number of jobs created out of processing mango in factory j in time period p
JOW_j	Number of jobs created out of handling waste in factory j
JOW_l	Number of jobs created out of handling waste in WRP l
$JOWP_l$	Number of fixed jobs created out of opening WRP l
JO_l	Number of jobs created out of processing mango waste in WRP l
JO_{t_1ij}	Number of jobs created out of shipping mango from supplier i to factory j using vehicle type t_1
JO_{t_2jk}	Number of jobs created out of shipping pulp from factory j to distributor k using vehicle type t_2
JO_{t_3jl}	Number of jobs created out of shipping waste from factory j to WRP l using vehicle type t_3
JO_{t_3lm}	Number of jobs created out of shipping pectin from WRP l to market m using vehicle type t_3
$JOInv_j$	Number of jobs created from holding inventory in factory j
$JOInv_l$	Number of jobs created from holding inventory in WRP l
JOM_i	Number of jobs created from mango cultivation at supplier location i

Resilience-Related Parameters

TTR_i	Time to recovery of supplier i after the disruption
TTR_j	Time to recovery of factory j after the disruption
TTR_l	Time to recovery of WRP l after the disruption
$SINV_i$	Time for survive for supplier i after the disruption from available inventory
$SINV_j$	Time for survive for factory j after the disruption from available inventory
$SINV_l$	Time for survive for WRP l after the disruption from available inventory

Other Parameters

D_{pk}	Forecasted pulp demand in distributor location k in time period p
D_{pm}	Forecasted pectin demand in market location m in time period p.
M	Maximum allowable count for opening factory.
N	Maximum allowable count for opening WRP.
CF_{pi}	Maximum capacity of supplier i in time period p.
SL_M	Maximum mango shelf-life.
SL_{MW}	Maximum mango-waste shelf-life.
$MaxIM_j$	Maximum inventory capacity for mango storage in the factory, j.
$MaxIP_j$	Maximum inventory capacity for pulp storage in factory j.
$MaxIMW_l$	Maximum inventory capacity for mango waste storage in the factory is l.
$MaxIRP_l$	Maximum inventory capacity for mango storage in WRP l.

Multi-Objective Optimisation Model

The proposed optimisation model has a mix of binary, integer and continuous decision variables. Further, four objective functions are formulated, of which three capture the economic, environmental and social dimensions of sustainability, and the last one captures the resilience of the FSC. As such, the proposed model is a 'multi-objective mixed integer linear programming model'. There is no non-linearity in the proposed model. The details of individual objective functions are explained below.

Objective Functions

The objective function (1) minimises the expected cost of the mango pulp FSC. This function captures all different components, including the cost of mango, different shipping involved, mango processing, handling waste, waste recovery and holding inventory, respectively.

Minimise, Obj1

$$\begin{aligned}
&\sum_p\sum_{t_1}\sum_i\sum_j m_{pt_1ij}.\mathrm{CM}_{pi} + \sum_p\sum_{t_1}\sum_i\sum_j m_{pt_1ij}.\mathrm{TCM}_{t_1ij} + \sum_p\sum_{t_2}\sum_j\sum_k tp_{pt_2jk}.\mathrm{TCP}_{t_2jk} \\
&+ \sum_p\sum_{t_3}\sum_j\sum_l tw_{pt_3jl}.\mathrm{TCW}_{t_3jl} + \sum_p\sum_{t_3}\sum_l\sum_m tr_{pt_3lm}.\mathrm{TCR}_{t_3lm} + \sum_j y_j.\mathrm{FCP}_j \\
&+ \sum_p\sum_j\sum_a q_{\mathrm{pja}}.\mathrm{VCP}_j + \sum_p\sum_j\sum_a\sum_{t_3}\sum_l \left(w_{pj} - tw_{pt_3jl} + \mathrm{wastem_{pja}}\right).\mathrm{HCW}_j \\
&+ \sum_l z_l.\mathrm{FCR}_l + \sum_p\sum_l\sum_b r_{\mathrm{plb}}.\mathrm{VCR}_l + \sum_p\sum_l\sum_b \mathrm{wastemw_{plb}}.\mathrm{HCW}_l \\
&+ \sum_p\sum_j\sum_a \mathrm{invm_{pja}}.\mathrm{ICM}_j + \sum_p\sum_j \mathrm{invp}_{pj}\,.\,\mathrm{ICP}_j \\
&+ \sum_p\sum_l\sum_a \mathrm{invmw_{plb}}.\mathrm{ICMW}_l + \sum_p\sum_l \mathrm{invrp}_{pl}.\mathrm{ICRP}_l
\end{aligned} \tag{1}$$

The objective function (2) minimises the emission (environmental dimension of sustainability) from all the different SC operations. This function captures the emission from the cultivation of mango, all different transportation operations, mango processing, pectin recovery and maintaining inventory, respectively.

Minimise, Obj2

$$\begin{aligned}&\sum_i\sum_j\sum_{t_1}\sum_p m_{pt_1ij}.\mathrm{EIM}_i + \sum_p\sum_{t_1}\sum_i\sum_j m_{pt_1ij}.\mathrm{EITM}_{t1ij} + \sum_p\sum_{t_2}\sum_j\sum_k tp_{pt_2jk}.\mathrm{EITP}_{t_2jk}\\&+ \sum_p\sum_{t_3}\sum_j\sum_l tw_{pt_3jl}.\mathrm{EITW}_{t_3jl} + \sum_p\sum_{t_3}\sum_l\sum_m tr_{pt_3lm}.\mathrm{EITR}_{pt_3lm}\\&+ \sum_p\sum_j\sum_a q_{\mathrm{pja}}.\mathrm{EIP}_j + \sum_p\sum_j\sum_a\sum_{t_3}\sum_l \left(w_{pj} - tw_{pt_3jl} + \mathrm{wastem}_{\mathrm{pja}}\right).\mathrm{EIMW}_j\\&+ \sum_p\sum_l\sum_b r_{\mathrm{plb}}.\mathrm{EIR}_l + \sum_p\sum_l\sum_b \mathrm{wastemw}_{\mathrm{plb}}.\mathrm{EIMW}_l\\&+ \sum_p\sum_j\sum_a \mathrm{invm}_{\mathrm{pja}}.\mathrm{EIIM}_{pj} + \sum_p\sum_j \mathrm{invp}_{pj}.\mathrm{EIIP}_{pj}\\&+ \sum_p\sum_l\sum_a \mathrm{invmw}_{\mathrm{plb}}.\mathrm{EIIMW}_{pl} + \sum_p\sum_l \mathrm{invrp}_{pl}.\mathrm{EIIRP}_{pl}\end{aligned} \tag{2}$$

The objective function (3) maximises the jobs created (social dimension of sustainability) from all the processes involved in the SC. This function captures the jobs created from the cultivation process, operating the factory for pulp production, operating the plant for pectin recovery, transportation across the entities and inventory handling, respectively.

Maximise, Obj3

$$\begin{aligned}&\sum_p\sum_{t_1}\sum_i\sum_j m_{pt_1ij}.\mathrm{JOM}_i + \sum_j y_j.\mathrm{JOPP}_j + \sum_p\sum_j\sum_a q_{pja}.\mathrm{JO}_{pj}\\&+ \sum_p\sum_j\sum_a\sum_{t3}\sum_l \left(w_{pj} - \mathrm{tw}_{pt_3jl} + \mathrm{wastem}_{\mathrm{pja}}\right).\mathrm{JOW}_j\\&+ \sum_l z_l.\mathrm{JOWP}_l + \sum_p\sum_l\sum_b r_{\mathrm{plb}}.\mathrm{JO}_{pl}\\&+ \sum_p\sum_l\sum_b \mathrm{wastemw}_{\mathrm{plb}}.\mathrm{JOW}_l + \sum_p\sum_{t_1}\sum_i\sum_j m_{pt_1ij}.\mathrm{JO}_{pt_1ij}\\&+ \sum_p\sum_{t_2}\sum_j\sum_k \mathrm{tp}_{pt_2jk}.\mathrm{JO}_{pt_2jk} + \sum_p\sum_{t_3}\sum_j\sum_l \mathrm{tw}_{pt_3jl}.\mathrm{JO}_{pt_3jl}\\&+ \sum_p\sum_{t_3}\sum_l\sum_m \mathrm{tr}_{pt_3lm}.\mathrm{JO}_{pt_3lm} + \sum_p\sum_j\sum_a \mathrm{invm}_{\mathrm{pja}}.\mathrm{JOInv}_j\\&+ \sum_p\sum_l\sum_b \mathrm{invmw}_{\mathrm{plb}}.\mathrm{JOInv}_l\end{aligned} \tag{3}$$

The objective function (4) captures the resilience of the SC using the two important measures of resilience – time to recovery and time to survive. As such, this function captures the time to recovery and time to survive when the disruption happens at the supplier's end, factory and recycling plant, respectively.

Maximise, Obj4

$$\sum_p \sum_i \text{invp}_{pi}.\text{SINV}_i - \sum_i x_i.\text{TTR}_i + \sum_p \sum_j \text{invp}_{pj}.\text{SINV}_j - \sum_j y_j.\text{TTR}_j + \sum_p \sum_l \text{inv}_{pl}.\text{SINV}_l - \sum_l z_l.\text{TTR}_l \tag{4}$$

Formulation of constraints

$$\sum_i x_i.\text{CF}_{pi} \geq \sum_{t1} \sum_i \sum_j m_{pt1ij} \ \forall \ \text{p} \tag{5}$$

$$m_{\text{pja}} = \sum_{t_1} \sum_i m_{pt_1ij} \ \forall \ \text{j, p, a} = 1 \tag{6}$$

$$m_{\text{pja}} = m_{p-1j\,a-1} - q_{p-1ja-1}.\text{MQ} \ \forall \ \text{j, p}, 1 < \text{a} \leq \text{SL}_\text{M} \tag{7}$$

$$\text{invm}_{\text{pja}} = m_{\text{pja}} - q_{\text{pja}}.\text{MQ} \ \forall \ \text{j, p, a} \tag{8}$$

$$\sum_a \text{invm}_{\text{pja}} \leq \text{MaxIM}_j \ \forall \ \text{j, p} \tag{9}$$

$$\text{wastem}_{\text{pja}} = \text{invm}_{\text{pja}} \ \forall \ \text{p, j, a} = \text{SL}_\text{M} \tag{10}$$

$$w_{pj} = \sum_a q_{\text{pja}}.\text{QoP} + \sum_a \text{wastem}_{\text{pja}}.\text{QoP} \ \forall \ \text{j, p} \tag{11}$$

$$\sum_a q_{\text{pja}} \leq \text{PV}_j.y_j \ \forall \ \text{j, p} \tag{12}$$

$$\sum_j y_j \leq \text{M} \tag{13}$$

$$\text{invp}_{pj} = \text{invp}_{p-1,j} + \sum_a q_{\text{pja}} - \sum_{t2} \sum_k \text{tp}_{pt_2jk} \ \forall \ \text{j, p} \tag{14}$$

$$\text{invp}_{pj} \leq \text{MaxIP}_j \ \forall \ \text{j, p} \tag{15}$$

$$\sum_{t_2} \sum_k \text{tp}_{pt_2jk} \leq \sum_a q_{\text{pja}} + \text{invp}_{p-1,j} \ \forall \ \text{j, p} \tag{16}$$

$$\sum_{l}\sum_{t_3} \mathrm{tw}_{pt_3jl} \leq w_{pj} \ \forall\ \mathrm{j, p} \tag{17}$$

$$\mathrm{mw_{plb}} = \sum_{t_3}\sum_{j} \mathrm{tw}_{pt_3jl} \ \forall\ \mathrm{l, p, b} = 1 \tag{18}$$

$$\mathrm{mw_{plb}} = \mathrm{mw}_{p-1\,l\,b-1} - r_{p-1\,l\,b-1}.\mathrm{WQ} \ \forall\ \mathrm{l, p,} 1 < \mathrm{b} \leq \mathrm{SL_{MW}} \tag{19}$$

$$\mathrm{invmw_{plb}} = \mathrm{mw_{p\,l\,b}} - r_{\mathrm{plb}}.\mathrm{WQ} \ \forall\ \mathrm{l, p, b} \tag{20}$$

$$\sum_{b} \mathrm{invmw_{plb}} \leq \mathrm{MaxIMW}_{l} \ \forall\ \mathrm{l, p} \tag{21}$$

$$\mathrm{wastemw_{plb}} = \mathrm{invmw_{plb}} \ \forall\ \mathrm{l, p, b} = \mathrm{SL_{MW}} \tag{22}$$

$$\sum_{b} r_{\mathrm{plb}} \leq \mathrm{PV}_{l}.z_{l} \ \forall\ \mathrm{l}, p \tag{23}$$

$$\sum_{l} z_{l} \leq N \tag{24}$$

$$\mathrm{invrp}_{pl} = \mathrm{invrp}_{\,p-1,l} + \sum_{b} r_{\mathrm{plb}} - \sum_{t3}\sum_{m} \mathrm{tr}_{pt3lm} \ \forall\ \mathrm{l, p} \tag{25}$$

$$\mathrm{invrp}_{pl} \leq \mathrm{MaxIRP}_{l} \ \forall\ \mathrm{l, p} \tag{26}$$

$$\sum_{t_3}\sum_{m} \mathrm{tr}_{pt_3lm} \leq \sum_{b} r_{\mathrm{plb}} \ \forall\ \mathrm{l, p} \tag{27}$$

$$\sum_{t_2}\sum_{j} \mathrm{tp}_{pt_2jk} + \mathrm{stktp}_{pk} = \mathrm{D_{pk}} \ \forall\ \mathrm{k, p} \tag{28}$$

$$\sum_{t_3}\sum_{l} \mathrm{tr}_{pt_3lm} + \mathrm{stktr_{pm}} \geq \mathrm{D_{pm}} \ \forall\ \mathrm{m, p} \tag{29}$$

$$x_{i}, y_{j}, z_{l} \in \{0, 1\} \tag{30}$$

$$\begin{gathered} m_{pt_1ij}, \mathrm{q_{pja}}, \mathrm{tp_{pt_2jk}}, \mathrm{w_{pj}}, \mathrm{tw_{pt_3jl}}, \mathrm{r_{plb}}, \mathrm{tr_{pt_3lm}}, \mathrm{invm_{pja}}, \mathrm{invp_{pj}}, \mathrm{wastem_{pja}}, \\ \mathrm{invmw_{plb}}, \mathrm{invrp_{pl}}, \mathrm{wastemw_{plb}}, \mathrm{m_{pja}}, \mathrm{mw_{plb}} \geq 0 \end{gathered} \tag{31}$$

Constraint (5) captures the capacity of mango supply. Constraints (6) and (7) capture the stock level of mango with a given shelf life. Constraint 6 captures the mangoes with shelf life = 1. Whereas constraint 7 captures the mango stock with age above 1 and less than or equal to its maximum shelf life, i.e. if any mangoes received in the previous periods and not processed and mangoes are within their maximum shelf life, then that total quantity is captured in constraint 7. In constraint (7), 'a' represents the age of a mango after it reaches the warehouse. Based on the data collected, we found that, generally, the mangoes are received before they actually ripen, and only in the warehouse does it ripen and then used for pulp extraction; hence, its age is calculated from the day it reaches the warehouse. Constraints (8) and (9) capture the inventory of mango and the maximum inventory limit for mango inventory. Constraints (10) and (11) capture the quantity of mango waste (peels) resulting from exceeding the maximum shelf life and pulp production. QoP in the equation represents the quantity of peels available in the waste. Constraints (12) and (13) restrict the maximum pulp production in each facility and the maximum number of facilities to open for pulp production. Constraints (14) and (15) capture the pulp inventory and its maximum limit. Constraints (16) and (17) represent the shipping of mango pulp and mango waste to the distributor and WRP, respectively. Constraints (18) and (19) capture the quantity of mango waste with a given shelf life. Constraints (20) and (21) capture the inventory of mango waste and restrict the maximum inventory that can be stored. Constraint (22) captures the waste resulting from exceeding the shelf life. Constraints (23) and (24) restrict the maximum pectin that can be recovered per plant and the number of WRPs that can be operated. Constraints (25) and (26) capture the pectin inventory and its maximum limit. Constraint (27) limits the quantity of pectin that can be shipped from each facility. Constraints (28) and (29) ensure that the demand for mango pulp and pectin is met. Constraints (30) and (31) define the nature of decision variables.

DESCRIPTION OF THE CASE OF INDIAN MANGO PULP FSC

In this study, we have considered the Indian mango pulp FSC. The data were collected from various stakeholders of the mango pulp FSC from various districts of Tamil Nadu in March–July 2019. The data were collected following semi-structured interviews with the key informants of the mango pulp producers, mango suppliers and transporters. The questionnaires are prepared to understand the operation of mango pulp FSC and to gather the data for solving the optimisation model. The representative SC network begins with 15 suppliers who supply their products to the processing plants. Eight such processing plants with either 12 or 24 metric tons per hour (MTPH) capacity process the mangoes into pulp with a yield of 50%. The pulp produced in these plans is then sent to seven distributors. The waste produced in the process is sent to five WRPs with a capacity of 10 MTPH each, which produce pectin from the waste with a yield of 25% (Banerjee et al., 2018). The recycled products are sent to five marketplaces.

Data regarding the WRP have been collected from experts in the industry and literature (Arora et al., 2018; Banerjee et al., 2018). The shelf life of 3 days is considered for both mango and waste. Further data regarding the sustainability parameters are obtained from Krishnan et al. (2022).

The resilience parameter – time to survive – has been estimated based on the number of days of inventory available to continue to supply products after any disruption happens at the processing plant or recycling plant. For example, if the processing plant has a capacity of 288,000 kg per day, then every one kg of inventory of pulp available can continue to provide the supply to the market for about 3.47E-6 days (=1/280,000) during the time of disruption. Similarly, the calculation is done for WRPs. In terms of time to recovery, the number of days it will take to recover the facilities after the disruption is estimated considering uniform distribution since the recovery time varies for different scenarios. The recovery time is estimated to be Uniform [7,10], Uniform [12,20] and Uniform [12,20] for suppliers, processing plants and WRPs, respectively.

RESULTS AND DISCUSSIONS

The methods available for solving multi-objective optimisation problems are classified into three types – a priori, interactive and a posteriori or generation methods, considering the phase where the decision-maker is involved in the decision-making process. In the a priori method, the decision-maker provides their preferences/weightage for multiple objectives before solving the problem, which does not allow the decision-maker to see all the alternatives and make the decision. In the case of the interactive method, the decision-maker is involved while solving the problem in iterations itself and provides their preferences. In this method, the decision-maker does not see all the alternatives, and the decision taken at every stage is based on whatever they saw in the previous iterations. This drawback is addressed in the posteriori method, where all the feasible solutions are found and presented to the decision-maker. Given this reason, in this study, we have used one of posteriori approach – the augmented ϵ-constraint to solve multi-objective problems (Mehrjerdi & Shafiee, 2021; Varsei & Polyakovskiy, 2017) because of its ability to provide a set of non-dominated solutions objectively.

In the first step, following the lexicographic approach, the payoff table is obtained. In the lexicographic approach, suppose the problem has three objective functions; first, the problem is solved with one objective function which is of more priority. Second, the first objective function is added as a constraint, with its right-hand side being the optimal solution obtained in the previous step. Similarly, the first and second objective functions are added as a constraint, with the right-hand side being its corresponding optimal solutions. This process is repeated by starting with the second and third objective functions. The payoff table is obtained at the end of this process. The payoff table helps to identify the range of each of the objective functions in front of the other objective functions.

In the second step, the range of each objective function is split into 'n' equal parts, and the bounds are obtained. Then, the priority objective function is solved by adding other objective functions as constraints, with its right-hand side value being equal to the bounds of the corresponding constraints. For a detailed explanation, readers are requested to read through the paper by Mavrotas (2009).

Following this solution methodology, in this study, the model is implemented in IBM ILOG CPLEX Studio IDE 22.1.0 in a desktop with a configuration of Intel Core i5 9th Generation 3GHz Processor with 16GB RAM.

The result presented in Table 4 clearly shows the presence of a trade-off between sustainability dimensions as well as between the resilience of the FSC. For example, when an organisation focuses only on improving the economic dimension of sustainability alone (C1), this results in increased environmental impact, reduced social benefit and reduced resilience of the FSC. Similarly, when the focus is only on improving the resilience (C4) of the FSC without considering its impact on the sustainability dimensions, then this negatively affects all three dimensions of sustainability. These results clearly show the importance of understanding the trade-off between sustainability dimensions and the interrelationship between sustainability dimensions and resilience.

Several other inferences are derived from this result. Figs. 2 and 3 show the quantity of mango procurement and the mango inventory at the processing plant. For example, under economic objective optimisation, more quantity of mangoes is procured and stocked if the expected price of mangoes is higher in the subsequent period, without considering the excess inventory's impact on other dimensions, the environmental dimension specifically. However, the mango procurement is completely reduced at the end of the planning cycle, and the inventory from previous periods is consumed. The social dimension of sustainability emphasises procuring the maximum possible quantity of mangoes and storing them in the inventory since holding inventory would also create job opportunities. Holding inventory typically requires employees to handle various tasks related to inventory management. Some of the job opportunities that can be created by holding inventory in the food industry include warehouse workers,

Table 4. The Payoff Table Obtained Following the Lexicographic Approach.

	Cost[@]	Emission*	Jobs[#]	Resilience[α]
Economic (C1)	13,270.49	145,439.14	381,195.39	1,344.9
Environmental (C2)	15,380.54	127,717.21	377,179.78	−313.1[β]
Social (C3)	14,440.44	154,024.57	603,490.83	331.9
Resilience (C4)	13,662.74	170,142.25	385,877.44	2,112.8

[@] Economic impact measured in terms of millions of INRs.
* Environmental emission measured in terms of tons of CO_2 eq.
# Social impact measured in terms of number of jobs created.
[α] Resilience measured in terms of number of days.
[β] Negative value indicates that the total time to survive is zero and the time for recovery is 313.1 days.

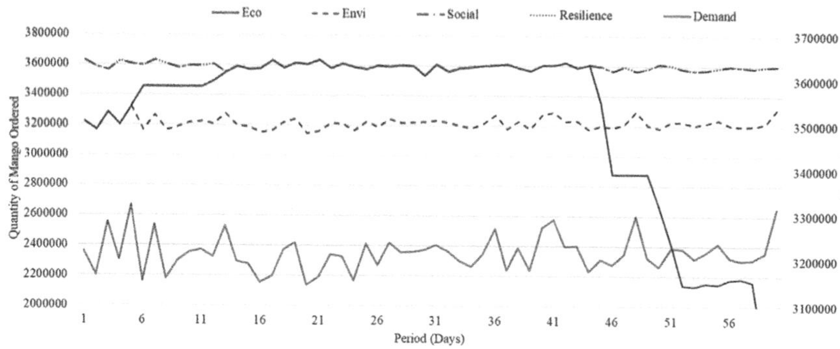

Fig. 2. Quantity of Mango Procurement Under Different Objectives.

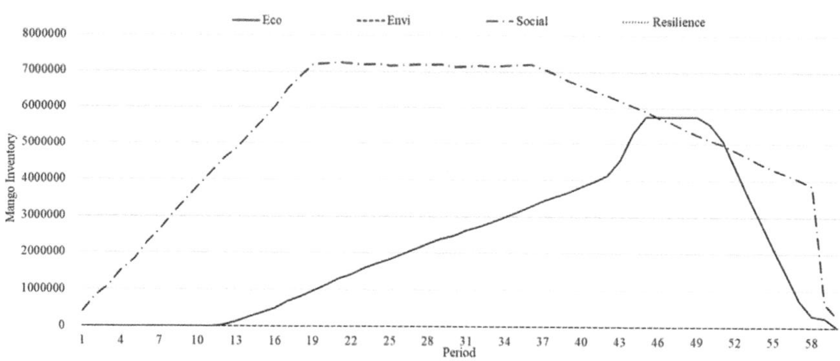

Fig. 3. Quantity of Mango Inventory Under Different Objectives.

inventory managers and quality control inspectors. Contradictory to economic and social objectives, the environmental dimension of sustainability discourages procuring excess quantity and stocking as inventory since holding and maintaining inventory also creates a negative environmental impact from energy consumed for lighting, temperature control and equipment operation.

Figs. 4 and 5 show the quantity of pulp production to meet the demand for pulp and the inventory of pulp maintained under different objective functions. Except under the social and resilience objective function optimisation, there is very minimal or no pulp inventory in all cases. Since holding inventory would help create job opportunities, mango pulp is stocked under a social dimension. Similar to the social dimension of sustainability, the resilience objective stocks the maximum possible pulp inventory since this would help improve the manufacturing facility's survival time during disruption or shutdown. In the case of economic objective, initially, the model suggests producing more amount of mango pulp; however, at the end of the planning horizon, the production of mango pulp is reduced, and the demands are met from the available inventory.

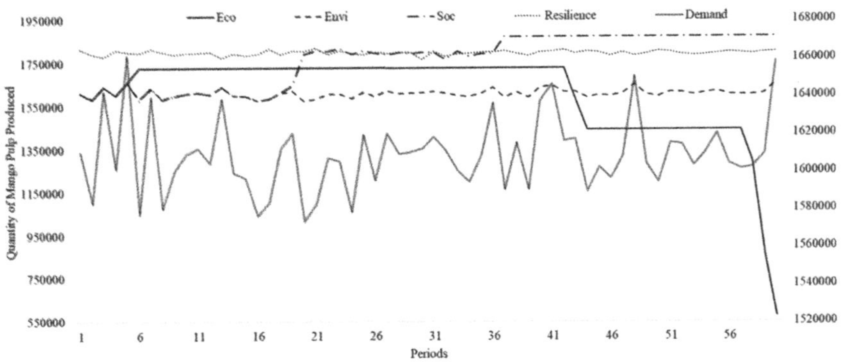

Fig. 4. Quantity of Mango Pulp Produced to Meet Pulp Demand Under Different Objectives.

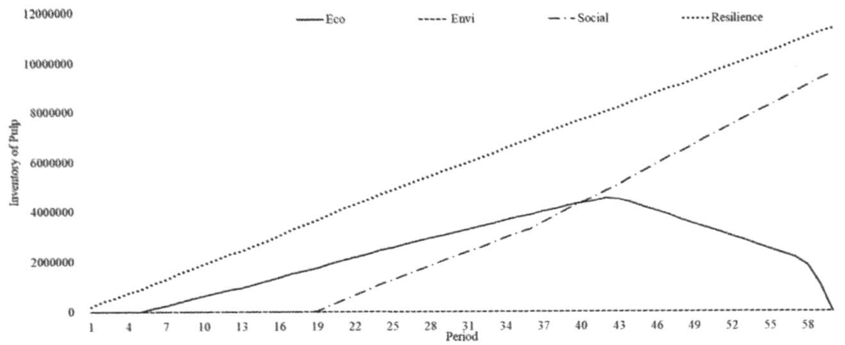

Fig. 5. Quantity of Mango Pulp Inventory Under Different Objectives.

From period 41, the quantity of mango pulp produced decreases because the excess inventory of mango pulp build-up until period 41 is used to meet the demand, and the pulp production is decreased gradually so as to reduce the cost of production and inventory. Whereas, when the focus is on social sustainability, the production is continued until the last period, and all the excess units produced are discarded as waste after the shelf life since production, inventory holding and waste disposal everything generate job opportunities, which is the prime focus of social sustainability.

Figs. 6 and 7 show the quantity of pectin produced at the WRP to meet the demand for pectin in the market and the quantity of pectin inventory stored under the resilience objective. Similar to the case of pulp, the quantity of pectin produced is almost equivalent to the pectin requirement except for the social and resilience objectives. In the case of resilience, the excess inventory is maintained in every period and used in the subsequent period. Otherwise, it is disposed of as waste at the end of its shelf life. In the case of social objective, the excess

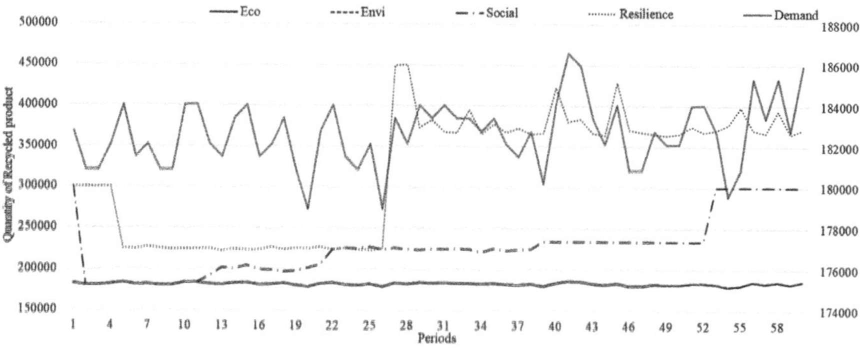

Fig. 6. Quantity of Pectin Produced Under Different Objectives.

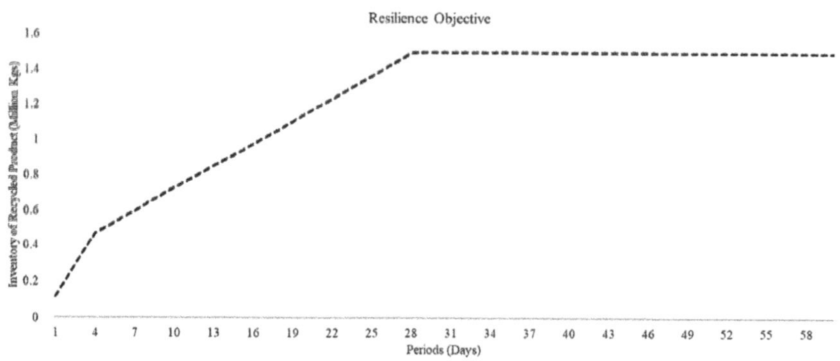

Fig. 7. Quantity of Inventory of Pectin Under Resilience Objective (Rest of the Objectives Carry No Inventory).

inventory is disposed of as waste at the end of the shelf life. Specifically, across all the scenarios, when the focus of the social objective is only on creating job opportunities, the processing plant and WRP generate a lot of waste since they create jobs from handling the waste. For example, in the processing plant alone, 5.3 million kgs of waste is generated while focusing only on social sustainability. Similarly, the resilience objective also generates 5.39 million kgs of waste. Towards recovering/utilising this large volume of waste, the WRP is considered in this study.

Further, although seven facilities are sufficient to meet the daily demand for the products, social and resilience objective function results emphasise opening all eight facilities and operating at less than maximum capacity since it creates job opportunities and helps in storing more inventory, respectively.

Since there is a clear trade-off between the objective functions, it is important to identify the interrelationship between the objective functions and show how an increase in one objective function affects the other objectives. This will help the decision-maker to take a balanced decision. Towards this, in the second step, non-dominated solutions are obtained. The FSC involves for-profit business organisations. Moreover, establishing the facilities involves cost, and the nature of any business is to minimise the cost incurred and still contribute to other dimensions of sustainability. Due to these reasons, the economic objective function has always been prioritised over other objective functions. Hence, the economic objective function is considered as a primary objective, and the rest of the objectives are added as constraints, with its right-side value being equal to the bounds obtained following the procedure explained before and suggested by Mavrotas (2009). In this study, the objective function ranges are split into four equal parts, and the bounds are obtained accordingly. We arrive at a set of non-dominated solutions, as shown in Table 5.

Table 5 shows the result of the economic objective function for different bounds of environmental, social and resilience constraints. For example, when the resilience constraint is constrained to take 2,112.8 days, environmental constraint to 254,337.481 CO_2 eq., and social dimension to 377,179.78 number of jobs, then the resulting economic objective function value is 13,663.62 million of INR. Similarly, the entire table can be inferred.

The above Table 5 reiterates that achieving the best of everything – all three dimensions of sustainability and resilience – is infeasible. As such, a set of feasible solutions, with possible minimum and maximum compromise on the environmental, social and resilience objectives, is obtained and presented. The table shows that, with more and more inventory maintained to improve resilience, the cost and environmental impact of holding and maintaining inventory also increases. However, the number of jobs created is increasing with resilience since more inventory maintenance requires more people to handle. Considering this trade-off, the decision-makers can choose a particular non-dominated solution presented in Table 5, depending on the level of sustainability and resilience that they wish to maintain or improve in their FSC.

THEORETICAL CONTRIBUTIONS AND MANAGERIAL IMPLICATIONS

Theoretical Contributions

FSC operation has a direct impact on all three dimensions of sustainability – economic, environmental and social (Soto-Silva et al., 2016). However, existing literature mainly focused on addressing the economic and environmental dimensions of sustainability (Jacob-John et al., 2022). This study contributes to the literature by capturing the social dimension of sustainability as well in addition to economic and environmental dimensions.

Further, existing literature highlights the importance of FSC resilience to ensure food security (Behzadi et al., 2020). Although there are studies on FSC resilience (Gholami-Zanjani, Jabalameli, et al., 2021; Gholami-Zanjani, Klibi, et al., 2021), the resilience models of those studies depend on the estimate of the

Table 5. Set of Non-Dominated Solution.

Resilience[α]	2,112.8 (n_4 = 0)				
Environmental*→ Social#↓	**254,337.481 (n_2 = 0)**	**222,682.401 (n_2 = 1)**	**191,027.322 (n_2 = 2)**	**159,372.242 (n_2 = 3)**	**127,717.163 (n_2 = 4)**
377,179.78 (n_3 = 0)	13,663.62[@]	13,663.62	13,662.74	15,358.73	Infeasible (Inf)
433,757.55 (n_3 = 1)	13,729.16	13,729.16	13,729.18	15,592.7	Inf
490,335.31 (n_3 = 2)	13,834.76	13,834.74	13,835.43	Inf	Inf
546,913.07 (n_3 = 3)	14,045.39	14,056.56	Inf	Inf	Inf
603,490.8 (n_3 = 4)	Inf	Inf	Inf	Inf	Inf
Resilience[α]	**1,506.35 (n_4 = 1)**				
Environmental*→ Social#↓	**254,337.481 (n_2 = 0)**	**222,682.401 (n_2 = 1)**	**191,027.322 (n_2 = 2)**	**159,372.242 (n_2 = 3)**	**127,717.163 (n_2 = 4)**
377,179.78 (n_3 = 0)	1,330,137	13,301.37	13,301.93	13,302.24	Inf
433,757.55 (n_3 = 1)	13,387.77	13,388.03	13,387.79	13,419.09	Inf
490,335.31 (n_3 = 2)	13,520.83	13,520.33	13,519.59	Inf	Inf
546,913.07 (n_3 = 3)	13,817.38	13,830.91	Inf	Inf	Inf
603,490.8 (n_3 = 4)	Inf	Inf	Inf	Inf	Inf
Resilience[α]	**899.94 (n_4 = 2)**				
Environmental*→ Social#↓	**254,337.481 (n_2 = 0)**	**222,682.401 (n_2 = 1)**	**191,027.322 (n_2 = 2)**	**159,372.242 (n_2 = 3)**	**127,717.163 (n_2 = 4)**
377,179.78 (n_3 = 0)	13,286.31	13,286.18	13,286.17	13,288.76	Inf
433,757.55 (n_3 = 1)	13,372.94	13,375.85	13,374.44	13,394.93	Inf
490,335.31 (n_3 = 2)	13,497.77	13,497.77	13,506.32	Inf	Inf
546,913.07 (n_3 = 3)	13,761.61	13,784.80	Inf	Inf	Inf
603,490.8 (n_3 = 4)	Inf	Inf	Inf	Inf	Inf
Resilience[α]	**293.5 (n_4 = 3)**				
Environmental*→ Social#↓	**254,337.481 (n_2 = 0)**	**222,682.401 (n_2 = 1)**	**191,027.322 (n_2 = 2)**	**159,372.242 (n_2 = 3)**	**127,717.163 (n_2 = 4)**
377,179.78 (n_3 = 0)	13,278.40	13,278.40	13,278.406	13,278.406	Inf

(Continued)

Table 5. (*Continued*)

Resilience[α]	2,112.8 ($n_4 = 0$)				
433,757.55 ($n_3 = 1$)	13,364.00	13,363.49	13,363.71	13,380.79	Inf
490,335.31 ($n_3 = 2$)	13,481.28	1.35E+10	13,486.59	13,683.01	Inf
546,913.07 ($n_3 = 3$)	13,758.45	13,767.06	16,270.48	Inf	Inf
603,490.8 ($n_3 = 4$)	Inf	Inf	Inf	Inf	Inf
Resilience[α]	**−313 ($n_4 = 4$)**				
Environmental*→	**254,337.481 ($n_2 = 0$)**	**222,682.401 ($n_2 = 1$)**	**191,027.322 ($n_2 = 2$)**	**159,372.242 ($n_2 = 3$)**	**127,717.163 ($n_2 = 4$)**
Social[#]↓					
368,694.6 ($n_3 = 0$)	13,278.40	13,291.44	13,291.44	13,291.44	15,380.53
427,393.6 ($n_3 = 1$)	13,373.10	13,377.80	13,377.80	13,374.60	Inf
486,092.7 ($n_3 = 2$)	13,502.97	13,502.97	13,502.97	13,661.89	Inf
544,791.8 ($n_3 = 3$)	13,752.51	13,815.88	14,290.26	Inf	Inf
603,490.8 ($n_3 = 4$)	Inf	Inf	Inf	Inf	Inf

@Economic impact measured in terms of millions of INRs.
*Environmental emission measured in terms of tons of CO_2 eq.
#Social impact measured in terms of number of jobs created.
[α]Resilience measured in terms of number of days.

probability of disruptions. However, such data are not always available for different SCs, and the disruption scenario could be a completely new one, hence requiring a different way of capturing the FSC resilience. Accordingly, in this study, time to recovery and time to survive have been used as a measure of resilience (Simchi-Levi et al., 2014). This measure doesn't require the probability of disruption data.

In addition, there is a lack of studies that capture the resilience of the FSC along with sustainability. This study is the first one to propose a model to capture the resilience and sustainability dimensions together and design the FSC. As such, this study addresses the call for papers by Elias et al. (2022) and Negri et al. (2021) to propose a multi-objective optimisation model considering both sustainability and resilience and assess their trade-offs.

Finally, to address the food waste-related issues and contribute to food waste literature, this study captured food WRPs as an additional entity of FSC and proposed an integrated model.

Managerial Implications

This study emphasises the importance of considering all sustainability dimensions and resilience while designing the FSC by showing the negative impacts created when the focus is restricted to only one (economic) objective alone, which firms typically focus on. For example, if the decision-maker completely focuses on improving the economic objective alone, from Table 4 (second row corresponding to cost), we can infer that the environmental emission is increasing by 13.87%, job opportunities are decreasing by 36.83% and resilience of the SC is decreasing by 36.35% from its corresponding optimal levels. Hence, the decision-maker should consider this negative impact and take a balanced decision. The non-dominant solution presented in Table 5 gives a detailed understanding of how a % change in individual objective function affects the cost. This table can be used by decision-makers in making a balanced judgement based on the level of sustainability and resilience they wish to achieve in their FSC.

The result of this study (Table 5) also highlights that with increasing resilience of the mango pulp FSC, the cost of the total SC is also increasing for the same level of emission and job opportunities. For example, when the resilience is increased from 899.9 to 1,506.35 days, i.e. a 40% increase, the cost increases by only ~0.113%, showing that the resilience of the mango pulp FSC can be improved with small additional costs. Such an increase in the resilience of the FSC would help the SC during times of disruptions and help an organisation to avoid shutting down production completely.

Lastly, in line with the Government of India's initiative – Waste to Wealth (Government of India, 2022) – if mango pulp industries plan to establish mango WRPs, the integrated model proposed in this study would be useful to optimally locate the facility and plan the production and distribution operations.

Overall, this study contributes to and advances the sustainability and resilience FSC literature and sustainability theory. Further, this study will help address the United Nations' 12th sustainable development goal – 'Responsible Production and Consumption' (UNDP, 2015), by providing an optimisation model to plan the SC decisions considering sustainability and resilience together and consume the resources responsibly.

CONCLUSION

Growing concern towards sustainability from consumers to government regulations makes it important to design the FSC network considering sustainability practices. In addition, the increase in disruptions resulting from climate change, pandemics, geopolitical issues and other causes emphasises the importance of building FSC as resilient. As such, developing an FSC that is sustainable and resilient is the need of the hour, and it is lacking in the literature. Towards addressing this research gap, this study aids in designing an FSC, taking into account all sustainability dimensions and resilience, using an optimisation model. The results demonstrate a distinct trade-off between sustainability and resilience. It provides a non-dominated solution that a decision-maker can use to make a balanced decision. This study also incorporates the WRP within the FSC towards addressing the food waste issue. Despite these contributions, this study has a set of limitations. First, job opportunity creation alone is considered a measure of the social dimension of sustainability. However, future studies could consider other aspects, such as local development, employee satisfaction and safety either using a social index or other measures to better represent the social sustainability of the FSC. Second, the proposed model considered all the parameters as deterministic. Future studies could capture the uncertainty associated with each of the parameters and develop an optimisation model. Third, this study only considered the SC of mango pulp. The SC of fresh mangoes is not considered. Future studies could consider integrating both these SCs. In addition to addressing these limitations, future studies could consider extending the proposed model to different resilient strategies and types of disruption scenarios.

REFERENCES

Ahmed, S., Chapple, L., Christ, K., & Osborne, S. (2022). Modern slavery risk disclosures in business operations and supply chains. *Advances in Environmental Accounting and Management*, *10*, 67–104. https://doi.org/10.1108/S1479-359820220000010005

Ajila, C. M., Aalami, M., Leelavathi, K., & Rao, U. J. S. P. (2010). Mango peel powder: A potential source of antioxidant and dietary fiber in macaroni preparations. *Innovative Food Science & Emerging Technologies*, *11*(1), 219–224. https://doi.org/10.1016/j.ifset.2009.10.004

Ajila, C., Naidu, K., Bhat, S., & Rao, U. (2007). Bioactive compounds and antioxidant potential of mango peel extract. *Food Chemistry*, *105*(3), 982–988. https://doi.org/10.1016/j.foodchem.2007.04.052

Allaoui, H., Guo, Y., Choudhary, A., & Bloemhof, J. (2018). Sustainable agro-food supply chain design using two-stage hybrid multi-objective decision-making approach. *Computers & Operations Research*, *89*, 369–384. https://doi.org/10.1016/J.COR.2016.10.012

Amorim, P., Meyr, H., Almeder, C., & Almada-Lobo, B. (2013). Managing perishability in production-distribution planning: A discussion and review. *Flexible Services and Manufacturing Journal*, *25*(3), 389–413. https://doi.org/10.1007/S10696-011-9122-3/FIGURES/2

Arora, A., Banerjee, J., Vijayaraghavan, R., MacFarlane, D., & Patti, A. F. (2018). Process design and techno-economic analysis of an integrated mango processing waste biorefinery. *Industrial Crops and Products*, *116*(February), 24–34.

Askham, T. (2019). Water-related disclosures by food producer companies in South Africa. *Advances in Environmental Accounting and Management*, *8*, 91–125. https://doi.org/10.1108/S1479-359820190000008005

Babbar, C., & Amin, S. H. (2018). A multi-objective mathematical model integrating environmental concerns for supplier selection and order allocation based on fuzzy QFD in beverages industry. *Expert Systems With Applications*, *92*, 27–38. https://doi.org/10.1016/J.ESWA.2017.09.041

Banasik, A., Kanellopoulos, A., Bloemhof-Ruwaard, J. M., & Claassen, G. D. H. (2019). Accounting for uncertainty in eco-efficient agri-food supply chains: A case study for mushroom production planning. *Journal of Cleaner Production*, *216*, 249–256. https://doi.org/10.1016/J.JCLEPRO.2019.01.153

Banerjee, J., Singh, R., Vijayaraghavan, R., MacFarlane, D., Patti, A. F., & Arora, A. (2018). A hydrocolloid based biorefinery approach to the valorisation of mango peel waste. *Food Hydrocolloids*, *77*, 142–151. https://doi.org/10.1016/j.foodhyd.2017.09.029

Behzadi, G., O'Sullivan, M. J., & Olsen, T. L. (2020). On metrics for supply chain resilience. *European Journal of Operational Research*, *287*(1), 145–158. https://doi.org/10.1016/J.EJOR.2020.04.040

Bhargava, R., & Bhargava, M. (2021, June 15). *The COVID-19 pandemic is creating a hunger catastrophe in India*. World Economic Forum. https://www.weforum.org/agenda/2021/06/covid-19-pandemic-hunger-catastrophe-india-poverty-food-insecurity-relief/

Bortolini, M., Faccio, M., Ferrari, E., Gamberi, M., & Pilati, F. (2016). Fresh food sustainable distribution: Cost, delivery time and carbon footprint three-objective optimization. *Journal of Food Engineering*, *174*, 56–67. https://doi.org/10.1016/J.JFOODENG.2015.11.014

Burgos, D., & Ivanov, D. (2021). Food retail supply chain resilience and the COVID-19 pandemic: A digital twin-based impact analysis and improvement directions. *Transportation Research Part E: Logistics and Transportation Review*, *152*, 102412. https://doi.org/10.1016/J.TRE.2021.102412

Carvalho, H., Barroso, A. P., MacHado, V. H., Azevedo, S., & Cruz-Machado, V. (2012). Supply chain redesign for resilience using simulation. *Computers & Industrial Engineering*, *62*(1), 329–341. https://doi.org/10.1016/j.cie.2011.10.003

Chopra, S., Meindl, P., & Meindl, P. (2016). *Supply chain management strategy, planning, and operation* (6th ed.). Pearson Education.

Costa, F. H. de O., de Moraes, C. C., da Silva, A. L., Delai, I., Chaudhuri, A., & Pereira, C. R. (2022). Does resilience reduce food waste? Analysis of Brazilian supplier-retailer dyad. *Journal of Cleaner Production*, *338*, 130488. https://doi.org/10.1016/J.JCLEPRO.2022.130488

Das, K. (2019). Integrating lean, green, and resilience criteria in designing a sustainable food supply chain planning model. *International Journal of Mathematical, Engineering and Management Sciences*, *4*(2), 259–275.

Devika, K., Jafarian, A., & Nourbakhsh, V. (2014). Designing a sustainable closed-loop supply chain network based on triple bottom line approach: A comparison of metaheuristics hybridization techniques. *European Journal of Operational Research*, *235*(3), 594–615. https://doi.org/10.1016/j.ejor.2013.12.032

Elias, A. A., Donadelli, F., Paiva, E. L., & Bacic Araujo, P. P. (2021). Analysing the complexities of sustainable wood supply chain in the Amazon: A systems thinking approach. *International Journal of Logistics Management*, *32*(4), 1481–1505. https://doi.org/10.1108/IJLM-07-2020-0276

Elias, A. A., Pepper, M., Anand, G., & Shukla, A. (2022). *Sustainable and resilient supply chain : Environmental accounting and management focus*. Advances in Environmental Accounting and Management.

Fahimnia, B., & Jabbarzadeh, A. (2016). Marrying supply chain sustainability and resilience: A match made in heaven. *Transportation Research Part E: Logistics and Transportation Review*, *91*, 306–324. https://doi.org/10.1016/j.tre.2016.02.007

Fahimnia, B., Jabbarzadeh, A., & Sarkis, J. (2018). Greening versus resilience: A supply chain design perspective. *Transportation Research Part E: Logistics and Transportation Review*, *119*, 129–148. https://doi.org/10.1016/J.TRE.2018.09.005

Fang, Y. P., & Zio, E. (2019). An adaptive robust framework for the optimization of the resilience of interdependent infrastructures under natural hazards. *European Journal of Operational Research*, *276*(3), 1119–1136. https://doi.org/10.1016/J.EJOR.2019.01.052

FAO. (2014). Sustainability pathways: Food loss and waste. *Food and Agriculture Organization of the United Nations*. https://www.fao.org/nr/sustainability/food-loss-and-waste/en/

FAO. (2020). *Emissions due to agriculture global, regional and country trends*.

Fresh Fruits – Worldwide. (2023, March). *Statista market forecast*. https://www.statista.com/outlook/cmo/food/fruits-nuts/fresh-fruits/worldwide

Ghadge, A., Kaklamanou, M., Choudhary, S., & Bourlakis, M. (2017). Implementing environmental practices within the Greek dairy supply chain drivers and barriers for SMEs. *Industrial Management and Data Systems*, *117*(9), 1995–2014. https://doi.org/10.1108/IMDS-07-2016-0270/FULL/PDF

Gholami-Zanjani, S. M., Jabalameli, M. S., Klibi, W., & Pishvaee, M. S. (2021). A robust location-inventory model for food supply chains operating under disruptions with ripple effects. *International Journal of Production Research*, *59*(1), 301–324. https://doi.org/10.1080/00207543.2020.1834159

Gholami-Zanjani, S. M., Klibi, W., Jabalameli, M. S., & Pishvaee, M. S. (2021). The design of resilient food supply chain networks prone to epidemic disruptions. *International Journal of Production Economics*, *233*, 108001. https://doi.org/10.1016/J.IJPE.2020.108001

Ghosh, N., & Bhowmick, S. (2022, May 30). Why India's food value-chain needs better risk management instruments amid Ukraine war. *Observer Research Foundation*, 1–4. shorturl.at/bfKS1.

Government of India. (2022). *Waste to wealth*. https://www.wastetowealth.gov.in/about-us

Govindan, K., & Gholizadeh, H. (2021). Robust network design for sustainable-resilient reverse logistics network using big data: A case study of end-of-life vehicles. *Transportation Research Part E: Logistics and Transportation Review*, *149*, 102279. https://doi.org/10.1016/J.TRE.2021.102279

Govindan, K., Jafarian, A., & Nourbakhsh, V. (2019). Designing a sustainable supply chain network integrated with vehicle routing: A comparison of hybrid swarm intelligence metaheuristics. *Computers & Operations Research*, *110*, 220–235. https://doi.org/10.1016/J.COR.2018.11.013

Gupta, M., Kaur, H., & Singh, S. P. (2021). Multi-echelon agri-food supply chain network design integrating operational and strategic objectives: A case of public distribution system in India. *Annals of Operations Research*, 1–58. https://doi.org/10.1007/S10479-021-04240-8/TABLES/12

Hutchins, M. J., & Sutherland, J. W. (2008). An exploration of measures of social sustainability and their application to supply chain decisions. *Journal of Cleaner Production*, *16*(15), 1688–1698. https://doi.org/10.1016/J.JCLEPRO.2008.06.001

Indian Fruits Pulp. (2023). *Mango pulp – Indian fruits pulp*. https://indianfruitspulp.com/mango-pulp/

Ivanov, D. (2018). Revealing interfaces of supply chain resilience and sustainability: A simulation study. *International Journal of Production Research*, *56*(10), 3507–3523. https://doi.org/10.1080/00207543.2017.1343507

Jabbarzadeh, A., Fahimnia, B., & Rastegar, S. (2019). Green and resilient design of electricity supply chain networks: A multiobjective robust optimization approach. *IEEE Transactions on Engineering Management*, *66*(1), 52–72. https://doi.org/10.1109/TEM.2017.2749638

Jabbarzadeh, A., Fahimnia, B., & Sabouhi, F. (2018). Resilient and sustainable supply chain design: Sustainability analysis under disruption risks. *International Journal of Production Research*, *56*(17), 5945–5968.

Jacob-John, J., D'Souza, C., Marjoribanks, T., & Singaraju, S. (2022). Sustainable development goals: A review of SDG 12.3 in food supply chain literature. *Benchmarking: An International Journal*, *30*(9), 3465–3481.

Krishnan, R., Agarwal, R., Bajada, C., & Arshinder, K. (2020). Redesigning a food supply chain for environmental sustainability – An analysis of resource use and recovery. *Journal of Cleaner Production*, *242*, 118374. https://doi.org/10.1016/J.JCLEPRO.2019.118374

Krishnan, R., Arshinder, K., & Agarwal, R. (2022). Robust optimization of sustainable food supply chain network considering food waste valorization and supply uncertainty. *Computers & Industrial Engineering*, *171*, 108499. https://doi.org/10.1016/J.CIE.2022.108499

Kummu, M., de Moel, H., Porkka, M., Siebert, S., Varis, O., & Ward, P. J. (2012). Lost food, wasted resources: Global food supply chain losses and their impacts on freshwater, cropland, and fertiliser use. *Science of the Total Environment*, *438*, 477–489. https://doi.org/10.1016/j.scitotenv.2012.08.092

León-Bravo, V., Caniato, F., & Caridi, M. (2021). Sustainability assessment in the food supply chain: Study of a certified product in Italy. *Production Planning & Control*, *32*(7), 567–584.

Lowe, M., Nadhanael, G. V., & Roth, B. N. (2021). India's food supply chain during the pandemic. *Food Policy*, *105*, 102162. https://doi.org/10.1016/J.FOODPOL.2021.102162

Maiyar, L. M., & Thakkar, J. J. (2019). Environmentally conscious logistics planning for food grain industry considering wastages employing multi objective hybrid particle swarm optimization. *Transportation Research Part E: Logistics and Transportation Review*, *127*, 220–248. https://doi.org/10.1016/j.tre.2019.05.006

Manteghi, Y., Arkat, J., Mahmoodi, A., & Farvaresh, H. (2021). A multi-period bi-level model for a competitive food supply chain with sustainability considerations. *Journal of Cleaner Production*, *325*, 129260. https://doi.org/10.1016/J.JCLEPRO.2021.129260

Martins, C. L., Melo, M. T., & Pato, M. V. (2019). Redesigning a food bank supply chain network in a triple bottom line context. *International Journal of Production Economics*, *214*, 234–247. https://doi.org/10.1016/J.IJPE.2018.11.011

Mavrotas, G. (2009). Effective implementation of the ϵ-constraint method in multi-objective mathematical programming problems. *Applied Mathematics and Computation*, *213*(2), 455–465.

Mehrjerdi, Y. Z., & Shafiee, M. (2021). A resilient and sustainable closed-loop supply chain using multiple sourcing and information sharing strategies. *Journal of Cleaner Production*, *289*, 125141. https://doi.org/10.1016/J.JCLEPRO.2020.125141

Mogale, D. G., Cheikhrouhou, N., & Tiwari, M. K. (2020). Modelling of sustainable food grain supply chain distribution system: A bi-objective approach. *International Journal of Production Research*, *58*(18), 5521–5544. https://doi.org/10.1080/00207543.2019.1669840

Mogale, D. G., Ghadge, A., Cheikhrouhou, N., & Tiwari, M. K. (2023). Designing a food supply chain for enhanced social sustainability in developing countries. *International Journal of Production Research*, *61*(10), 3184–3204. https://doi.org/10.1080/00207543.2022.2078746

Mohammadi Bidhandi, H., Mohd Yusuff, R., Megat Ahmad, M. M. H., & Abu Bakar, M. R. (2009). Development of a new approach for deterministic supply chain network design. *European Journal of Operational Research*, *198*(1), 121–128. https://doi.org/10.1016/J.EJOR.2008.07.034

Munoz, A. (2015). On the quantification of operational supply chain resilience. *International Journal of Production Research*, *53*(22), 6736–6751. https://doi.org/10.1080/00207543.2015.1057296

Nayeri, S., Ali Torabi, S., Tavakoli, M., & Sazvar, Z. (2021). A multi-objective fuzzy robust stochastic model for designing a sustainable-resilient-responsive supply chain network. *Journal of Cleaner Production*, *311*, 127691. https://doi.org/10.1016/j.jclepro.2021.127691

Negri, M., Cagno, E., Colicchia, C., & Sarkis, J. (2021). Integrating sustainability and resilience in the supply chain: A systematic literature review and a research agenda. *Business Strategy and the Environment*, *30*(7), 2858–2886. https://doi.org/10.1002/bse.2776

Pratichi. (2022). *Staying alive: COVID-19 and public services in West Bengal.*

Pullman, M. E., Maloni, M. J., & Carter, C. R. (2009). Food for thought: Social versus environmental sustainability practices and performance outcomes. *Journal of Supply Chain Management*, *45*(4), 38–54. https://doi.org/10.1111/j.1745-493X.2009.03175.x

Rajakal, J. P., Ng, D. K. S., Tan, R. R., Andiappan, V., & Wan, Y. K. (2021). Multi-objective expansion analysis for sustainable agro-industrial value chains based on profit, carbon and water footprint. *Journal of Cleaner Production*, *288*, 125117. https://doi.org/10.1016/J.JCLEPRO.2020.125117

Ramos, T. R. P., Gomes, M. I., & Barbosa-Póvoa, A. P. (2014). Planning a sustainable reverse logistics system: Balancing costs with environmental and social concerns. *Omega*, *48*, 60–74. https://doi.org/10.1016/J.OMEGA.2013.11.006

Reynolds, C. J., Buckley, J. D., Weinstein, P., & Boland, J. (2014). Are the dietary guidelines for meat, fat, fruit and vegetable consumption appropriate for environmental sustainability? A review of the literature. *Nutrients*, *6*(6), 2251–2265. https://doi.org/10.3390/nu6062251

S&P Global. (2020). The world is looking beyond India for supplies of mango purée. https://www.spglobal.com/commodityinsights/en/ci/research-analysis/special-report-the-world-is-looking-beyond-india.html

Sabouhi, F., Jabalameli, M. S., & Jabbarzadeh, A. (2021). An optimization approach for sustainable and resilient supply chain design with regional considerations. *Computers & Industrial Engineering*, *159*, 107510. https://doi.org/10.1016/J.CIE.2021.107510

Salehi, S., Zare Mehrjerdi, Y., Sadegheih, A., & Hosseini-Nasab, H. (2022). Designing a resilient and sustainable biomass supply chain network through the optimization approach under uncertainty and the disruption. *Journal of Cleaner Production*, *359*, 131741. https://doi.org/10.1016/j.jclepro.2022.131741

Samadi, A., Mehranfar, N., Fathollahi Fard, A. M., & Hajiaghaei-Keshteli, M. (2018). Heuristic-based metaheuristics to address a sustainable supply chain network design problem. *Journal of Industrial and Production Engineering*, *35*(2), 102–117. https://doi.org/10.1080/21681015.2017.1422039

Sarkis, J. (2020). Supply chain sustainability: Learning from the COVID-19 pandemic. *International Journal of Operations & Production Management*, *41*(1), 63–73. https://doi.org/10.1108/IJOPM-08-2020-0568/FULL/PDF

Sazvar, Z., Mirzapour Al-e-hashem, S. M. J., Baboli, A., & Akbari Jokar, M. R. (2014). A bi-objective stochastic programming model for a centralized green supply chain with deteriorating products. *International Journal of Production Economics*, *150*, 140–154. https://doi.org/10.1016/j.ijpe.2013.12.023

Sazvar, Z., Tafakkori, K., Oladzad, N., & Nayeri, S. (2021). A capacity planning approach for sustainable-resilient supply chain network design under uncertainty: A case study of vaccine supply chain. *Computers & Industrial Engineering*, *159*, 107406. https://doi.org/10.1016/j.cie.2021.107406

Seuring, S., & Müller, M. (2008). From a literature review to a conceptual framework for sustainable supply chain management. *Journal of Cleaner Production*, *16*(15), 1699–1710. https://doi.org/10.1016/J.JCLEPRO.2008.04.020

Simchi-Levi, D., Kaminsky, P., & Simchi-Levi, E. (2004). *Managing the supply chain: Definitive guide*. Tata McGraw-Hill Education.

Simchi-Levi, D., Schmidt, W., & Wei, Y. (2014). From superstorms to factory fires: Managing unpredictable supply-chain disruptions. *Harvard Business Review*, *92*(1–2), 96–101.

Simchi-Levi, D., Schmidt, W., Wei, Y., Zhang, P. Y., Combs, K., Ge, Y., Gusikhin, O., Sanders, M., & Zhang, D. (2015). Identifying risks and mitigating disruptions in the automotive supply chain. *Interfaces*, *45*(5), 375–390. https://doi.org/10.1287/INTE.2015.0804/ASSET/IMAGES/LARGE/INTE.2015.0804-F08.JPEG

Soto-Silva, W. E., Nadal-Roig, E., González-Araya, M. C., & Pla-Aragones, L. M. (2016). Operational research models applied to the fresh fruit supply chain. *European Journal of Operational Research*, *251*(2), 345–355.

Stevens, P. (2021, March 29). Suez Canal is moving, but the supply chain impact could last months. *CNBC*, 5. https://www.cnbc.com/2021/03/29/suez-canal-is-moving-but-the-supply-chain-impact-could-last-months.html. Accessed on March 10, 2023.

Stone, J., & Rahimifard, S. (2018). Resilience in agri-food supply chains: A critical analysis of the literature and synthesis of a novel framework. *Supply Chain Management*, *23*(3), 207–238. https://doi.org/10.1108/SCM-06-2017-0201/FULL/PDF

Taleb, N. N. (2007). The Black Swan: The impact of the highly improbable. *Business Economics*, *44*(2). https://doi.org/10.1057/BE.2009.6

Taleizadeh, A. A., Ahmadzadeh, K., Sarker, B. R., & Ghavamifar, A. (2022). Designing an optimal sustainable supply chain system considering pricing decisions and resilience factors. *Journal of Cleaner Production*, *332*, 129895. https://doi.org/10.1016/j.jclepro.2021.129895

Tsai, W. H., & Hung, S. J. (2009). A fuzzy goal programming approach for green supply chain optimisation under activity-based costing and performance evaluation with a value-chain structure. *International Journal of Production Research*, *47*(18), 4991–5017. https://doi.org/10.1080/00207540801932498

UN. (2022). *Stop food loss and waste, for the people, for the planet*. United Nations. https://www.un.org/en/observances/end-food-waste-day

UNDP. (2015). *Sustainable development goals | UNDP*. United Nations Development Program.

Vali-Siar, M. M., & Roghanian, E. (2022). Sustainable, resilient and responsive mixed supply chain network design under hybrid uncertainty with considering COVID-19 pandemic disruption. *Sustainable Production and Consumption*, *30*, 278–300. https://doi.org/10.1016/J.SPC.2021.12.003

Validi, S., Bhattacharya, A., & Byrne, P. J. (2014). A case analysis of a sustainable food supply chain distribution system – A multi-objective approach. *International Journal of Production Economics*, *152*, 71–87. https://doi.org/10.1016/J.IJPE.2014.02.003

Varsei, M., & Polyakovskiy, S. (2017). Sustainable supply chain network design: A case of the wine industry in Australia. *Omega*, *66*, 236–247.

Yavari, M., & Geraeli, M. (2019). Heuristic method for robust optimization model for green closed-loop supply chain network design of perishable goods. *Journal of Cleaner Production*, *226*, 282–305. https://doi.org/10.1016/j.jclepro.2019.03.279

Zahiri, B., Zhuang, J., & Mohammadi, M. (2017). Toward an integrated sustainable-resilient supply chain: A pharmaceutical case study. *Transportation Research Part E: Logistics and Transportation Review*, *103*, 109–142. https://doi.org/10.1016/j.tre.2017.04.009

Zhu, Z., Chu, F., Dolgui, A., Chu, C., Zhou, W., & Piramuthu, S. (2018). Recent advances and opportunities in sustainable food supply chain: A model-oriented review. *International Journal of Production Research*, *56*(17), 5700–5722. https://doi.org/10.1080/00207543.2018.1425014

Zobel, C. W. (2011). Representing perceived tradeoffs in defining disaster resilience. *Decision Support Systems*, *50*(2), 394–403. https://doi.org/10.1016/J.DSS.2010.10.001

DISCLOSURES: DRIVING SUPPLY CHAIN SUSTAINABILITY THROUGH ACCOUNTING

Sheetal Deo[a], Matthew Pepper[a,b], Anura De Zoysa[a] and Ciorstan Smark[a]

[a]*University of Wollongong, Australia*
[b]*Rajagiri Business School, Kochi, India*

ABSTRACT

Discourse concerning the most effective way for enterprises to offset environmental impacts is well established. While certain approaches like the Triple Bottom Line (TBL) have gained widespread acceptance, other initiatives like introducing the Carbon Tax in Australia have not been successful. This study examines the practical implementation of two environmental accounting models, the TBL and Carbon Tax, analysing their benefits and drawbacks and focusing on their application within the Australian accounting system. Using discourse and content analysis within two case studies of two different sectors – the banking sector (Westpac) and the manufacturing sector (BlueScope), this research contributes to the discourse concerning the implementation of such disclosures and how models such as the TBL and Carbon Tax initiative could be effectively used in practice. The results show that the implementation of the TBL was more widely adopted and seen as a positive factor in determining the company's environmental impact as viewed by investors. The Carbon Tax was initially adopted less frequently until modifications were made to allow for voluntary compliance. This was due to the misalignment of the cost of the tax with the financial priorities of each sector. Furthermore, the study suggests that a more comprehensive approach that leverages the strengths of both models to complement each other within an integrated framework may be the best solution for organisations seeking a more systemic approach to environmental disclosures and offsetting in their supply chain network.

Keywords: Environmental accounting; supply chain; carbon tax; triple bottom line; banking sector; manufacturing sector

Sustainable and Resilient Supply Chain
Advances in Environmental Accounting & Management, Volume 12, 49–64

ISSN: 1479-3598/doi:10.1108/S1479-359820240000012007

INTRODUCTION

The concept of environmental accounting is a complex and multifaceted topic, with numerous models and guidelines available for incorporating sustainability into accounting practices (Lieder & Markard, 2018). The United Nations Sustainable Development Goals (UN SDGs), the Triple Bottom Line (TBL) and the International Organization for Standardization (ISO) Suite are just a few examples of these models (Watanabe, 2020). Despite the importance of objective standards in accounting, the implementation of a carbon tax to account for a company's carbon footprint poses a significant challenge, as it requires a deep understanding of how to integrate this cost across different industries without negatively affecting consumers (Bai & Min, 2019). The research paper aims to evaluate the effectiveness of including the concept of carbon tax within the dimensions of a TBL within the financial statements. This paper aims to evaluate the effectiveness of the implementation of a carbon tax and the third bottom line in accounting financial reporting. Barriers that are faced in environmental accounting/carbon tax are highlighted in consideration with the practical implications on supply chain management. Thus, proper application of environmental accounting is essential to ensure that it provides meaningful and accurate information about a company's sustainability performance.

This paper uses content and discourse analysis to explore the inclusion of environmental accounting disclosures of a carbon tax and the third bottom line from 2009 to 2020 for the two case studies. Institutional theory serves as the theoretical lens employed to examine the content and discourse analysis results. Attempts to implement carbon tax within Australia were unsuccessful in the measurement scheme. It can be observed that if we blend different areas with environmental accounting and their financial reporting, such as taking concepts from the third-bottom line, we may successfully communicate more widely to the environmental stakeholder requirements both externally and within the company's needs.

Ultimately, this paper seeks an alternative to existing measures of Carbon Tax, which can be construed as punitive or inequitable by certain stakeholders or industry sectors. This is recognised as the gap in the literature. Not many journal articles have observed the way in which the carbon tax has been interpreted and whether this interpretation is effective and relevant. Consequently, the authors argue for a more blended approach that incorporates the third-bottom line with carbon tax elements in an effort to provide guidance for a more systemic and sustainable approach to supply chain-wide sustainability reporting and navigate barriers to implementation.

The research question proposed is the effectiveness of the treatment of the carbon tax measure in financial from the banking and manufacturing sector and, furthermore, the triple bottom line (TBL).

The chapter is organised as follows: The literature review is included in Section 'Literature Review'. Section 'Methodology' presents the research methodology, and analysis, findings and discussion of results are included in Section 'Results'.

Finally, the conclusions and implications of the study are included in Section 'Discussion'.

LITERATURE REVIEW

Fundamentally, '[A]ccounting provides the most important corporate system of information collection and analysis. This is reflected in the notion of being held "accountable", which means that someone has the duty to give an explanation for how resources have been used' (Schaltegger & Burritt, p. 32).

Environmental Accounting + EEA (Environmental Economic Accounting) (Disclosure: Third Bottom-Line)

Environmental accounting extends a notion incorporating and accounting for environmental factors and providing a set of guidelines that should be included in a company's financial statements, thus, introducing the 'third-bottom line' concept (the first line being income and the second being expenses) (Andrew et al., 2010). The third bottom line indicates the importance of the environment by being included in these publicly available financial statements. Another reason for the inclusion of this 'third-bottom line' was in line with the outcomes of accounting itself – to be able to have this information readily available in one place (financial statements) for all stakeholders. The 'Third Bottom Line' refers to the idea of measuring a company's social and environmental performance in addition to its financial performance, often represented by a third 'bottom line' on a financial statement. The 'Triple Bottom Line' is a more comprehensive framework that encompasses three interrelated components: economic, social, and environmental performance. It is seen as a more holistic way of measuring a company's overall performance and impact, beyond just financial results. Therefore, even if this information was not required by a stakeholder, the availability of this information provided a more comprehensive picture and increased visibility to the wider stakeholder group, which in turn may lead to different decision-making outcomes for a company given the more comprehensive overview. An example of this examined in this paper is the banking sector. Previously, this sector would not need to report on environmental factors.

> There is a growing interest and awareness in environmental responsibility, owing to increasing societal awareness of social and environmental issues. This in turn has resulted in an increase of academic publications on the topic, which have adopted different perspectives. The majority of this research has focussed on the analysis of social and environmental reports (SER), in search of the theoretical statements that justify these practices. Mata et al. (2018, p. 1198)

In doing so, it becomes accountable to stakeholders both across and external to the supply chain that may not have a vested interest in the banking sector itself but can use these financial data about the environmental presence of the business and, therefore, help inform decisions regarding whether or not investing within the business is a worthwhile strategy. This incentive has been '[F]uelled by stakeholder interest, including those of investors...' (Lokuwaduge & de Silva, 2020, p. 36).

The usage of a third bottom line has resulted in a framework to help decision-making within factors of the accounting and the environment. 'Environmental-Economic Accounting (EEA) is a framework for organising statistical information to help decision-makers better understand how the economy and the environment interact' (EEA, 2019).

> An incentive to provide this information to stakeholders is the opportunity to show the company's way in resourcefully using their influence for the better of the community. EEA (2019) and Mata et al. (2018)

All of the above factors contribute to the idea of how environmental accounting has been encapsulated through the evolution and adoption of the 'third bottom-line' in various locally based financial statements. This is an example of a positive instrument that helps navigate the environmental footprints of companies through reporting.

Environmental Accounting (Disclosure: Carbon Tax)

The idea of the third bottom line in the context of environmental accounting reporting is further extended by the notion and example of 'carbon tax' (Clean Energy Act, 2011; NSW Department of Planning and Environment, 2022). The incentive of having a tax on carbon is to provide a baseline for businesses to produce fewer carbon emissions (Zhang et al., 2016). Metcalf and Weisbach (2009, p. 1) state:

> [T]the purpose of such a tax, which we will generally refer to as a carbon tax, is to internalise externalities associated with anthropogenic climate change. Without a carbon tax, individuals face a distorted set of prices. Activities that result in carbon emissions are relatively too cheap because individuals will not consider the costs the emissions impose on others, including on future generations. A tax forces individuals to consider the full set of consequences from emissions. Metcalf and Weisbach (2009, p. 1).

Given this understanding of its purpose, carbon tax is a good idea in theory and a:

> ...promising tool for discouraging the greenhouse gas emissions that cause climate change. In principle, a well-designed tax could reduce the risk of climate change, minimise the cost of emissions reductions, encourage innovation in low-carbon technologies, and raise new public revenue. But designing a real-world carbon tax poses significant challenges. Marron and Toder (2014, p. 563).

In Australia, a carbon tax was introduced by the Gillard Labour government in 2011 as part of the Clean Energy Act 2011 (Clean Energy Act, 2011; NSW Department of Planning and Environment, 2022). This chapter examines two organisations, Westpac Banking Corporation and BlueScope Steel Limited. Both organisations included the concept of environmental accounting through the inclusion of carbon tax within their financial reporting. The purpose of the carbon tax was to counteract Australia's carbon emissions for the future:

> The Australian government introduced a carbon pricing scheme or 'carbon tax' through the Clean Energy Act 2011, which came into effect on 1 July 2012. This was one of the initiatives to control emissions in the country, with the intention that polluters would pay a certain amount as tax per tonne of carbon that they released into the atmosphere. Each year, selected entities were required to surrender one emissions unit for every tonne of carbon dioxide equivalent (CO2-e) they produced (Centre for Public Impact a BCG Foundation, 2022).

Introduced as a guideline for institutions/companies to counteract their carbon footprint, by having a requirement within financial statements to disclose this, the tax element is formed through measurement of carbon emissions and applied as:

> The carbon price of AUD23 per tonne was to apply to around 500 of the nation's biggest polluters from 1 July 2012, and would transition to a cap-and-trade emissions trading scheme on 1 July 2015, linking Australia to international carbon markets. The law was intended to transform the Australian economy and provide support to low- and middle-income households as it cut pollution and grew the economy (Centre for Public Impact a BCG Foundation, 2022).

Various limitations have been observed in the function and application of carbon tax. The first limitation was the measurement of carbon tax and its accuracy in calculating these figures (Andrew et al., 2010; Marron & Toder, 2014; Qian et al., 2020), which are based on a rate for each industry sector. For example, Westpac will have a different calculation as opposed to BlueScope and in theory, as BlueScope is a manufacturing company it should have a higher carbon footprint and resulting carbon tax expense. This questions the consistency of the tax rate application itself and the self-evaluation method of this rate. The self-evaluation method is meant to make the application of the tax easier on the company to calculate, but this raises the questions: are companies in differing sectors able to self-reflect appropriately to account for this tax expense, or can the calculation be misinterpreted, thus its application in differing sectors is not reflected correctly (Arvidsson & Dumay, 2022; Lokuwaduge & de Silva, 2020, 2022).

The second limitation is the concept of voluntary inclusion of the third bottom line and, intrinsically, the carbon tax expense. Due to the practical implications of how to mandate the carbon tax, after its introduction, this tax was added to the financial statements as a voluntary disclosure, which leads to how accounting is contributing to a subjective narrative. For example, this tax was meant to focus on or target companies with higher carbon footprints, but in its practical application, this was not feasible as companies were not honest in their calculations. In doing so, some companies passed on this additional tax to their consumers (Andrew et al., 2010; Hines, 1988; Lokuwaduge & de Silva, 2022). Consequently, this 'additional tax' is included within financial statements as a voluntary inclusion, which satisfies the need from stakeholders and communities to address the issue of accounting for the environmental contributing factors such as carbon footprints. Additionally, it also questions how the company does not actually pay this tax expense; thus technically their bottom line is not affected financially, and therefore 'if they exist, then, even without you recognising them, they are real' (Hines, 1988, p. 252 and Moses & Tauringana, 2022).

The third limitation is that of the concept of 'greenwashing'. Greenwashing is a process by which companies provide misleading information on their products that claim they are environmentally sustainable, and therefore, the company's impact is minimal to the environment (Porter & Kramer, 2006). The way in which both accounts of environmental accounting and the instrument of carbon tax have contributed to this concept is through the suggestion that the companies may suggest '[R]eductions in pollution, waste, carbon emissions, or energy use, for example, may be documented for specific divisions or regions but not for the company as a whole' (Porter & Kramer, 2006, p. 3; Elias, 2022).

It can be observed that whilst there were good intentions in the reporting and disclosure of the carbon tax, it did not lead to an effective mechanism for companies to abide by. The error fell within the calculations of this tax and the impact the tax was having on institutions that may not have borne the expenses as much, but consequently were doing so as per their financial statements such as the banking sector in comparison to the manufacturing sector. In practice, it was interpreted as a punitive measure and, therefore, as an unintended consequence, clearly influenced the behaviour of reporting to circumvent or minimise taxation.

Impact on Supply Chain

An analysis of available literature regarding Sustainable Supply Chain Management (SSCM) by Elias et al. (2021), identifies the need for a more comprehensive and holistic understanding of the 'connections between barriers that affect SSCM adoption', also highlighting that 'The links between stakeholders and performance outcomes…require further investigation' (Elias et al., 2021, p. 1485). The impact of financial instruments concerned with environmental accounting (such as carbon tax) on the broader supply chain is a critical dimension of such a holistic view and can be twofold. Firstly, any form of taxation inevitably exerts a discernible impact on the revenue and profit margins of supply chain partners and stakeholders, thereby contributing to the resilience discourse through financial lenses. Secondly and perhaps particularly from the manufacturer's perspective, 'the unit cost of the low-carbon product' (Zhang et al., 2020, p. 1; Zhou et al., 2020; Wachira & Mathuva, 2022) may well increase, thereby also impacting revenue streams. However, the intensity of production is not affected only through the market trends for the product to be manufactured (Chen, 2021; Zhang et al., 2020). It has also been suggested that to negate any negative financial ramifications of the carbon tax within the supply chain, government incentives should be taken into consideration where a 'carbon cost-sharing contract' (Yuyin & Jinxi, 2018, p. 675; Moses et al., 2022) can be entered into by manufacturing companies. This will impact the way in which carbon tax calculations affect the units of measurement and help to subside the taxation expense by sharing the cost within the same set of manufacturing types. An incentivised approach would also aid in the stewardship of correct and proper reporting rather than organisations seeking to circumvent full tax liabilities through investment in taxation planning (see Zolotoy et al., 2021).

The impact of carbon emissions is of great environmental concern, but the inclusion and implementation of such a tax effect not only an increasing cost to the supply side stakeholders but will also then affect an increasing cost to the end user (Chen, 2021; Gilbert & Weisbach, 2009; Wang et al., 2017). Therefore, critical evaluation and review of such a programme is required, that embraces a systemic view of the supply chain, focusing on how such a programme may be successfully implemented to reduce emissions but also be able to pragmatically minimise any impact on financial health for organisations and end-users. An idea put forward would be to provide an analysis for this trade-off between costs and emissions and then negotiate into a bargaining agreement whereby the government can put in some sanctions to help with the costs, so the end user does not consume it all (Chen, 2021; Fahimnia et al., 2014).

In Australia, companies are required to disclose their environmental impacts as part of their annual reporting to the Australian Securities and Investments Commission (ASIC). These disclosures can include information on greenhouse gas emissions, energy and water usage and waste management.

The implications of these disclosures for supply chains in Australia include increased transparency and accountability for companies' environmental performance. This can lead to pressure on companies to improve their environmental performance and reduce their environmental impact, both in their own operations and in their supply chains. Additionally, these disclosures can also provide useful information for investors and other stakeholders, who can use this information to make more informed decisions about the companies they invest in or do business with (Ahmed et al., 2022; Dacin et al., 2002; Oyewo et al., 2022; Sardanelli et al., 2022).

However, it's worth noting that the Australian regulations for environmental disclosures are not as strict as in some other countries, so the level of detail and accuracy of the information provided may vary. Additionally, companies may be able to use creative accounting to present their performance in a better light than it actually is. Hence, our research serves as a critical milestone in understanding the intricate interplay of environmental disclosures, carbon taxes, and the TBL approach within the Australian context, reinforcing the broader discourse on fostering Sustainable and Resilient Supply Chains.

Enhanced transparency and heightened accountability, intrinsic to environmental disclosures, serve as catalysts, exerting substantial pressure on enterprises to elevate their environmental performance, an essential underpinning of supply chain resilience. The compelling financial incentives from carbon taxes propel companies toward adopting environmentally cleaner and more sustainable practices, thereby fortifying the bedrock of supply chain resilience. Consequently, organisations witness a reduction in greenhouse gas emissions, more judicious utilisation of energy and water resources, and the implementation of robust waste management systems. The mandatory disclosure of environmental impacts empowers stakeholders, including investors, customers, and regulatory bodies, facilitating more informed decision-making regarding their engagement with or investment in these enterprises.

Carbon taxes can also play a role in improving supply chains by putting a price on carbon emissions. This creates a financial incentive for companies to reduce their emissions and invest in clean energy and technology, which can lead to more sustainable supply chains (Okwuosa, 2022). The TBL approach goes beyond the traditional financial bottom line and takes into account the social and environmental impacts of a company's operations and supply chain. By considering these three bottom lines, companies can make decisions that benefit not only their financial performance but also the Society and the environment. This gap in the literature is that few journal articles have observed how the carbon tax has been interpreted and whether this interpretation is adequate and relevant. This paper also evaluates how this impacts the TBL within the banking and manufacturing sectors.

In summary, within our investigation, we have identified a significant gap in the existing body of literature – a noticeable absence of scholarly inquiry into the nuanced interpretation of the carbon tax and its relevance in contemporary discourse. This research lacuna underscores the distinctive contribution of our study, which not only delves into the intricacies of financial implications but also examines their interdependence with the TBL framework, specifically within the banking and manufacturing sector. Our investigation, which closely scrutinises the intricate interplay among financial instruments, environmental disclosures, and the holistic ethos of the TBL, significantly enriches the ongoing discourse concerning the resilience of supply chains, particularly in response to the ever-evolving environmental dynamics and regulatory landscapes.

METHODOLOGY

An analysis is formed to explain the reasons as to what extent guidelines are implemented and reasons as to why they may not have been implemented initially. The design of the research and the analysis is to examine to what extent carbon tax reporting has been undertaken within the banking and manufacturing sectors in their financial reporting. Two case study organisations, BlueScope (manufacturing) and Westpac (banking) were reviewed in their respective annual reports for 2009 and 2020. The case study organisations were chosen because the Carbon Tax was initially implemented in 2009, and 2020 was selected as a comparison for when the carbon tax was not relevant anymore within financial reports (from 2013 onwards). These companies are also two of the largest industry sectors in Australia and were outspoken during the implementation of the Carbon Tax. Within the contexts of each financial statement for Westpac and BlueScope, we reviewed the inclusion of the carbon tax disclosure and its impact on the financial statement. The reasoning behind choosing Westpac and BlueScope is to capture the essence of how two different sectors, such as a financial institution such as Westpac and a manufacturing company such as BlueScope, convey the inclusion of a carbon tax with the overriding factor of environmental accounting within their financial statement. From this, the analysis can interpret the influence/hindrance this has on the overall nature of the financial statements and whether this inclusion of a third-bottom line factor is contributing to a 'well-rounded' company in either sector. Discourse and content analysis are then used to highlight how both companies identify with how they interpret the disclosure of both a carbon tax and third-bottom line. These methods allowed the research to examine and develop a deeper understanding of the financial statements within the two companies using the companies' available financial data.

The methodology undertaken will be a combination of discourse and content analysis. Though the use of discourse and content analysis methods seems contradictory in their application, the use of both provides a comprehensive approach to how the data is interpreted. Content analysis follows a methodical approach to the data, whereas discourse analysis allows for an interpretive and subjective approach to occur by examining the text intricately through the usage of words and how they add to the report. Using discourse and content analysis in conjunction with each other provides an intricate approach to how the research can be explored.

The first interpretive method used in the paper is discourse analysis. Discourse analysis, as discussed by Phillips and Jorgensen (2002), is the study of discourse (text, speech) and analysis of what is said and written. It assumes that the influence of the discourse is greater than the participants in it, and that these participants are aware of it (Patton, 2014; Phillips & Jorgensen, 2002). Discourse analysis examines the way in which the interpretation of the carbon tax guideline is implemented within the company's financial reports over the two years of 2009 and 2020. Hence, a composite examination of the different understandings within the reports is conducted. It examines if there is ambiguity contained in the way in which definitions are written and then interpreted or if it is due to external factors such as budgets and time that prevented councils from implementing the guidelines.

The second method used is content analysis. Content analysis applies a systematic approach to the data analysis. Whereas discourse allows for interpretation within the definition to suit the context, content analysis is a mere version of word counting within the text. The interpretation is done at the discourse level. Content analysis is a technique that studies the written material and reduces it to meaningful units using carefully applied rules (Beck et al., 2010; Glasser & Strauss, 2012; Krippendorff, 2004; Patton, 2014). In the context of this research, content analysis involves a systematic reading of the financial reports from both Westpac and BlueScope, which utilises the guidelines from the carbon tax guideline and examines the way in which certain words, such as carbon and environmental, are applied in their financial reports. Though a content analysis approach has a methodical style in the way in which words and texts can be categorised and then further evaluated to find a distinctive feature, it has an interpretive nature, which allows meaning to be formed through this methodical analysis. This affects the data analysis simultaneously by providing an examination of a quantitative approach by observing how the financial reports have taken precautions by implementing the carbon tax guidelines within the company's financial reports. The qualitative approach outlines how specific concepts have been used in the report and whether these concepts apply to the local council context.

RESULTS

The analysis is broken up into two specific areas of analysis. Firstly, the examination of the data was taken from the perspective of searching for key terms such as 'carbon, environment/al, tax, accounting and supply', within the financial statements of Westpac and BlueScope. From this, an interpretation analysis will be conducted on how many times and to what effect these terms are used within the two reports over the 2-year cycles of 2009 (this was when the proposed carbon tax was to be introduced within the reports) and 2020 (after 2009, it was discussed that the carbon tax was ineffective in measuring the rate of carbon and therefore, the tax will not be included within the financials, and the use of a 'third-bottom' line was now voluntary) (Andrew et al., 2010). The second part of the analysis was to investigate the actual usage or inclusion of a carbon tax calculation component and how they calculated this function. From this, the paper will endeavour to see the differences between the year that carbon tax was introduced in 2009 and the year in which carbon tax inclusion was not compulsory but highly recommended in 2020.

Within the context of this research, two elements of disclosure within environmental accounting were examined. These were the third bottom line and carbon tax. From this, the findings for the third bottom line were that it was implemented as part of contextual overhaul within accounting financial reporting, to include the environment as a factor for stakeholders to consider when considering investment within a company.

Similarly, to navigate and minimise our carbon footprint, the carbon tax was meant to achieve a similar outlook, but due to the financial ramifications of it and the consequential effect on the company's profits, it did not have a similar implementation and accepted presence within the financial reporting. This was due to this particular instrument being hard to measure and effectively accounting for all sectors (banking and manufacturing) similarly. It was also difficult to correctly measure the effect of carbon within each industry. From the report analysis, Westpac sometimes had more of a carbon outlay than BlueScope (measured on a monthly basis), which does not reflect in the sector in which both companies individually reside. From this, it can also be observed that when implementing the carbon tax, the barriers faced within the calculations and the outlay of these expenses within the company's finances were not accurately tested within the financial space before implementation; when applying it, the gaps started to appear.

However, in relation to how the third-bottom line was implemented, this was communicated as a factor that stakeholders could use to invest in not just the company and its financials (short term) but also what the company was doing for the environment and itself (long-term). The incentives were similar, both contributing to lessening the depletion of a company's footprint within the environment, but dissimilar in the approach which the government promoted and eventually, the application of carbon tax was not applicable within all sectors as easily as once assumed. This shares a coinciding ideal that the institution of the government relays ideas, but once implemented, these ideas can either be adopted effectively or need to be changed to be adopted, as seen with a carbon tax, the voluntary reporting without the financial consequences of a tax has been widely accepted. This is due to, the ingraining of deeper sociological barriers and questioning why an institution like a bank may need to outline its response to a carbon tax. And if it's required, how can they actually account for it being in an institution that does not readily actually produce carbon within that sector.

A consideration should be made at having a hybrid of the two third-bottom line and carbon tax, whereby, an element of a voluntary disclosure would be made within the financial statements. Therefore, this will show the stakeholders what the company could have incurred and allow them to also show the stakeholders what they are doing to negate such emissions.

Overall, the findings indicate that the implementation of the TBL, within the context of carbon tax, was call to action as opposed to understanding the underlying implications of it. Because this implementation did not have a financial impact on their bottom-line, the inclusion of this was a more societal answer to environmental accountability than actually the understanding of the impact the business is making on the environment.

DISCUSSION

The concept of environmental accounting is a societally driven method to account for the environment within the financial statements of organisations. Conceptually, the inclusion of such information makes absolute sense against a background of increasing stakeholder awareness of important environmental issues. However, as seen through the presented findings, in practice, it is a hard concept to adopt and implement effectively due to the different needs and requirements of different industry sectors.

The concept of greenwashing, as defined by Porter and Kramer (2006), involves presenting idealistic principles of environmental accounting, which are often disconnected from the realities of business operations. This can lead to misleading financial reporting that is justified by societal expectations rather than actual business performance. For instance, the reporting and disclosure of carbon tax can result in vastly different measurements between the banking and manufacturing industries, potentially leading to understated performance and negatively skewed income reporting even when the performance was not actually negative in a given year. This is seen through the way in which both companies present the carbon tax figures in a separate line contained within the TBL and, furthermore, the profit and loss statement. This, in a way, highlights the fact that they have taken it into consideration, but it also highlights that this incentive does not actually portray any real ramifications to both the companies' actual bottom-line.

It was also observed that the application and measurability of carbon tax must also be further considered. Existing models do not suit all industry sectors and therefore may lead to unintended consequences such as greenwashing or lobbying against its use. It can be seen from the findings that, comparatively, the manufacturing sector will have the most carbon output. Given the physical nature of the outputs and processes of manufacturing, this may be easier to accept than within more service-based contexts such as the banking and finance sector. It is argued that different carbon measurements should be made to counteract the differences in industry sector.

The issue of unequal carbon measurements between different industry sectors has been addressed by researchers, who argue that standardisation is necessary to counteract the inconsistencies in carbon reporting. For example, a study by Jenkins and Yakovleva (2011) suggests that 'different industries have different carbon footprints and therefore, a one-size-fits-all approach to carbon reporting is not appropriate'. This highlights the need for sector-specific measurements to ensure accountability and provide a fair comparison between similar industries. Similarly, a report by Unerman and O'Dwyer (2010) states that 'without standardised carbon measurements, the implementation of the carbon tax within financial calculations will vary greatly between industries and may not accurately reflect their true carbon footprint'. These findings support the idea that carbon measurements must be tailored to the needs of each industry to accurately reflect their performance and minimise the risk of greenwashing. This is again observed by the discrepancy in the figures between the two industries and how they measure it. For example, the figures in the banking sector seem to be a higher figure of carbon tax. However, this should be the case for the manufacturing industry.

Another aspect for consideration is the enforceability and accountability of such a practice. If this idea of environmental accounting is based on societal needs, it should also account for industrial needs as well. For example, it needs to be considered the effectiveness of reporting carbon emissions figures for each industry type, such as the banking sector, and what values they require to report.

In light of the carbon tax, it was not effective within the needs of industry. Therefore, this reporting has now become voluntary. This is a reflection of the implementation of a deeper discussion on how barriers are formed between societal needs and industry obligations, how these barriers can be removed through better comprehensive accountability through narrative and not taxation enforceability based on a government calculation for it and how frameworks can be implemented to account for each industrial and societal needs.

When adopting an environmental accounting lens to consider the whole supply chain, supply chain members (and stakeholders) must carefully consider the potential impact (both positive and negative) of any individual instrument. Emerging from the recent disruptions of the last two to three years, it is well known that transparency and traceability are significant issues in supply chains, whether local or global in nature. A renewed focus and discourse on the practical applicability of environmental accounting techniques such as those discussed may provide a partial solution to such systemic problems (Hines, 1988). With renewed momentum and societal focus on key issues such as environmental impact and sustainability, new mechanisms for environmental accounting and disclosure, such as a hybridised TBL-carbon tax framework, may be used to guide supply chains to map and consider their entire structure and networks through a different lens (Chen et al., 2020). Such an approach, using environmental or emission-based metrics, could be used to work towards a more systemic view of supply chain footprints and the total environmental footprint for specific products or outputs. This could also form the basis for a 'total environmental cost' index, using the systemic view to manage emissions and environmental impact across the whole supply chain network.

However, such an approach would need to be strictly regulated to avoid any unintended consequences, such as a supply chain network discharging the accountability of a particularly high-emitting partner organisation by offsetting their outputs with the inclusion of low-emitting supply chain partners. Such an approach would complement traditional approaches to supply chain mapping and may even lead to more traditional improvement outcomes such as 'better, faster cheaper'. For example, when analysed through a lens of environmental impact, functions such as manufacturing, logistics or warehousing could well experience increases in efficiency or quality as lower emitting/environmental impact solutions are implemented.

CONCLUSION

In conclusion, this study has explored the intricate interplay between environmental disclosures and financial statements, shedding light on their significant implications for supply chain sustainability and resilience. This research has addressed the broader thematic context of Sustainable and Resilient Supply Chains, aligning with the overarching concerns of contemporary business and environmental discourse.

The theoretical insights gleaned from our investigation centred on integrating the carbon tax and the TBL framework within corporate financial practices. Notably, the TBL approach demonstrated greater acceptance due to its lesser financial impact compared to the carbon tax, reflecting the stakeholder demand for transparent insights into a company's environmental footprint and corresponding mitigation strategies – a critical facet of supply chain resilience.

We acknowledge the limitation of our study, primarily its focus on two sectors, banking and manufacturing. The need for comprehensive research across diverse sectors to enhance our understanding of supply chain resilience within the context of environmental disclosures is evident.

In summary, this research emphasises the pivotal role of environmental accounting in contemporary financial discourse and its potential impact on supply chain management. As environmental concerns intersect with financial considerations, our findings highlight the importance of exploring strategies seamlessly integrating environmental accounting. By mitigating the financial implications associated with environmental disclosures, we can facilitate their broader adoption across various facets of financial accounting, thus contributing to the overarching goal of fostering Sustainable and Resilient Supply Chains.

Furthermore, our study underscores the value of both voluntary and involuntary disclosure frameworks in response to growing societal demands for sustainability practices. Nonetheless, the accuracy and precision of environmental calculations in financial reports remain areas requiring continued attention, particularly to benefit accounting and supply chain professionals. Establishing transparent feedback mechanisms remains vital regardless of the chosen environmental accounting framework. These mechanisms effectively communicate the progress of sustainability initiatives and their role in achieving strategic priorities, ultimately contributing to the realisation of Sustainable and Resilient Supply Chains.

REFERENCES

Ahmed, S., Chapple, L., Christ, K., & Osborne, S. (2022). Modern slavery risk disclosures in business operations and supply chains. In V. Tauringana & O. Moses (Eds.), *Environmental sustainability and agenda 2030. Advances in environmental accounting & management* (Vol. 10, pp. 67–104). Emerald Publishing Limited.

Andrew, J., Kaidonis, M. A., & Andrew, B. (2010). Carbon tax: Challenging neoliberal solutions to climate change. *Critical Perspectives on Accounting*, *21*(7), 611–618.

Arvidsson, S., & Dumay, J. (2022). Corporate ESG reporting quantity, quality and performance: Where to now for environmental policy and practice? *Business Strategy and the Environment*, *31*(3), 1091–1110.

Bai, J., & Min, Y. (2019). Environmental accounting and carbon tax policy. *International Journal of Economics, Commerce and Management*, *7*(2), 1–7.

Beck, A. C., Campbell, D., & Shrives, P. J. (2010). Content analysis in environment reporting research: Enrichment and rehearsal of the method in a British – German context. *The British Accounting Review*, *42*, 207–222.

Centre for Public Impact a BCG Foundation. (2022). https://www.centreforpublicimpact.org/case-study/carbon-tax-australia#:~:text=The%20Australian%20government%20introduced%20a,development%20of%20clean%20energy%20technologies. Accessed on 30 August 2022.

Chen, S. (2021). The technical impacts of the carbon tax in China. *Discover Sustainability*, *2*, 51. https://doi.org/10.1007/s43621-021-00060-9

Chen, X., Yang, H., Wang, X., & Choi, T. M. (2020). Optimal carbon tax design for achieving low carbon supply chains. *Annals of Operations Research*, 1–28.

Clean Energy Act. (2011). *Clean Energy Act*. https://www.legislation.gov.au/Details/C2011A00131. Accessed on 30 August 2022.

Dacin, T. M., Goodstein, J., & Richard, W. S. (2002). Institutional theory and institutional change: Introduction to the special research forum. *Academy of Management Journal*, *45*(1), 45–57.

Elias, A. A. (2022). Multi-stakeholder participation for achieving sustainable development goals: A systems thinking approach. In V. Tauringana & O. Moses (Eds.), *Environmental sustainability and agenda 2030. Advances in environmental accounting and management* (Vol. 10, pp. 45–65). Emerald Publishing Limited.

Elias, A. A., Donadelli, F., Paiva, E. L., & Bacic Araujo, P. P. (2021). Analysing the complexities of sustainable wood supply chain in the Amazon: A systems thinking approach. *International Journal of Logistics Management*, *32*(4), 1481–1505. https://doi.org/10.1108/IJLM-07-2020-0276

Environmental-Economic Accounting (EEA). (2019). https://eea.environment.gov.au/#:~:text=Environmental%2DEconomic%20Accounting%20(EEA)%20is%20a%20framework%20for%20organising,economy%20and%20the%20environment%20interact

Fahimnia, B., Sarkis, J., Choudhury, A., & Eshragh, A. (2014). Tactical supply chain planning under a carbon tax policy scheme: A case study. *International Journal of Production Economics*, *164*, 206–215.

Gilbert, E. M., & Weisbach, D. A. (2009). The design of a carbon tax. *University of Chicago Public Law & Legal Theory Working Paper*, No. 254.

Glasser, B. G., & Strauss, A. L. (2012). The discovery of grounded theory: Strategies for qualitative research. http://books.google.com.au/books?hl=en&lr=&id=rtiNK68Xt08C&oi=fnd&pg=PP1&dq=grounded+theory+article&ots=UVtTYiXDYI&sig=bV_O1yHdtVxizRezkCT7H l6Ja1k#v=onepage&q=grounded%20theory%20article&f=false. Accessed on 30 August 2022.

Hines, R. D. (1988). Financial accounting: In communicating reality, we construct reality. *Accounting, Organisations and Society*, *13*(3), 251–261.

Jenkins, H., & Yakovleva, N. (2011). Corporate social and environmental reporting: A review of the literature and a longitudinal study of UK disclosure. *Accounting, Auditing & Accountability Journal*, *24*(1), 20–44.

Krippendorff, K. (2004). *Content analysis introduction to its methodology*. Sage Publications, Inc.

Lieder, C., & Markard, J. (2018). Innovations in environmental accounting: Current trends and future directions. *Journal of Cleaner Production*, *195*, 23–33.

Lokuwaduge, C. S., & de Silva, K. (2020). Emerging corporate disclosure of environmental social and governance (ESG) risks: An Australian study. *Australasian Accounting, Business and Finance Journal*, *14*(2), 35–50.

Lokuwaduge, C. S., & de Silva, K. M. (2022). ESG risk disclosure and the risk of green washing. *Australasian Accounting, Business and Finance Journal*, *16*(1), 146–159.

Marron, D. B., & Toder, E. J. (2014). Tax policy issues in designing a carbon tax. *The American Economic Review: Papers & Proceedings*, *104*(5), 563–568.

Mata, C., Fiahlo, A., & Eugenio, T. (2018). A decade of environmental accounting reporting: What we know? *Journal of Cleaner Production*, *198*, 1198–1209.

Metcalf, G. E., & Weisbach, D. A. (2009). The design of a carbon tax. University of Chicago Public Law & Legal Theory Working Paper No. 254.

Moses, O., Nnam, I. J., Olaniyan, J. D., & Tariquzzaman, A. (2022). Sustainable development goals (SDGS): Assessment of implementation progress in BRICS and MINT. In V. Tauringana & O. Moses (Eds.), *Environmental sustainability and agenda 2030. Advances in environmental accounting & management* (Vol. 10, pp. 11–44). Emerald Publishing Limited.

Moses, O., & Tauringana, V. (2022). Environmental sustainability and the progress towards agenda 2030. In V. Tauringana & O. Moses (Eds.), *Environmental sustainability and agenda 2030. Advances in environmental accounting & management* (Vol. 10, pp. 1–9). Emerald Publishing Limited.

NSW Department of Planning and Environment. (2022). https://www.planning.nsw.gov.au/Policy-and-Legislation/Renewable-Energy. Accessed on 30 August 2022.

Okwuosa, I. I. (2022). Examining disclosure of contribution towards SDG-6 and its motivation among Nigeria's premium board companies. In V. Tauringana & O. Moses (Eds.), *Environmental sustainability and agenda 2030. Advances in environmental accounting & management* (Vol. 10, pp. 135–157). Emerald Publishing Limited.

Oyewo, B., Tawiah, V., & Zakari, A. (2022). Actualising agenda 2030 through sustainability accounting: Evidence from the Nigerian manufacturing sector. In V. Tauringana & O. Moses (Eds.), *Environmental sustainability and agenda 2030. Advances in environmental accounting & management* (Vol. 10, pp. 105–133). Emerald Publishing Limited.

Patton, M. Q. (2014). *Qualitative research and evaluation methods*. SAGE Publications Ltd.

Phillips, L., & Jorgensen, M. W. (2002). *Discourse analysis as theory and method*. SAGE Publications Ltd.

Porter, M. E., & Kramer, M. R. (2006). The link between competitive advantage and corporate social responsibility. *Harvard Business Review*, 78–94.

Qian, W., Suryani, A. W., & Xing, K. (2020). Does carbon performance matter to market returns during climate policy changes? Evidence from Australia. *Journal of Cleaner Production*, *259*, 121.

Sardanelli, D., Bittucci, L., Mirone, F., & Marzioni, S. (2022). An integrative framework for supply chain rating: From financial-based to ESG-based rating models. *Total Quality Management and Business Excellence*, 1–20.

Unerman, J., & O'Dwyer, B. (2010). Corporate social responsibility and financial performance: A review of the evidence. *Accounting, Auditing & Accountability Journal*, *23*(1), 9–42.

Wachira, M. M., & Mathuva, D. M. (2022). Corporate environmental reporting in sub-Saharan Africa: A literature review and suggestions for further research. In V. Tauringana & O. Moses (Eds.),

Environmental sustainability and agenda 2030. Advances in environmental accounting & management (Vol. 10, pp. 159–182). Emerald Publishing Limited.

Wang, C., Wang, W., & Hunag, R. (2017). Supply chain enterprise operations and government carbon tax decisions considering carbon emissions. *Journal of Cleaner Production*, *152*, 271–280.

Watanabe, Y. (2020). Environmental accounting models: A review and comparison. *Sustainability*, *12*(15), 5309.

Yuyin, Y., & Jinxi, L. (2018). The effect of governmental policies of carbon taxes and energy-saving subsidies on enterprise decisions in a two-echelon supply chain. *Journal of Cleaner Production*, *181*, 675–691.

Zhang, H., Li, P., Zheng, H., & Zhang, Y. (2020). Impact of carbon tax on enterprise operation and production strategy for low-carbon products in a co-opetition supply chain. *Journal of Cleaner Production*, *287*, 1–11.

Zhang, Z., Zhang, A., Wang, D., Li, A., & Song, H. (2016). How to improve the performance of carbon tax in China? *Journal of Cleaner Production*, *142*, 2060–2072.

Zhou, X., Wei, X., Lin, J., Tian, X., Lev, B., & Wang, S. (2020). Supply chain management under carbon taxes: A review and bibliometric analysis. *Omega*, *98*, 1–16.

Zolotoy, L., O'Sullivan, D., Martin, G. P., & Wiseman, R. M. (2021). Stakeholder agency relationships: CEO stock options and corporate tax avoidance. *Journal of Management Studies*, *58*, 782–814. https://doi.org/10.1111/joms.12623

SUPPLY CHAIN DISRUPTIONS AND THEIR IMPACT ON ENERGY SECTOR DURING COVID-19

Lijo John, Wojciech D. Piotrowicz and Aino Ruggiero

Hanken School of Economics, Finland

ABSTRACT

The impact of COVID-19 on the lives of people and businesses across the globe was devastating. While governments across the world had undertaken a slew of measures to control the spread of the COVID-19 virus within their geography, many of these measures had long and unintended consequences. The restrictions imposed by the governments on the movement of people and goods across the world brought supply chains to a grinding halt. This study identifies the cascading effects of supply chain disruptions (SCDs) on the energy sector and thereby on the security of supply of energy from a European Union perspective. Since these systems are closely integrated and the impact of COVID-19 needs to be analysed at a much broader level, this study uses a systems-thinking approach to study the effect of SCDs on energy services. The study develops a causal loop model to gain further insight into how SCDs caused by COVID-19 affected the coping capabilities of society and how critical services were affected. Furthermore, the study puts forth certain policy recommendations for both businesses and governments to prepare for and protect against a similar situation in the future.

Keywords: Qualitative systems model; COVID-19; energy supply chain; supply chain disruptions; system dynamics; disaster management; group model building

INTRODUCTION

Recent trends and developments in supply chains, such as the increase in the outsourcing of manufacturing and research and development to suppliers, the

Sustainable and Resilient Supply Chain
Advances in Environmental Accounting & Management, Volume 12, 65–92

Published under exclusive licence by Emerald Publishing Limited
ISSN: 1479-3598/doi:10.1108/S1479-359820240000012009

reduction of supplier base to gain competitive advantage and reduction in inventory and lead time buffers for improving efficiency, have created lean and interconnected supply chains that are often vulnerable to disruptions (Hasani & Khosrojerdi, 2016; Ivanov et al., 2016; Rezapour et al., 2017). Furthermore, the integrated nature of supply chains indicates that it is not possible to manage the disruptions and risks associated with these disruptions within a single stage; there can often be a ripple effect across the supply chain due to disruptions (Dolgui et al., 2018). This has been the concern of businesses for a long time, and industry efforts to combat supply chain disruptions (SCDs) have focused on formulating either supply chain–wide or company-specific strategies (Ivanov et al., 2018). However, recent COVID-19-induced SCDs indicate that global supply chains are still vulnerable to disruptions and can potentially have long-lasting impacts on multiple global economies simultaneously (Moosavi et al., 2022; Pujawan & Bah, 2022).

SCD is an unexpected event that stops or slows the normal flow of material with potentially negative consequences to supply chain members (Chopra & Sodhi, 2004). At a broad level, SCDs are usually classified based on their causes, such as acts of nature (e.g. flooding, earthquakes, hurricanes and pandemics). While this cause-based classification identifies the underlying reasons for these disruptions, it is often much more useful to further classify them based on various other factors. This has led to multiple classifications of SCDs. Ivanov et al. (2017) classified SCD based on the level or echelon at which the disruption has occurred: production-based disruption, supply-based disruption and transportation disruption. Chopra and Sodhi (2014) classified SCD based on the causes of disruption. They identified that SCDs can be caused by disasters, delays in commerce systems, forecasts, intellectual property, procurement, receivables, inventory and capacity. Other classifications for SCDs are based on frequency of occurrence (Tang et al., 2014), nature and their source of origin (Christopher et al., 2011) and who they affect, from broad to specific (Dolgui & Ivanov, 2021).

The impact of SCDs has also been studied in detail in the supply chain literature. The main impacts on businesses can be broadly classified into operational, marketing and financial (Katsaliaki et al., 2021). Operational impacts may include, for example, a failure to meet the end customer demand because of product unavailability, partially fulfiled orders, late deliveries, logistic challenges, the use of alternative transportation sources for product deliveries and higher administrative costs (Jabbarzadeh et al., 2018; Wagner & Neshat, 2012). Some of the marketing impacts due to SCDs include an increase in customer complaints, damage to brand reputation, loss of customers, breach of supplier contracts, penalties associated with breach of contracts and failure to meet legal or regulatory requirements (Ponomarov & Holcomb, 2009). Financial impacts include, for example, loss of sales and revenue, reduced market share, production shutdown and reduction in asset utilisation (Ivanov, 2017).

However, what has been lacking in studies related to SCDs is their impact on the security of the supply of critical services, such as energy. The International Energy Agency (IEA) is mandated to promote energy security among 29 member countries. Member countries include European states such as Austria, Belgium,

Czech Republic, Denmark, Estonia, Finland, France, Germany, Greece, Hungary, Iceland, Italy, Norway, Poland, Portugal, Spain, Sweden and Switzerland (IEA, 2014). According to the IEA, energy security means that energy sources are available uninterruptedly and at an affordable price. In the short term, the energy system must be able to react to supply and demand risks. Sources of risks can be further categorised as technical, human-made and natural. Technical risk sources include, for example, failure of transmission lines, power plants or transformers. In contrast, human-made risks include demand fluctuations, withholding of suppliers, terrorism, wars and export embargos. Natural risks include risks such as natural disasters and the depletion of fossil fuel stock. Technology advancements, shifting market trends and environmental issues all contribute to the ongoing evolution of the risk environment for the energy sector (Larsen et al., 2017).

SCDs caused by COVID-19 had far-reaching impacts on energy security. Many energy companies experienced the dual shock of the rapidly changing demand profile of consumers and the demand itself. SCDs also affected energy generation capabilities and energy generation capacity. For instance, China produces more than 60% of the world's solar panels and accounts for nearly 58% of world's wind turbine production capacity. It also supplies roughly 75% of the world's lithium-ion batteries, among many other components (Nahm & Urpelainen, 2022). With disruptions in the supply chain, clean energy projects have been on hold for several months, and many of them have been stalled indefinitely. This was primarily due to challenges in procurement, manufacturing, assembly, shipping and logistics, which were affected due to the shutdown because of COVID-19 (Henze, 2022). This had an unintended impact on sustainable energy production, and once again, fossil fuels started to gain traction as sources of energy (Henze, 2022).

To summarise the preceding discussion, COVID-19 has shed light on the intricate relationship between the security of the supply of energy and SCDs. In the modern world, products and services depend on the intricate supply chain network (SCN) connecting buyers, sellers and consumers. Any disruption in the supply chain often has far-reaching impacts. While previous studies on SCDs have primarily focused on business and commercial aspects, the societal impact of these disruptions has received much less attention. In this line of thought, the impact of SCD caused by COVID-19 on the security of the supply of energy was brought to the attention of policymakers and energy companies. Any disruption of energy services causes a severe societal impact and might even be detrimental to people's lives, as observed during the COVID-19 peaks. This study aims to address this gap in the literature by exploring the impact of SCDs due to COVID-19 on the security of the energy supply. The study further aims to identify the major impacts of SCDs on the energy supply chain. Finally, the study also aims to identify how the security of the supply of energy is connected to the coping capability of society towards a crisis such as COVID-19.

CONTEXT OF THE STUDY

Security of Supply in the European Union

Energy policy is a shared competence between the European Union and its Member States. Security of supply (of energy) is one of the five mutually reinforcing dimensions of the EU's Energy Union strategy. To a certain extent, a common energy policy has existed since the beginning of the European integration process. Concrete developments towards a single EU energy market, however, began in the 1990s (Wilson & Doberva, 2019). Fig. 1 summarises the various directives in the EU that deal with supply security.

The legislative focus on supply security came into existence in the aftermath of a series of terrorist attacks in the first part of the 21st century. In response to these attacks, the European Council asked for the preparation of an overall strategy to protect critical infrastructure. They identified that the risk of another potentially catastrophic terrorist attack that can affect critical infrastructure is high (Lazari, 2014). However, the consequences of such an attack on the industrial control systems of critical infrastructure could vary widely. The call identified that critical infrastructures consist of physical and information technology facilities, networks, services and assets that, if disrupted or destroyed, would have a serious impact on the health, safety, security or economic well-being of citizens and the effective functioning of governments in the Member States. Critical infrastructures extend across many sectors of the economy, including banking and finance, transport and distribution, energy, utilities, health, food supply and communications, as well as key government services. Some critical elements in these sectors are not, strictly speaking, 'infrastructure' but are, in fact, networks or supply chains that support the delivery of an essential product or service (EU, 2004).

In 2005, Justice and Home Affairs called for a final proposal for the European Programme for Critical Infrastructure Protection (EPCIP). The general objective of the EPCIP was to improve the protection of critical infrastructures in the EU by creating an EU framework concerning the protection of critical infrastructures. The framework consisted of a procedure for the identification and designation of European Critical Infrastructures (ECIs), measures designed to facilitate the implementation of EPCIP, support for Member States concerning National Critical Infrastructures (NCI), contingency plans to ensure security of supply and accompanying financial measures (EU, 2006).

While the protection of ECIs began as a counterterrorism measure, the Member States realised that an all-hazard approach would be beneficial to ensure the safety and effective functioning of ECIs (Pursiainen, 2009). Under this approach, anthropogenic technological threats and natural disasters should also be considered for the critical infrastructure protection plan, but the threat of terrorism should be given priority. As a first step, it was decided to identify and designate ECIs and assess their needs to improve their protection. The 2008 EU directive concentrated on the energy and transport sectors to ensure their security and operations (EU, 2008). The ECI directive (2008) also mentioned that each Member State should come up with operator security plans or equivalent

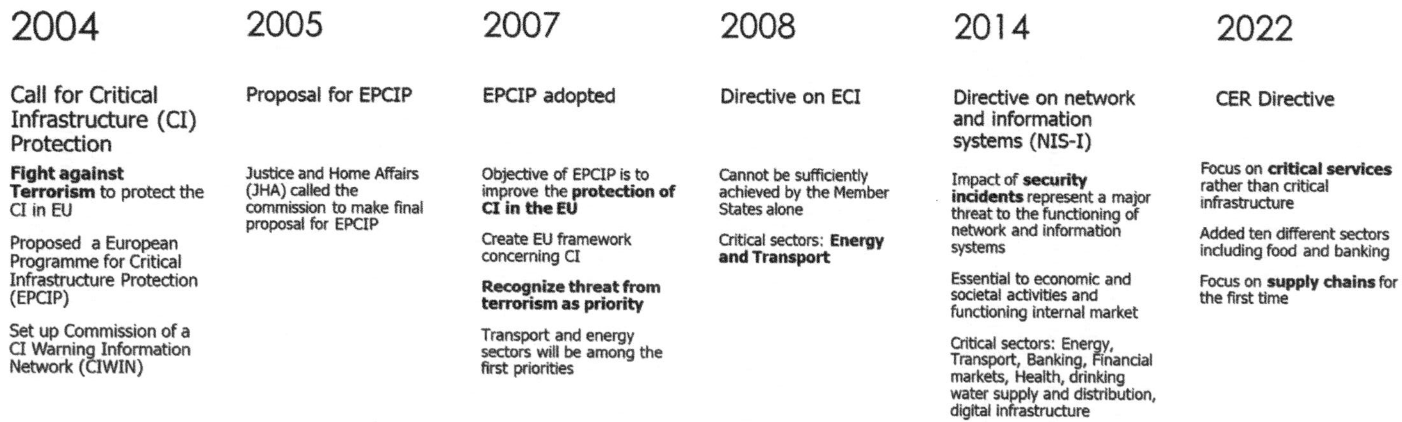

Fig. 1. Evolution of Security of Supply in the EU. *Source:* Authors.

measures comprising an identification of important assets, a risk assessment and the identification, selection and prioritisation of counter measures and procedures in all designated ECIs (EU, 2008).

In 2016, the EU passed another directive called the Directive on security of network and information systems (NIS-I). NIS-I identified that networks, information systems and services play a vital role in society. Their reliability and security are essential to economic and societal activities and the functioning of the internal market (Fantin et al., 2021). NIS-I expanded the purview from just energy and transport to other sectors, including banking, financial markets, health, drinking water supply and distribution and digital infrastructure. In addition to cross-sectoral factors, the NIS-I also discussed sector-specific factors that should be considered to determine whether an incident would have a significant disruptive effect on the provision of an essential service (EU, 2016).

In the wake of the COVID-19 pandemic, the ECI directive (2008) was revisited to evaluate standing, considering new challenges. A 2019 evaluation of the ECI directive (2008) concluded that existing European and national measures of each Member States face challenges in enabling operators to address the operational challenges they face. Furthermore, the interdependent nature of vulnerabilities often leads to a complex risk landscape within which multiple critical infrastructures operate. Some of the most pertinent reasons were, first, that operators are not fully aware of or do not fully understand the implications of the dynamic risk landscape within which they operate. Second, resilience efforts diverge significantly between Member States and sectors. Third, similar types of entities are recognised as being critical by some Member States but not by others, meaning that comparable entities receive varying degrees of official capacity-building support (in the form of, e.g. guidance, training and exercise organisation), depending on where they operate in the EU, and are subject to different requirements (EU, 2020).

The new Critical Entities Resilience (CER, 2022) framework identifies that given the increasing interconnection among infrastructures, networks and operators delivering essential services across the internal market, it is necessary to fundamentally switch the current approach from protecting specific assets towards reinforcing the resilience of the critical entities that operate them. Thus, the implication of this is clear – a disruption affecting the service provision by one operator in one sector has the potential to generate cascading effects on service provision in other sectors and potentially in other Member States or across the entire EU. Keeping this in mind, the new CER directive (2022) focuses on preventing incidents from occurring through disaster risk reduction and climate adaptation measures; ensuring adequate physical protection of sensitive areas, facilities and other infrastructure, including fencing, barriers, perimeter monitoring tools and routines, as well as detection equipment and access controls; resisting and mitigating the consequences of incidents, including the implementation of risk and crisis management procedures and protocols and alert routines; and recovering from incidents, including business continuity measures and the identification of alternative supply chains (EU, 2020).

One of the key aspects of the new CER directive (2022) was identifying the role supply chains play in ensuring the operation of the ECI. The EU identified that major crises, such as the COVID-19 pandemic, have shown the importance of ensuring the security of the supply chain and have demonstrated how its disruption can have a negative economic and societal impact across a large number of sectors and across borders. Therefore, Member States were directed to consider the effects on the supply chain, to the extent possible, when determining the extent to which other sectors and subsectors depend on the essential service provided by a critical entity. The directive specifically stated that Member States will take adequate measures to recover from incidents, duly considering business continuity measures and the identification of alternative supply chains, in order to resume the provision of the essential service (EU, 2022).

LITERATURE REVIEW

The disruption of supply chains during the COVID-19 period is a well-documented fact. The impact of these disruptions has been phenomenal and has spread through national and international boundaries, cascading across various sectors. This section summarises the impact of COVID-19 on energy consumption and the impact of COVID-19-led SCDs on the energy industry in the EU.

Supply Chain Disruptions

The impacts of COVID-19 on supply chains were far more disruptive than any localised disaster would have. The pandemic-induced disruptions have three specific characteristics that make them distinct. First, the pandemic had a long-term disruption and was unpredictable in its scaling (Dai et al., 2021). Second, the pandemic caused simultaneous disruption propagation in the supply chain (i.e. the ripple effect) and epidemic outbreak propagation in the population (i.e. pandemic propagation) (Ivanov, 2022). Finally, the pandemic also caused disruptions in supply, demand and logistics infrastructure (Diop, 2020). These characteristics were not unique to COVID-19 but were observed previously in Severe Acute Respiratory Syndrome, Middle East Respiratory Syndrome, Ebola and swine flu outbreaks (Dasaklis et al., 2012).

In the past few decades, supply chains have moved towards efficiency and cost reduction. One way to improve the efficiency of supply chains is to leverage economies of scale, reduce safety stock and focus on the sole source of suppliers to be strategically integrated into supply chain planning (Parmigiani et al., 2011). With improvements in data-capturing mechanisms and data analytics, centralised supply chain planners get better insights into the supply chain process in real time. Armed with computational power for better visibility into the supply chain process, managers across the world were able to save billions of dollars through supply chain process optimisation. However, the major side effect of these optimisations was that the supply chains became extremely fragile and would break down even at the slightest disruption since not enough cushions were built into the process (Ivanov et al., 2016). This was most evident during the COVID-19 pandemic, when supply chains were under severe stress owing to supply and demand shocks (Atkinson et al., 2020). A report by the corporate data analytics firm Dun and Bradstreet (2020) says that 51,000 companies around the world have one or more direct suppliers in Wuhan (the epicentre of the COVID-19 outbreak) and at least 5 million companies around the world have one or more tier-two suppliers in the Wuhan region, where COVID-19 was first discovered. Moreover, 938 Fortune 1000 companies have tier-one or tier-two suppliers in the Wuhan region (Dun & Bradsteet, 2020).

SCD severity is influenced by design characteristics and mitigation capabilities, highlighting the need for resilience planning and business continuity planning (Craighead et al., 2007). Mitigating SCDs requires implementing process management, information sharing and partner and service provider relationship management, with the depth and breadth of security initiatives depending on top management mindfulness, operational complexity, product risk and coupling (Speier et al., 2011). SCD propagation is driven by disruption nature, structure, dependence and managerial decision-making (Scheibe & Blackhurst, 2018). Disruption at one point in the supply chain also has a cascading effect across the entire SCN. The propagation of a disruption across the SCN and its associated impact is called the ripple effect. A ripple effect is distinct from the well-known bullwhip effect. This manifests when the impact of an SCD cannot be localised or contained in one part of the supply chain and cascades downstream, resulting in a high-impact effect on supply chain performance (Dolgui et al., 2018). The ripple effect is initiated by a severe disruption and describes the propagation of the impact of this SCD downstream, for example, in terms of the propagation of the disruption of the demand fulfilment capabilities of the supply network because of a severe disruption. In more severe cases, the ripple effect can cause some nodes and arcs in the SCN to become temporarily dysfunctional (e.g. due to a material shortage and capacity loss) (Dolgui et al., 2018).

To understand the supply chain ripple effect, it is imperative to understand risk propagation in the SCN. In practice, a disruption to an SCN often begins locally, with a trigger event affecting any one or a group of nodes in the network usually located within the same vicinity. This impact spreads to other firms (or nodes) through their relationships. Consequently, the impact might propagate to parts of the network through a set of cascading impacts and affect nodes that are far from the origin of the impact (Scala & Lindsay, 2021). The extent to which the impact propagates in the supply network is also a testament to the resilience of the network (Li & Zobel, 2020). Dolgui et al. (2018) discussed the main reasons for the systemic vulnerabilities that make SCNs more prone to the ripple effect when presented with a disruption in any or multiple nodes within the SCN. These reasons can be broadly classified into four main categories: sourcing strategy risks, production planning risks, inventory management risk and control risk. Fig. 2 summarises the main risks.

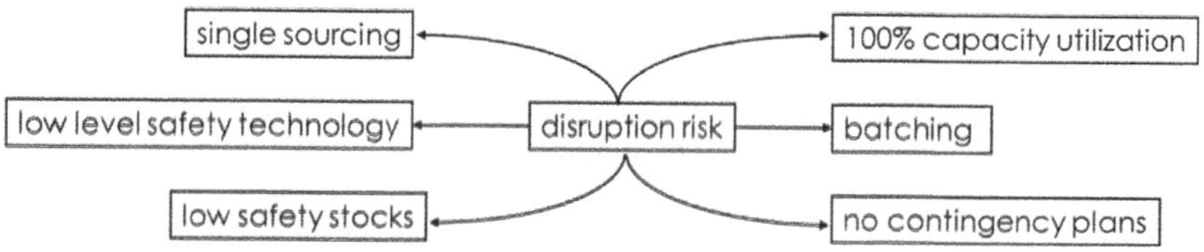

Fig. 2. Main Reasons for Ripple Effect in Supply Chain Network. *Source:* Dolgui et al. (2018).

SCDs and the Energy Sector

Energy supply chains are essential assets in modern societies. A disruption in the energy supply chain can have tremendous impacts on the quality of life we have; hence, the safety and security of the production and distribution of energy products is often a major concern of all national governments. While supply chains face the risk of disruption due to endogenous and exogenous factors, energy supply chains are often affected catastrophically by exogenous risks (Urciuoli et al., 2014). These exogenous risks include, for example, terrorist attacks, natural disasters, wars and piracy. Furthermore, due to the extensive network of suppliers abroad, energy supply chains could be disrupted due to any of the exogenous risks. Managing the disruption caused by exogenous factors is a highly important activity for energy industry executives. Multiple strategies for managing energy SCDs have been discussed in the literature. These include diversification of suppliers (Tørhaug, 2008) and network re-engineering (Christopher et al., 2011) by diversifying the supplier network base and creating a global sourcing risk management culture. In contrast to diversification, Melacini et al. (2011) argued in favour of centralising supply chains to improve the lead time and reliability of supply chains. Urciuoli et al. (2014) identified that in practice, energy supply chain managers do not rely on a risk management approach to handle SCDs caused by exogenous factors but on management strategies and information sharing. These typically include safety stocks to handle emergencies and diversification of suppliers based on factors such as geography, quality of product supplied, type of country or region, transport capabilities available and price. Energy companies also focus on developing multiple long- and short-term contracts and investing in manufacturing capabilities to ensure that they have the flexibility to use different types of raw materials.

SCD in the Energy Sector Due to COVID-19

COVID-19-induced disruptions have had a major impact on companies dealing with the production and distribution of energy across the world (Zahraee et al., 2022). Although COVID-19 was an exogenous disrupter, it had an impact on the demand and supply sides of the energy supply chain. The nationwide lockdowns led to an unprecedented reduction in the demand for energy across the world, excessive supply of raw material used in the energy sector and an unexpected change in the demand profile of energy consumption (Zakeri et al., 2022). The impact on the energy sector, in turn, has had a tremendous impact on other sectors. For instance, households, industries, hospitals and transportation consume energy to upkeep their operations.

Furthermore, plummeting oil prices expanded the scope of cheap oil-based energy generation, which impeded renewable energy development. The shift to low-carbon production and renewable energy was to be halted temporarily around the world. Meanwhile, a Bloomberg study predicted that solar power would decline, as policymakers were more concerned with battling the impact of COVID-19 on their economies than building new plants and agreeing on renewable energy growth goals (Manzanedo & Manning, 2020). Green energy ventures are also facing instability as a direct result of COVID-19 after the global pandemic. Wind producers GE, Vestas and Siemens Gaemsa were preparing to close their factories. The shortage of construction components, such as inverters and modules, pushed up costs by as much as 15% in some markets (Priya et al., 2021). Payment defaults were also causing ripple effects on the entire renewable energy market. A shortage of working capital dried up funds for short-term routine operating liabilities (Priya et al., 2021).

The lockdown-led restrictions across the world had a significant effect on the energy consumption pattern, and the distribution of energy usage shifted a great deal. For instance, industrial energy usage was reduced significantly, while domestic energy consumption saw a marked increase. Due to a reduction in the energy consumption for transportation, industrial manufacturing and other economic activity, oil prices fell to a record low (Carvalhaes et al., 2020).

Many countries saw a sudden reduction in energy consumption in the commercial and industrial sectors (Table 1). In the United Kingdom, energy consumption dropped to as low as 20% of normal usage during the weekend in comparison to over weekdays at the height of the COVID-19 lockdown (Wilson et al., 2020). The sudden reduction in electricity consumption has led to a significant deviation in voltages due to the capacitive elements in the transmission line that generate reactive power (Carmon et al., 2020). This abnormally low consumption of electricity affected the management and control of the generation

Table 1. Energy Demand Development (Based on Jiang et al., 2021).

	Growth in Energy Demand (%)	
Region	2019	2020
EU	−1.9	−10.9
USA	−0.6	-9
Japan	−2.9	−7.8
Korea	−0.3	−6.8
India	0.9	−4.1
China	3.4	−4.1
South East Asia	3.4	−3.4
Africa	2.9	−3

of power units and led to high fluctuations in the voltage and frequency of the electric current. These fluctuations, in turn, affected the resilience and reliability of the entire system (Carmon et al., 2020) and required shutting down power generation units. Since electricity consumption was exceptionally low, the system operator had to shut down conventional power plants until consumption returned to normal. However, several large power plants cannot be fully reactivated in a brief time, once shut down for a few days. This means that in the case of a contingency, such as a failure in a generation unit or an unexpected load deviation, backup units with a short start-up time are used, which are usually more expensive and polluting options. Furthermore, there may be delays in the synchronisation of these units to the grid, making it difficult for the system operator to supply demand during peak requirements (Carmon et al., 2020).

The most visible impact of COVID-19 was the energy market collapse. The price of the Brent crude fell from US $69 a barrel (6 January 2020) to under US $23 (30–31 March 2020) before partially recovering to around US $32 (13 April 2020) because of deep production cuts by OPEC plus countries (Duffy & Disis, 2020). Cross-border travel limitations, supply insufficiencies, quarantines and Capex reductions had a pronounced effect on the European energy service market, which is heavily dependent on its international workforce and efficient flow of goods and services between nations. A vast majority of the European Oil Field service, in Norway and the United Kingdom, lost purchases worth around $4.5 billion within the segments of maintenance, modifications and operations, drilling rigs and well services. It is estimated that about 1,000 small- and mid-sized suppliers in the United Kingdom and Norway have become insolvent or have been acquired by companies upstream (Bajic, 2020).

Impact on Renewable Energy

Renewable energy sources can be primarily classified into solar power, wind energy, hydro energy and others. The solar energy industry was the worst affected by SCDs. China is known to be the largest solar photovoltaic cell manufacturing country in the world and accounts for almost 80% of all solar cells and modules manufactured globally. The pandemic brought the production of the components used in renewable energy systems to a halt (Kanda & Kivimaa, 2020). As a result of lockdown disruptions in supply, there was a major decrease in solar energy supplements.

Table 2 shows that there was a steady increase in the proportion of renewable energy usage during the pandemic. However, this can be, in essence, a little misleading if the entire picture is not considered. As shown in Table 2, the percentual growth of renewable energy sources has decreased in 2020 compared to 2019. Therefore, the increase in the percentage of energy used from renewable energy sources does not come directly from the actual increase of renewables but is due to the total decrease in energy consumption as a result of pandemic-induced lockdown. The reasons for this reduction in the growth of energy sources from renewable energy sources are multifold. First, the sharp economic downturn caused by the pandemic had a significant impact on

Table 2. The Projected Change Rates of Energy Types Across 2019–2020 (Based on Jiang et al., 2021).

		Growth Rate (%)		
Energy Type	Change Rate	Type of Renewable	2019	2020
Renewables	0.79	Hydropower	2.4	0.7
Nuclear	−2.52	Bioenergy	7.8	2.8
Gas	−4.99	Wind	11.9	11.7
Coal	−7.73	Solar PV	22.3	16.1
Oil	−9.12	Others	7.1	2.8
Total energy	−6.05	All renewables	6.5	4.6

renewable energy. With reduced financing and government funding for market incentives, renewable energy investment has raised serious concerns among developers. In Germany, which is one of the leading renewable energy producers in the world, the decreasing overall level of energy demand negatively affects pricing schemes for renewable energy production and carbon trading. Furthermore, the sudden halt of the manufacturing process across the world led to major disruptions in the global renewable energy supply chain (Ivanov & Dolgui, 2021). SCDs and halting nonessential manufacturing activities have caused significant delays in the deployment of renewable energy projects. China, the leading supplier of solar photovoltaic cells, experienced a widespread shutdown of its factories due to the COVID-19 outbreak. Finally, the grid integration of new renewable energy projects was postponed due to a delay in distribution system operators' noncritical operations (Energy Community and Energy, 2020). Power companies adapted their operations in response to the fallouts from the pandemic by putting aside new investment projects, tightening budgets, cutting unnecessary spending and reassessing project implementation and investment priority, which collectively resulted in major impacts on global renewable energy production in the near term (Hoang et al., 2021).

The preceding discussion summarises SCDs and their impact on the energy sector in general and in particular due to COVID-19. While previous studies have investigated the impact of SCDs primarily from the perspective of a firm, studies on the impact of SCD on energy supply chains are sparse. Furthermore, very few studies have focused on SCDs in the energy sector caused by exogenous factors, such as the COVID-19 pandemic. While the exogenous risk to SCDs often affects the supply side of the energy supply chain, COVID-19 had both supply- and demand-side impacts on the energy supply chains. In addition, the impact of COVID-19 on the energy supply chain affected the strategic nature of the industry, especially with respect to its position on renewable energy and the nature of the SCN. Therefore, a deeper understanding of how COVID-19 has affected the energy supply chain and the impact of COVID-19 on the supply chain is warranted.

SYSTEMS THINKING

The fields of systems thinking bring three important patterns of thought to this study: (1) thinking dynamically, (2) thinking in feedback loops and (3) thinking endogenously (Sterman, 1994). Thinking dynamically means considering issues as they have evolved and will manifest themselves in the future. The behaviour over time (BOT) plot is one of the main tools for facilitating dynamic thinking. Drawing these BOT plots across time enables researchers and policymakers to shift their attention from a phenomenon as a discrete dramatic event to an ongoing process or phenomenon (Howick et al., 2006). The reasoning in feedback loops is centred on circular causality or the expected long-lasting ripple effects of system players' activities (Richardson & Andersen, 1995). Feedback loops are a source of visibility in policy resistance. Planners have the chance to circumvent the innate tendencies of competitive systems by discovering, reinforcing and balancing feedback loops that are active or latent in the system structure. Thinking endogenously is the most powerful part of systems thinking. Although it develops from the feedback concept, it serves as its foundation (Anderson & Johnson, 1997; Forrester, 1968). Thinking endogenously extends the border that normally surrounds our thinking about a problem to the point where underlying causes are perceived as connected in circular causal loops with internal forces over which we may have some control rather than as autonomous forces from the outside. Many disparate schools of thought are motivated by 'systems thinking', but at their foundation, they are all focused on identifying endogenous drivers of system activity.

Systems thinking has been used as a tool to study complex interactions in supply chain research. Within the supply chain context, the system is defined as 'a whole consisting of two or more parts (1) each of which can affect the performance or properties of the whole, (2) none of which can have an independent effect overall, and (3) no subgroup of which can have an independent effect on the whole. In brief, then, a system is a whole that cannot be divided into independent parts or subgroups of parts' (Ackoff, 1994, p. 175). In the same vein, Ackoff (2010) defined systems thinking as looking at relationships (rather than unrelated objects), connectedness, process (rather than structure), the whole (rather than just its parts), the patterns (rather than the contents) of a system and context (Ackoff, 2010). This view of systems thinking aligns with the supply chain function, in which various aspects of the supply chain need to relate to an established process to communicate with various parts of the supply chain to fulfil consumers' demands (Wilden et al., 2022). Given the complexities of modern-day supply chains, systems thinking has recently received much attention. Advocating for systems thinking, Jackson (2020) argued that systems thinking could have helped respond to COVID-19 in the United Kingdom, specifically the systems thinking frames of reference used to address some of the supply chain–related challenges (e.g. personal protective equipment). While not referring to systems thinking directly, Sarkis et al. (2020) took a systems view to critique the weaknesses in the supply chain and promote resilience measures, in addition to detailed lessons learnt from a post-COVID perspective. Elias et al. (2021) used systems thinking to holistically analyse the complexities involved in the adoption of a sustainable wood supply chain in Amazon and to develop strategic interventions to improve the system. However, COVID-19-led SCD has generated many important insights into supply chain resilience as a research paradigm and has been criticised for missing opportunities to learn from other fields (Wieland et al., 2023). Nikookar et al. (2021) argued that adaptations or even radical transformations may well be required in order not only to survive but also to flourish in an era characterised by factors such as geopolitical, social, epizootic, climate and biodiversity crises. According to Wieland et al. (2023), supply chains are not only complex adaptive systems but also have close connections with social, economic, ecological and political contexts within which they are embedded. Thus, supply chains are much more fluid in nature and cannot be expected to operate as engineering systems.

This study aims to understand the impact of COVID-19 on SCDs. The subsequent impact on the energy sector has all the characteristics that make it ideal for the use of systems thinking and qualitative system models using causal loop modelling. These characteristics are as follows:

- The problems are dynamic (developing over time).
- The root causes of the dynamics are not clear.
- Different stakeholders have different perceptions.
- Past solutions have not worked; solutions that fail to consider how the system will respond will fail to produce desirable long-term results.
- Implementing change will require aligning powerful stakeholders around policies that they agree have the highest likelihood of long-term success (Senge, 1997).

The next section summarises the overall methodological approach employed in this study.

METHODOLOGICAL FRAMEWORK

System dynamics, a research approach based on systems thinking, often uses group model building (GMB) to identify complex relationships between various entities and subsystems (Vennix, 1999). GMB helps guide problem definition, system conceptualisation, model building and refinement and model use. GMB has been the favoured approach for the system dynamist for three main reasons: first, to capture the required knowledge in the mental models through the various stakeholders; second, to increase the chances of implementation of model results; third, to enhance the stakeholder learning process (Vennix et al., 1997). GMB exercises allow stakeholders to voice their individual perceptions of reality and help them develop a shared mental model of their perceptions as a group (Elias, 2016).

For this study, an exploratory approach using the GMB method was adopted to gain an understanding of the complex nature of SCDs due to COVID-19 and its impact on the energy sector (Rouwette et al., 2002). Due to the exploratory nature of the research, the discussions were semi-structured to enable the researchers to discover the varying causal influences that the participants perceived to occur in practice (Graham et al., 1992). The subsequent sections broadly explain the main parts of the research process. The research process was divided into four main steps as described below (Hovmand et al., 2012).

(1) The first step included an initial literature review and identification of the main impact on the energy sector due to SCDs caused by COVID-19. The main findings of this stage are summarised in the Literature Review section of this study.
(2) The second stage involved initial data collection based on a questionnaire developed by the gatekeepers, which was shared with the sCience and human factOr for Resilient sociEty (CORE) consortium members to gather insights into the impacts of SCD on the energy sector due to COVID-19. The data collection for this stage was carried out during an annual conference among CORE partners in Vienna in September 2022. The structure of the questionnaire, with open-ended questions, was first introduced to the attendees and then subsequently shared with them. The questionnaire captured the direct and indirect impacts of lockdown, beginning of unlocking (with certain restrictions) and beginning of back to normalcy on energy sectors. Subsequently, after the annual conference, the questionnaire was shared with the rest of the consortium members who were not present at the annual meeting.
(3) The third stage involved a GMB workshop in Helsinki, in which the participants developed an initial set of relationships between the variables and helped identify an initial set of relationships. As part of initiating GMB, experts in HUMLOG were contacted and invited to be part of GMB. The HUMLOG Institute was established in 2008, after 2 years of close collaboration and exchanges between several schools, universities and institutes within the Nordic countries. It is a joint institute between the Hanken School of Economics and the National Defence University in Finland and is hosted at the Hanken School of Economics in Helsinki. Subsequently, the variables and relationships were evaluated, and the final model was developed after multiple rounds, as suggested by Andersen and Richardson (1997).
(4) The fourth stage involved final model building and validation, where the model was shared with members of the CORE consortium project. The causal loop model developed in GMB was shared with the consortium members to seek their input in validating and further refining the model. The feedback received was incorporated into the final model.

RESULTS AND DISCUSSION

Based on the discussion in the GMB session, the impact of COVID-19 on supply chains and how SCDs have affected the energy sector are discussed. The first part of this section summarises the general impact of COVID-19 and SCD caused by lockdowns as preventive measures for societal coping capabilities. The second part of this section specifically delves into the impact of SCD on the energy sector.

Impact of SCD on the Overall Well-Being of Society

The impact of COVID-19 on supply chains was critical, owing to the disruptions. As COVID-19 cases across the world increased, almost all governments responded by cutting down the interactions among their populace, and as a result, various forms of lockdowns or restrictions were put in place (Coccia, 2021). Some of them included extreme levels of lockdowns, where no one could move within or across the boundaries of the nation, and in some other cases, conditional restrictions were imposed on the movement of people. However, the general impact of the increase in the number of COVID-19 cases was the surge of restrictions limiting the movement of people and goods. The direct impact of these restrictions was, thus, not just the disruption in the flow of the people but also on that of the goods and services and thereby on the level of economic activity. This had a profound impact on supply chains across the globe and led to massive disruptions (Vo & Tran, 2021).

While the governments recognised this as a potential impact of rapid lockdowns, the impact of SCDs was far-reaching, especially on critical services. For instance, the lockdowns led to the sudden drop in the shipments of various goods, including raw materials, semi-finished parts and finished goods across industries (Arunmozhi et al., 2021; Raj et al., 2022). This was further aggravated by the fact that the lockdown-induced fall in economic activities led to either job loss or a reduction in the average wage across multiple sectors (Deshpande & Ramachandran, 2020). Combined with higher inflation and supply disruptions, the overall coping capacity of many individuals and households was significantly affected (Erokhin & Gao, 2020).

While the conditions during the lockdown were similar for everyone (in most countries), the impact was not uniform. Multiple studies (see Burlina & Rodrigues-Pose (2023), for detailed exposition) have identified that the impact of pandemics and income inequality are closely related, and this was the same for COVID-19. Households' decrease in access to work and education are two of the most important drivers of the reduction in well-being, both in the short and medium terms (Mahmud & Riley, 2021; Zoch et al., 2022). Having said that, the impact was not the same across the EU. It was observed that the countries with the greatest degree of deprivation are a group of Eastern European countries: Bulgaria, Latvia, Serbia, Lithuania and Cyprus. On the other hand, some Nordic countries, such as Norway and Finland – together with Croatia – are those with the lowest degree of deprivation (Ayala et al., 2022). This disproportionality within social groups had further adverse effects on vulnerabilities across society, where the already disadvantaged were further and disproportionately affected by lockdowns and subsequent SCDs and their impact on critical services (Jesus et al., 2021; Moore et al., 2021). With an increase in cases across the geographies, many administrations resorted to further clamping down and extending the restrictions. This further tightening of the restrictions added to the already existing conditions that had led to the disproportionate impact of COVID-19.

Causal Model of SCD and the Energy Sector

Total energy consumption in any economy is the sum of industrial energy consumption and household energy consumption. Energy generation and transmission processes are also based on consumption patterns. The sudden reduction in economic activities had a significant impact on the energy sector, especially on the profitability and energy generation capabilities of energy companies. This reduction in total energy consumption combined with SCDs has also affected the revenue of energy companies, which in turn has affected the profitability of the companies and thereby any investments in both maintenance and green energy transitions. Fig. 3, given below, captures the essence of the discussion.

Total energy consumption within an economy depends on both domestic and industrial consumption (Zhong et al., 2021). Usually, peak industrial loads and domestic loads are different. Residential customers usually have moderate energy consumption during daytime hours, with a minor increase in the morning and a peak demand around dinnertime. On weekends, the energy consumption of residential customers is generally higher, while the afternoon peak is substantially lower (Ayón et al., 2017). On the other hand, peak load in commercial buildings tends to occur during the late afternoon or early evening hours when businesses are operating at full capacity and people are using more electricity (Darwazeh et al., 2022). The highest peak load in industries typically occurs during the daytime, specifically during late morning and early afternoon hours. This is when

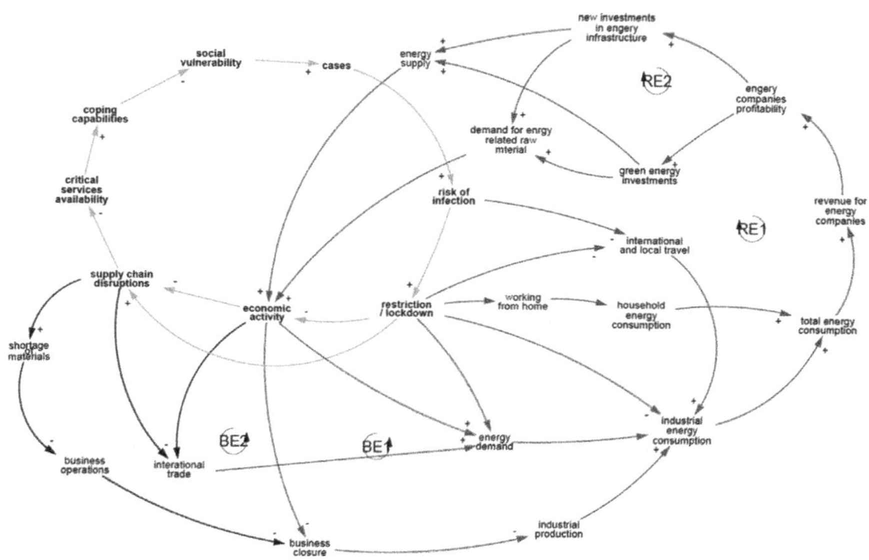

Fig. 3. Effect of Supply Chain Disruption on the Energy Sector.

industrial activities are at their peak and demand for electricity and other resources is typically highest (Ashok & Banerjee, 2000). However, due to the lockdown, the peak industrial and commercial building load was significantly reduced in the morning hours, and the domestic load was distributed across the day (Krarti & Aldubyan, 2021). Furthermore, while there was some increase in the domestic load due to remote working, which was popular during the lockdown, it was not significant enough to match industrial demand (Krarti & Aldubyan, 2021). This change in energy consumption pattern had two significant impacts. First, the total revenue generated by the energy companies had significantly reduced, while maintenance expenses had gone up (Pilloni et al., 2022). The second impact of the change in consumption patterns was the need to depend more on non-renewable sources of energy (He & Zhang, 2022).

Since majority of the revenue for energy companies come directly from industrial consumption, a significant drop in industrial consumption led to a loss of revenues for many energy companies (Zhong et al., 2020). This was a particularly difficult time for smaller energy companies, especially those that did not have their own generational capabilities but acted mostly as intermediaries between large energy companies and consumers (Busch & Hansen, 2021). During this time, there was a significant consolidation of the energy providers since many companies could not manage their revenue deficit and had to be merged with other energy companies. With reduced electricity demand from the commercial and industrial sectors, utilities have experienced a decline in revenue. This has made it difficult for them to cover fixed costs and investments in infrastructure upgrades. Some utilities have had to implement cost-cutting measures or seek financial assistance to maintain operations (Zhong et al., 2020). This contributed to redundancies in these companies, adding to unemployment (Poyner, 2020).

Another significant impact on the bottom line of energy companies was the increase in maintenance expenses for grid reliability and resilience. Companies have had to ensure that the electricity supply remains stable and uninterrupted, especially with the increased reliance on digital technologies for remote work and education. The industry has also had to adapt to the challenges posed by remote operations and maintenance, emphasising the need for a robust and flexible grid infrastructure (Zhong et al., 2020). Since transmission and generation capabilities are tuned to consumption patterns, any sudden change in this consumption pattern requires load balancing across transmission lines (Lopes et al., 2007). Load balancing exercises are extremely time consuming as well as intense processes that cannot be conducted without any planning. It was observed that energy companies had to restructure their load balancing across transmission lines, which affected their maintenance schedule and created stress on the lines, thereby requiring more maintenance than expected (Handfield et al., 2020).

The SCDs and non-availability of spare parts affected maintenance schedules and caused many companies to be unable to operate at 100% capacity. Energy companies faced challenges in obtaining replacement parts and equipment, leading to longer downtime for repairs and maintenance activities. This put additional strain on grid reliability and resilience, especially during a time when the electricity supply was crucial for supporting remote work, education and healthcare (Elavarasan et al., 2020). In Fig. 3, RE1 represents the reinforcing loop under pre-COVID conditions, while BE1 represents the balancing loop capturing the impact of restrictions and a slowdown in economic activities due to COVID.

Since the profitability of the energy companies had reduced significantly, almost all energy companies and governments reduced or stopped funding for green energy transitions. There were two primary reasons for this. First, COVID-19 affected the renewable energy sector in various ways. Construction delays and SCDs slowed down the development of renewable energy projects (Olabi et al., 2022). Additionally, the economic downturn caused by the pandemic led to reduced investments in renewables (Zhong et al., 2020). Second, the pandemic prompted discussions about the future of the energy industry and the need for a more sustainable and resilient energy system. Many governments and policymakers started considering the role of overall change in the usage of energy in economic recovery plans. This led to policy changes and initiatives aimed at accelerating the energy transition and supporting renewable energy projects (Hoang et al., 2021).

The multiple components required for solar power generation, including solar panels, are primarily manufactured in China. For renewable energy projects, SCDs have resulted in delays in the construction and commissioning of wind farms, solar power plants and other renewable energy installations (Deshwal et al., 2021). The closure of factories and restrictions on international trade have led to shortages of key components such as solar panels, wind turbines and batteries. This has slowed the expansion of renewable energy capacity and hindered the achievement of renewable energy targets. Combined with SCDs and a lack of funding for the green energy transition, the energy generated through green energy sources was significantly reduced during COVID times (Zhong et al., 2020). Furthermore, many governments and energy companies decided to freeze any major investments in the energy sector until the situation stabilised (Hoang et al., 2021). This is captured by the reinforcing loop RE2 and the balancing loop BE2 in Fig. 3. Loop RE2 is a positively reinforcing loop without being affected by COVID-19, while loop BE2 is the balancing loop, which captures the impact of COVID-19 and the associated disruption in the supply chain and international trade.

POLICY IMPLICATIONS

The impact of COVID-19 on the lives of people and businesses across the world has been devastating. While COVID-19 itself had direct effects on people's health and lives, much of the damage across the globe was indirectly due to lockdowns and restrictions, which in turn led to SCDs simultaneously causing both demand and supply shocks (Guan et al., 2020). This section discusses some of the policy implications that both businesses and governments could take into consideration to protect themselves against similar SCDs in the future.

The challenge businesses face is to make their supply chains more resilient without damaging their competitiveness (Chopra & Sodhi, 2004). Multiple studies have focused on finding the balance between making a supply chain resilient towards risks while ensuring that profitability is not compromised (see Pettit et al., 2013, for a detailed discussion). To meet this challenge, managers should first understand the sources of their vulnerabilities and then consider a series of steps that can be taken to ensure that these vulnerabilities do not cause future disruptions. The business-level policy implications are as follows:

Identify hidden risks: Modern products often incorporate critical and sophisticated components sourced from various suppliers across the globe. This makes it extremely difficult for a single firm to have both the technological and manufacturing capabilities to produce complex products entirely alone (Pescaroli & Alexander, 2018). To gain a competitive advantage, companies depend on suppliers that specialise in specific components. While this may be beneficial in terms of having a competitive advantage, it creates vulnerabilities within the system. Hence, firms are vulnerable because of a single supplier's dependence on a critical component. This can be seen in BE2 in Fig. 3, where a shortage of raw material can be avoided by building a larger and more diverse supplier base. The businesses must do complete risk mapping of their supply chain, identify where the risks lie, build redundancies within the supply chain, ensure that risk is distributed over a set of players and is concentrated neither horizontally nor vertically within the supply chain.

Managing net working capital: One of the main reasons for the bankruptcy of many small businesses was the lack of working capital since small businesses operate on small amounts of working capital. This is often due to long periods of cash receivables and relatively smaller periods of cash payables. As the financial function works on accounts payable and receivable, supply chain leaders should focus on freeing up cash that is locked in other parts of the value chain. This could include reducing the finished goods inventory and unlocking value within processes through strong governance. Furthermore, firms should focus on improving logistics through smarter fleet management. Most importantly, firms should test their financial situation and evaluate their level of resilience in terms of how much pressure they can handle in the case of an SCD. This is evident in both RE1 and BE1. Previous studies have shown that in the energy industry, a firm's growth rate causes a decrease in the level of working capital management measures. This may imply that although growing firms invest primarily in fixed assets, working capital is not their priority (Jaworski & Czerwonka, 2022). Furthermore, it can also be seen that the growing cash flow in the energy industry has often been prioritised to be invested in capital assets rather than working capital management. Thus, during revenue drops in the COVID-19 lockdowns, the energy companies had large amounts of capital assets that needed both maintenance and debt servicing, with little revenue to manage their operations. This led to major retracting in the energy sector. Thus, because the energy industry comes under critical resources within a society, public policies and the government can play an important role in setting guidelines, especially in working capital management, to ensure that such challenges are not faced in the future.

Keeping markets open for international trade: One of the main challenges during the peak COVID-19 was the unpredictable changes in the rules and regulations as well as the scope of their application by every government, which led to confusion and created difficulties for companies to adapt to the changes (Curran et al., 2021). This also contributed to the SCD, as shown in Fig. 3, in loops BE2 and RE2. For companies to be able to manage their operations and build resilience into the supply chain, they need policies and regulations to be stable, transparent and predictable in nature (Tomalska, 2022). While the majority of measures are probably justifiable, there were nevertheless many whose coverage or nature was such that a justification under Articles XX or XXI of World Trade Organization law was debatable. The banning of exports is an extreme measure, which is a relatively rare global trading system unless there is a global embargo. However, COVID-19 seems to have changed this. During peak lockdowns, we saw widespread recourse to export bans, sometimes with no published end date (ECIPE, 2020). Governments should focus on creating both predictability and transparency with rules and regulations and on ensuring that information is made available in a timely and transparent manner. Towards this, governments should reinforce confidence and commitment to rule-based trading to address gaps that might have led to trade tensions. Finally, governments should focus on creating coordinated efforts between various national and international governments and firms to develop common approaches for the simplified procurement and supply of essential commodities (OECD, 2021).

Governments should also establish policies for putting guardrails in the form of a risk-reduction framework within which businesses operate. This helps in stability and continuity for business operations, boosts investor confidence, helps in streamlining regulatory compliance, fosters innovations and growth and finally helps make the business resilient to global changes. Some of the policy steps governments should undertake are as follows:

Develop national-level risk assessment tools to identify risk: Governments should develop risk management frameworks at both national and local governance levels that include a supply chain perspective. Governments should focus on identifying different types of risks, especially supply chain risks pertaining to essential goods and services (Patrucco & Kähkönen, 2021). Risk identification should not be limited to the supply chains but should comprise the entire value chains. Governments should focus on creating efficient regulations through international cooperation to ensure the free movement of goods. Mechanisms should be put in place to detect and anticipate crises by monitoring vulnerabilities and risks in supply chains, including an international exchange of information and early warning signals.

Develop policies to minimise exposure to shocks: The focus of government should be to minimise shocks by ensuring the availability and accessibility of critical services to their citizens. This entails an efficient operation of infrastructures through trade, procurement and regulatory flexibility. Ensuring the resilience of critical infrastructures during shocks underpins the flow of goods, services and people (Meehan et al., 2016). Keeping in line with the recent CER 2022 directive by the EU, the focus should shift from asset protection to ensuring systemic resilience, owing to the increased interconnectedness and interdependence between infrastructure assets and various critical sectors. This should be ensured through a long-term strategic vision for infrastructure and the implementation of a government approach to managing threats. The focus should be on promoting evidence-informed decision-making to ensure that infrastructure is regularly maintained and strengthened for resilience.

CONCLUSIONS

We live in an extensively interconnected world with the ability to source, manufacture and consume products from different parts of the world. This is possible because of the interconnected network of supply chains that operate continuously throughout the year. In the past, the impact of SCDs on businesses has been studied in detail. However, their impact on the lives of common people and thereby societal vulnerability has not received much attention. The recent COVID-19-led SCDs across the world have brought this to the attention of both business owners and policymakers. The importance of supply chains in the modern world cannot be overstated.

Previous studies, while having studied exogenous risks from SCDs, usually do not consider both supply- and demand-side risks caused by SCDs. This study offers a novel outlook into the role of exogenous risks from SCDs, especially in the energy sector, which can have both supply and demand implications. Furthermore, the study uses a systems thinking approach to develop a holistic view of how SCDs produce ripple effects on the energy industry. The study also offers practical suggestions in the form of policy implications, which can be used by both practitioners and policymakers to develop policies to prevent the effects of SCDs caused by events such as COVID-19 on the energy sector in the future. While this study offers a holistic perspective using systems thinking, more empirical research needs to be conducted to quantify the real impact of SCDs across the energy value chain.

This study was carried out as part of Work Package 4, Task 4.3, under the CORE project, to study the impact of SCDs due to COVID-19 on creating social vulnerabilities. This was explored through the impact of SCDs on the energy sector. Since this sector is critical to the functioning of society, it is imperative to ensure that it functions without disruption. The study also explores how SCDs affected the operational capabilities of the energy sector and how they influenced both short-term and long-term operational capabilities. The study also suggests policy recommendations for both businesses and governments to protect themselves against system-wide SCDs in the future.

ACKNOWLEDGEMENT

This study is undertaken as a part of Work Package 4, under the CORE project funded by the European Union's Horizon 2020 research and innovation program under grant agreement no. 101021746.

REFERENCES

Ackoff, R. L. (1994). Systems thinking and thinking systems. *System Dynamics Review*, *10*(2–3), 175–188.

Ackoff, R. L. (2010). *Systems thinking for curious managers*. Triarchy Press.

Andersen, D. F., & Richardson, G. P. (1997). Scripts for group model building. *System Dynamics Review: The Journal of the System Dynamics Society*, *13*(2), 107–129.

Anderson, V., & Johnson, L. (1997). *Systems thinking basics: From concepts to causal loops*. Pegasus Communications.

Arunmozhi, M., Kiran Kumar, R., & Srinivasa, B. A. (2021). Impact of COVID-19 on global supply chain management. In *Managing supply chain risk and disruptions: Post COVID-19* (pp. 1–18). Springer International Publishing.

Ashok, S., & Banerjee, R. (2000). Load-management applications for the industrial sector. *Applied Energy*, *66*(2), 105–111.

Atkinson, C. L., McCue, C., Prier, E., & Atkinson, A. M. (2020). Supply chain manipulation, misrepresentation, and magical thinking during the COVID-19 pandemic. *The American Review of Public Administration*, *50*(6–7), 628–634.

Ayala, L., Bárcena-Martín, E., Cantó, O., & Navarro, C. (2022). COVID-19 lockdown and housing deprivation across European countries. *Social Science & Medicine*, *298*, 114839.

Ayón, X., Gruber, J. K., Hayes, B. P., Usaola, J., & Prodanović, M. (2017). An optimal day-ahead load scheduling approach based on the flexibility of aggregate demands. *Applied Energy*, *198*, 1–11.

Bajic, D. (2020). More than 200 European oilfield service providers face bankruptcy. *Project Cargo Journal*. https://www.projectcargojournal.com/offshore/2020/03/18/more-than-200-oilfield-services-providers-face-bankruptcy/. Accessed on 23 December 2022.

Burlina, C., & Rodríguez-Pose, A. (2023). Inequality, poverty, deprivation and the uneven spread of COVID-19 in Europe. *Regional Studies*, 1–22. https://doi.org/10.1080/00343404.2023.2172390

Busch, H., & Hansen, T. (2021). Building communities in times of crisis-Impacts of the COVID-19 pandemic on the work of transition intermediaries in the energy sector. *Energy Research & Social Science*, *75*, 102020.

Carmon, D., Navon, A., Machlev, R., Belikov, J., & Levron, Y. (2020). Readiness of small energy markets and electric power grids to global health crises: Lessons from the COVID-19 pandemic. *IEEE Access*, *8*, 127234–127243.

Carvalhaes, T., Markolf, S., Helmrich, A., Kim, Y., Li, R., Natarajan, M., ... & Chester, M. (2020). COVID-19 as a harbinger of transforming infrastructure resilience. *Frontiers in Built Environment*, *6*, 148.

Critical Entities Resilience (CER). (2022). Directive (EU) 2022/2557 of the European Parliament and of the on the resilience of critical entities and repealing council directive 2008/114/EC. https://eur-lex.europa.eu/eli/dir/2022/2557/oj. Accessed on December 12, 2023.

Chopra, S., & Sodhi, M. S. (2004). Managing risk to avoid supply-chain breakdown. *MIT Sloan Management Review*, *46*(1), 53–61.

Chopra, S., & Sodhi, M. S. (2014). Reducing the risk of supply chain disruptions. *MIT Sloan Management Review*, *55*(3), 73–80.

Christopher, M., Mena, C., Khan, O., & Yurt, O. (2011). Approaches to managing global sourcing risk. *Supply Chain Management: International Journal*, *16*(2), 67–81.

Coccia, M. (2021). The relation between length of lockdown, numbers of infected people and deaths of Covid-19, and economic growth of countries: Lessons learned to cope with future pandemics similar to Covid-19 and to constrain the deterioration of economic system. *Science of the Total Environment*, *775*, 145801.

Craighead, C. W., Blackhurst, J., Rungtusanatham, M. J., & Handfield, R. B. (2007). The severity of supply chain disruptions: Design characteristics and mitigation capabilities. *Decision Sciences*, *38*(1), 131–156.

Curran, L., Eckhardt, J., & Lee, J. (2021). The trade policy response to COVID-19 and its implications for international business. *Critical Perspectives on International Business*, *17*(2), 252–320.

Dai, T., Zaman, M. H., Padula, W. V., & Davidson, P. M. (2021). Supply chain failures amid Covid-19 signal a new pillar for global health preparedness. *Journal of Clinical Nursing, 30*(1–2), e1.

Darwazeh, D., Duquette, J., Gunay, B., Wilton, I., & Shillinglaw, S. (2022). Review of peak load management strategies in commercial buildings. *Sustainable Cities and Society, 77*, 103493.

Dasaklis, T. K., Pappis, C. P., & Rachaniotis, N. P. (2012). Epidemics control and logistics operations: A review. *International Journal of Production Economics, 139*(2), 393–410.

Deshpande, A., & Ramachandran, R. (2020). *Is COVID-19 'The Great Leveler'? The critical role of social identity in lockdown-induced job losses (No. 622)*. GLO Discussion Paper.

Deshwal, D., Sangwan, P., & Dahiya, N. (2021). How will COVID-19 impact renewable energy in India? Exploring challenges, lessons and emerging opportunities. *Energy Research & Social Science, 77*, 102097.

Diop, M. (2020). What can AI tell us about COVID-19's impact on infrastructure? https://blogs.worldbank.org/ppps/what-can-ai-tell-us-about-covid-19s-impact-infrastructure. Accessed on 23 December 2022.

Dolgui, A., & Ivanov, D. (2021). Ripple effect and supply chain disruption management: New trends and research directions. *International Journal of Production Research, 59*(1), 102–109.

Dolgui, A., Ivanov, D., & Sokolov, B. (2018). Ripple effect in the supply chain: An analysis and recent literature. *International Journal of Production Research, 56*(1–2), 414–430.

Duffy, C., & Disis, J. (2020). *PEC+ reaches deal to cut oil production by 9.7 million barrels per day*. CNN Business. https://edition.cnn.com/2020/04/12/energy/opec-deal-production-cut/index.html. Accessed on 23 December 2022.

Dun and Bradstreet. (2020). https://foreignpolicy.com/2020/03/04/blindsided-on-the-supply-side/. Accessed on 10 February 2023.

ECIPE. (2020, June 8). The state of international free trade with Dan Ikenson. *Global Economy Podcast, 30*. https://ecipe.org/wp-content/uploads/2020/06/Podcast-w_D-Ikenson.mp3. Accessed on 14 November 2023.

Elavarasan, R. M., Shafiullah, G. M., Raju, K., Mudgal, V., Arif, M. T., Jamal, T., ... & Subramaniam, U. (2020). COVID-19: Impact analysis and recommendations for power sector operation. *Applied Energy, 279*, 115739.

Elias, A. A. (2016). Analysing the stakes of stakeholders in research and development project management: A systems approach. *R&D Management, 46*(4), 749–760.

Elias, A. A., Donadelli, F., Paiva, E. L., & Bacic Araujo, P. P. (2021). Analysing the complexities of sustainable wood supply chain in the Amazon: A systems thinking approach. *International Journal of Logistics Management, 32*(4), 1481–1505.

Energy Community and Energy. (2020). Annual implementation report 2020. https://www.energy-community.org/dam/jcr:0af3b17a-3759-4a23-a2ef-3134784e217c/EnC_IR2020.pdf. Accessed on 12 December 2023.

Erokhin, V., & Gao, T. (2020). Impacts of COVID-19 on trade and economic aspects of food security: Evidence from 45 developing countries. *International Journal of Environmental Research and Public Health, 17*(16), 5775.

European Union (EU). (2022). Directive (EU) 2022/2557 of the European Parliament and of the Council of 14 December 2022 on the resilience of critical entities and repealing Council Directive 2008/114/EC. https://eur-lex.europa.eu/eli/dir/2022/2557/oj. Accessed on 14 November 2023.

European Union. (2004). Communication from the commission to the council and the European parliament – Critical infrastructure protection in the fight against terrorism. Online. https://eur-lex.europa.eu/legal-content/GA/TXT/?uri=CELEX:52004DC0702

European Union (EU). (2006). Communication from the commission to the European parliament, the council, the European economic and social committee and the committee of the regions contingency plan for ensuring food supply and food security in times of crisis. https://eurlex.europa.eu/legal-content/EN/TXT/HTML/?uri=CELEX:52021DC0689. Accessed on December 12, 2023.

European Union. (2008). *Council Directive 2008/114/EC of 8 December 2008 on the identification and designation of European critical infrastructures and the assessment of the need to improve their protection*. Official Journal of the European Union.

European Union (EU). (2016). Directive on security of network and information systems (NIS Directive) EU cybersecurity policy. https://www.europarl.europa.eu/RegData/etudes/BRIE/2020/654198/EPRS_BRI(2020)654198_EN.pdf. Accessed on December 12, 2023.

European Union. (2020). Proposal for a Directive of the European Parliament and of the Council on the resilience of critical entities. Online. https://eur-lex.europa.eu/legal-content/EN/TXT/?uri=CELEX%3A52020PC0829

Fantin, S., Bergholm, J., & Royer, S. (2021). Securing critical infrastructures through research: EU law, policy and ethics. *Cyber-Physical Threat Intelligence for Critical Infrastructures Security, 107.*

Forrester, J. W. (1968). Market growth as influenced by capital investment. *Industrial Management Review, 9*(2), 83–105.

Graham, A. K., Morecroft, J. D., Senge, P. M., & Sterman, J. D. (1992). Model-supported case studies for management education. *European Journal of Operational Research, 59*(1), 151–166.

Guan, D., Wang, D., Hallegatte, S., Davis, S. J., Huo, J., Li, S., ... & Gong, P. (2020). Global supply-chain effects of COVID-19 control measures. *Nature Human Behaviour, 4*(6), 577–587.

Handfield, R., Finkenstadt, D. J., Schneller, E. S., Godfrey, A. B., & Guinto, P. (2020). A commons for a supply chain in the post-COVID-19 era: The case for a reformed strategic national stockpile. *The Milbank Quarterly, 98*(4), 1058–1090.

Hasani, A., & Khosrojerdi, A. (2016). Robust global supply chain network design under disruption and uncertainty considering resilience strategies: A parallel memetic algorithm for a real-life case study. *Transportation Research Part E: Logistics and Transportation Review, 87*, 20–52.

He, Y., & Zhang, Z. (2022). Non-renewable and renewable energies, and COVID-19 pandemic: Do they matter for China's environmental sustainability? *Energies, 15*(19), 7143.

Henze, V. (2022). Renewable energy sector defies supply chain challenges to hit a record first-half for new investment. *Bloomberg*. https://about.bnef.com/blog/renewable-energy-sector-defies-supply-chain-challenges-to-hit-a-record-first-half-for-new-investment/

Hoang, A. T., Nižetić, S., Olcer, A. I., Ong, H. C., Chen, W. H., Chong, C. T., ... & Nguyen, X. P. (2021). Impacts of COVID-19 pandemic on the global energy system and the shift progress to renewable energy: Opportunities, challenges, and policy implications. *Energy Policy, 154*, 112322.

Hovmand, P. S., Andersen, D. F., Rouwette, E., Richardson, G. P., Rux, K., & Calhoun, A. (2012). Group model-building 'scripts' as a collaborative planning tool. *Systems Research and Behavioral Science, 29*(2), 179–193.

Howick, S., Ackermann, F., & Andersen, D. (2006). Linking event thinking with structural thinking: Methods to improve client value in projects. *System Dynamics Review: The Journal of the System Dynamics Society, 22*(2), 113–140.

International Energy Agency (IEA). (2014). ENERGY SUPPLY SECURITY Emergency Response of IEA Countries 2014. https://iea.blob.core.windows.net/assets/73908149-4d6e-4f10-b626-d55c60ab3bd7/ENERGYSUPPLYSECURITY2014.pdf. Accessed on December 21, 2023.

Ivanov, D. (2017). Simulation-based ripple effect modelling in the supply chain. *International Journal of Production Research, 55*(7), 2083–2101.

Ivanov, D. (2022). Viable supply chain model: Integrating agility, resilience, and sustainability perspectives – Lessons from and thinking beyond the COVID-19 pandemic. *Annals of Operations Research, 319*(1), 1411–1431.

Ivanov, D., Das, A., & Choi, T. (2018). New flexibility drivers for manufacturing, supply chain and service operations. *International Journal of Production Research, 56*(10), 3359–3368.

Ivanov, D., & Dolgui, A. (2021). OR-methods for coping with the ripple effect in supply chains during COVID-19 pandemic: Managerial insights and research implications. *International Journal of Production Economics, 232*, 107921.

Ivanov, D., Dolgui, A., Sokolov, B., & Ivanova, M. (2017). Literature review on disruption recovery in the supply chain. *International Journal of Production Research, 55*(20), 6158–6174.

Ivanov, D., Pavlov, A., Dolgui, A., Pavlov, D., & Sokolov, B. (2016). Disruption-driven supply chain (re)-planning and performance impact assessment with consideration of pro-active and recovery policies. *Transportation Research Part E: Logistics and Transportation Review, 90*, 7–24.

Jabbarzadeh, A., Fahimnia, B., & Sabouhi, F. (2018). Resilient and sustainable supply chain design: Sustainability analysis under disruption risks. *International Journal of Production Research, 56*(17), 5945–5968.

Jackson, M. C. (2020). How we understand 'complexity' makes a difference: Lessons from critical systems thinking and the Covid-19 pandemic in the UK. *Systems, 8*(4), 52.

Jaworski, J., & Czerwonka, L. (2022). Which determinants matter for working capital management in energy industry? The case of European Union economy. *Energies, 15*(9), 3030.

Jesus, T. S., Bhattacharjya, S., Papadimitriou, C., Bogdanova, Y., Bentley, J., Arango-Lasprilla, J. C., ... & Refugee Empowerment Task Force, International Networking Group of the American Congress of Rehabilitation Medicine. (2021). Lockdown-related disparities experienced by people with disabilities during the first wave of the COVID-19 pandemic: Scoping review with thematic analysis. *International Journal of Environmental Research and Public Health, 18*(12), 6178.

Jiang, P., Van Fan, Y., & Klemeš, J. J. (2021). Impacts of COVID-19 on energy demand and consumption: Challenges, lessons and emerging opportunities. *Applied Energy, 285*, 116441.

Kanda, W., & Kivimaa, P. (2020). What opportunities could the COVID-19 outbreak offer for sustainability transitions research on electricity and mobility? *Energy Research & Social Science, 68*, 101666.

Katsaliaki, K., Galetsi, P., & Kumar, S. (2021). Supply chain disruptions and resilience: A major review and future research agenda. *Annals of Operations Research, 319*, 965–1002.

Krarti, M., & Aldubyan, M. (2021). Review analysis of COVID-19 impact on electricity demand for residential buildings. *Renewable and Sustainable Energy Reviews, 143*, 110888.

Larsen, E. R., Osorio, S., & van Ackere, A. (2017). A framework to evaluate security of supply in the electricity sector. *Renewable and Sustainable Energy Reviews, 79*(January 2016), 646–655.

Lazari, A. (2014). *European critical infrastructure protection*. Springer International Publishing.

Li, Y., & Zobel, C. W. (2020). Exploring supply chain network resilience in the presence of the ripple effect. *International Journal of Production Economics, 228*, 107693.

Lopes, J. P., Hatziargyriou, N., Mutale, J., Djapic, P., & Jenkins, N. (2007). Integrating distributed generation into electric power systems: A review of drivers, challenges and opportunities. *Electric Power Systems Research, 77*(9), 1189–1203.

Mahmud, M., & Riley, E. (2021). Household response to an extreme shock: Evidence on the immediate impact of the Covid-19 lockdown on economic outcomes and well-being in rural Uganda. *World Development, 140*, 105318.

Manzanedo, R. D., & Manning, P. (2020). COVID-19: Lessons for the climate change emergency. *Science of the Total Environment, 742*, 140563.

Meehan, J., Ludbrook, M. N., & Mason, C. J. (2016). Collaborative public procurement: Institutional explanations of legitimised resistance. *Journal of Purchasing and Supply Management, 22*(3), 160–170.

Melacini, M., Creazza, A., & Perotti, S. (2011). Analysis of supply chain planning centralisation for multinational companies. *International Journal of Logistics Systems and Management, 9*(4), 478–500.

Moore, S. E., Wierenga, K. L., Prince, D. M., Gillani, B., & Mintz, L. J. (2021). Disproportionate impact of the COVID-19 pandemic on perceived social support, mental health and somatic symptoms in sexual and gender minority populations. *Journal of Homosexuality, 68*(4), 577–591.

Moosavi, J., Fathollahi-Fard, A. M., & Dulebenets, M. A. (2022). Supply chain disruption during the COVID-19 pandemic: Recognizing potential disruption management strategies. *International Journal of Disaster Risk Reduction, 75*, 102983.

Nahm, J., & Urpelainen, J. (2022). *The US should treat climate policy as economic policy*. Brookings. https://www.brookings.edu/articles/the-us-should-treat-climate-policy-as-economic-policy/

Nikookar, E., Varsei, M., & Wieland, A. (2021). Gaining from disorder: Making the case for antifragility in purchasing and supply chain management. *Journal of Purchasing and Supply Management, 27*(3), 100699.

OECD. (2021). COVID-19 and a new resilient infrastructure landscape, OECD policy responses to coronavirus (COVID-19). https://www.oecd.org/coronavirus/policy-responses/covid-19-and-a-new-resilient-infrastructure-landscape-d40a19e3/. Accessed on 23 December 2022.

Olabi, V., Wilberforce, T., Elsaid, K., Sayed, E. T., & Abdelkareem, M. A. (2022). Impact of COVID-19 on the renewable energy sector and mitigation strategies. *Chemical Engineering & Technology*, *45*(4), 558–571.

Parmigiani, A., Klassen, R. D., & Russo, M. V. (2011). Efficiency meets accountability: Performance implications of supply chain configuration, control, and capabilities. *Journal of Operations Management*, *29*(3), 212–223.

Patrucco, A. S., & Kähkönen, A. K. (2021). Agility, adaptability, and alignment: New capabilities for PSM in a post-pandemic world. *Journal of Purchasing and Supply Management*, *27*(4), 100719.

Pescaroli, G., & Alexander, D. (2018). Understanding compound, interconnected, interacting, and cascading risks: A holistic framework. *Risk Analysis*, *38*(11), 2245–2257.

Pettit, T. J., Croxton, K. L., & Fiksel, J. (2013). Ensuring supply chain resilience: Development and implementation of an assessment tool. *Journal of Business Logistics*, *34*(1), 46–76.

Pilloni, M., Kádár, J., & Abu Hamed, T. (2022). The impact of COVID-19 on energy start-up companies: The use of global financial crisis (GFC) as a lesson for future recovery. *Energies*, *15*(10), 3530.

Ponomarov, S. Y., & Holcomb, M. C. (2009). Understanding the concept of supply chain resilience. *International Journal of Logistics Management*, *20*(1), 124–143.

Poyner, B. (2020). Energy community DSOs committed to keeping lights on during COVID-19 crisis. https://www.energy-community.org/news/Energy-Community-News/2020/04/21.html. Accessed on 23 December 2022.

Priya, S. S., Cuce, E., & Sudhakar, K. (2021). A perspective of COVID-19 impact on global economy, energy and environment. *International Journal of Sustainable Engineering*, *14*(6), 1290–1305.

Pujawan, I. N., & Bah, A. U. (2022, January). Supply chains under COVID-19 disruptions: Literature review and research agenda. *Supply Chain Forum: International Journal*, *23*(1), 81–95.

Pursiainen, C. (2009). The challenges for European critical infrastructure protection. *European Integration*, *31*(6), 721–739.

Raj, A., Mukherjee, A. A., de Sousa Jabbour, A. B. L., & Srivastava, S. K. (2022). Supply chain management during and post-COVID-19 pandemic: Mitigation strategies and practical lessons learned. *Journal of Business Research*, *142*, 1125–1139.

Rezapour, S., Farahani, R. Z., & Pourakbar, M. (2017). Resilient supply chain network design under competition: A case study. *European Journal of Operational Research*, *259*(3), 1017–1035.

Richardson, G. P., & Andersen, D. F. (1995). Teamwork in group model building. *System Dynamics Review*, *11*(2), 113–137.

Rouwette, E. A., Vennix, J. A., & Mullekom, T. V. (2002). Group model building effectiveness: A review of assessment studies. *System Dynamics Review: The Journal of the System Dynamics Society*, *18*(1), 5–45.

Sarkis, J., Dewick, P., Hofstetter, J. S., & Schröder, P. (2020). Overcoming the arrogance of ignorance: Supply-chain lessons from COVID-19 for climate shocks. *One Earth*, *3*(1), 9–12.

Scala, B., & Lindsay, C. F. (2021). Supply chain resilience during pandemic disruption: Evidence from healthcare. *Supply Chain Management: An International Journal*, *26*(6), 672–688.

Scheibe, K., & Blackhurst, J. (2018). Supply chain disruption propagation: A systemic risk and normal accident theory perspective. *International Journal of Production Research*, *56*(1–2), 43–59.

Senge, P. M. (1997). The fifth discipline. *Measuring Business Excellence*, *1*(3), 46–51.

Speier, C., Whipple, J., Closs, D., & Voss, M. (2011). Global supply chain design considerations: Mitigating product safety and security risks. *Journal of Operations Management*, *29*, 721–736.

Sterman, J. (1994). Learning in and about complex systems. *System Dynamics Review*, *10*(2±3), 291–330.

Tang, S. Y., Gurnani, H., & Gupta, D. (2014). Managing disruptions in decentralized supply chains with endogenous supply process reliability. *Production and Operations Management*, *23*(7), 1198–1211.

Tomalska, A. (2022). Preparing critical infrastructure for the future: Lessons learnt from the Covid-19 pandemic. *Security and Defence Quarterly*, *39*(3), 21–32.

Tørhaug, M. (2008). Petroleum supply vulnerability due to terrorism at North Sea Oil and Gas infrastructures. *Protection of Civilian Infrastructure From Acts of Terrorism NATO Security Through Science and Series*, 73–84.

Urciuoli, L., Mohanty, S., Hintsa, J., & Gerine Boekesteijn, E. (2014). The resilience of energy supply chains: A multiple case study approach on oil and gas supply chains to Europe. *Supply Chain Management: An International Journal, 19*(1), 46–63.

Vennix, J. A. (1999). Group model-building: Tackling messy problems. *System Dynamics Review: The Journal of the System Dynamics Society, 15*(4), 379–401.

Vennix, J. A., Andersen, D. F., & Richardson, G. P. (1997). Special issue on group model building. *System Dynamics Review, 13*(2).

Vo, T. D., & Tran, M. D. (2021). The impact of Covid-19 pandemic on the global trade. *International Journal of Social Science and Economics Invention, 7*(1), 1–7.

Wagner, S. M., & Neshat, N. (2012). A comparison of supply chain vulnerability indices for different categories of firms. *International Journal of Production Research, 50*(11), 2877–2891.

Wieland, A., Stevenson, M., Melnyk, S. A., Davoudi, S., & Schultz, L. (2023). Thinking differently about supply chain resilience: What we can learn from social-ecological systems thinking. *International Journal of Operations & Production Management, 43*(1), 1–21.

Wilden, D., Hopkins, J., & Sadler, I. (2022). The prevalence of systems thinking in supply chain management: A systematic literature review. *Systemic Practice and Action Research, 35*(4), 491–526.

Wilson, A., & Doberva, A. (2019). Energy supply and security, BRIEFING on EU policies – Delivering for citizens. https://www.europarl.europa.eu/RegData/etudes/BRIE/2018/630275/EPRS_BRI(2018)630275_EN.pdf

Wilson, N. G., Sharma, S., & Bassett, T. (2020, April). Here's how energy demand has changed during the UK's lockdown. [online]. https://www.weforum.org/agenda/2020/04/we-analysed-electricity-demand-and-found-coronavirus-has-turned-weekdays-into-weekends/. Accessed on 23 December 2022.

Zahraee, S. M., Shiwakoti, N., & Stasinopoulos, P. (2022). Agricultural biomass supply chain resilience: COVID-19 outbreak vs. sustainability compliance, technological change, uncertainties, and policies. *Cleaner Logistics and Supply Chain, 4*, 100049.

Zakeri, B., Paulavets, K., Barreto-Gomez, L., Echeverri, L. G., Pachauri, S., Boza-Kiss, B., ... & Pouya, S. (2022). Pandemic, war, and global energy transitions. *Energies, 15*(17), 6114.

Zhong, W., Song, J., Yang, W., Fang, K., & Liu, X. (2021). Evolving household consumption-driven industrial energy consumption under urbanization: A dynamic input-output analysis. *Journal of Cleaner Production, 289*, 125732.

Zhong, H., Tan, Z., He, Y., Xie, L., & Kang, C. (2020). Implications of COVID-19 for the electricity industry: A comprehensive review. *CSEE Journal of Power and Energy Systems, 6*(3), 489–495.

Zoch, G., Bächmann, A. C., & Vicari, B. (2022). Reduced well-being during the COVID-19 pandemic – The role of working conditions. *Gender, Work and Organization, 29*(6), 1969–1990.

EMPLOYEE LEARNING AGILITY AS AN ANTECEDENT OF KNOWLEDGE SHARING IN THE SUPPLY CHAIN: AN EXAMINATION THROUGH THE LENS OF CONSERVATION OF RESOURCE THEORY

Shalendra Satish Kumar, Karalaini Tubuna, Avisekh Asish Lal, Rajneel Ravinesh Prasad and Shiu Lingam

Fiji National University, Fiji

ABSTRACT

Based on the conservation of resource (COR) theory, this study explores employees' learning agility (ELA) as an antecedent of knowledge sharing behaviour, specifically in the supply chain environment. However, such discretionary behaviour can be negatively affected by the prevalence of psychological contract breaches. According to COR theory, employees' resources (knowledge, ability and skills) act as motivational factors that employees strive to protect, retain and at the same time invest in favour of obtaining more resources. On the other hand, when resource loss weighs more than resource gain, an individual agitated with resource depletion will minimise resource loss by decreasing their effort for future displays of resources. A random sample of 418 participants from the public sector in the Fiji Islands yielded a sample of 418 participants. The proposed model was analysed through structural equation modeling (SEM) to determine its fit. The analysis supports the proposed theoretical framework, providing a new dimension for ELA as an unexplored phenomenon for knowledge sharing behaviour (KSB) in the supply chain. The

Sustainable and Resilient Supply Chain
Advances in Environmental Accounting & Management, Volume 12, 93–114

Published under exclusive licence by Emerald Publishing Limited
ISSN: 1479-3598/doi:10.1108/S1479-359820240000012010

study specifically draws the attention of policymakers on industry, innovation and infrastructure (SDG09), where immediate actions are needed to create resilient supply chain management through ELA. Research shows that agile employees can easily adapt to unexpected changes, actively participate in discussions and quickly contribute to innovative and creative solutions. KSB can be further developed through a culture of learning and sharing, rewards for KSB, psychological support and upholding its promised obligations through regular communication, establishing a more resilient supply chain management.

Keywords: Employee learning agility; knowledge sharing behaviour; psychological contract breach; conservation of resource theory; resilient supply chain

INTRODUCTION

Knowledge is regarded as an essential organisational resource necessary to achieve competitive advantages (Schiuma et al., 2012). Fundamentally, knowledge sharing is a process of sharing task-related ideas and information and providing constructive suggestions to members of the organisation (Kogut & Zander, 1992; Wang & Noe, 2010). Interestingly, knowledge is one of the most fundamental resources for performance, and many organisations encourage their employees to share their knowledge to create value for sub-suppliers and even rival companies through supplier networks, communities of practice and knowledge management systems. As a result, knowledge sharing in the supply chain is an intriguing topic to research for various reasons: First, knowledge sharing can help businesses make better decisions by giving them access to a broader range of information and expertise. This can lead to more informed decision-making, which can enhance efficiency, profitability and customer satisfaction (Zeraati et al., 2020). In line with Kaufman's (1997, p. 14) perspective, knowledge sharing is characterised by its capacity to 'remove communication barriers and eliminate redundancies through monitoring, coordinating and controlling processes.' Second, knowledge sharing can help decrease costs by removing duplication of work, increasing efficiency and uncovering cost-saving options. For example, by sharing best practice knowledge, firms can avoid reinventing the wheel, save money on training and development costs and reduce the level of complexity (Chakraborty & Tan, 2013; Damien, 2005; Gong et al., 2013; Nonaka & Takeuchi, 1995). Third, organisations can benefit from knowledge sharing by gaining access to new ideas and insights. This can result in the development of new products and services, the improvement of existing products and services and the discovery of new market opportunities (Li et al., 2019). Furthermore, this approach implies that knowledge sharing can lead to personal growth and foster increased collaboration, trust and greater interaction between network actors. As a result, scholars have called for more exploration of how knowledge sharing can be managed within integrated supply chain processes and become drivers of sustained competitive advantage (Akkermans et al., 1999, Gold et al., 2010; Wang & Noe, 2010; Wasko & Faraj, 2005).

The Sustainable Development Goals (SDGs) established by the United Nations serve as a framework for achieving sustainable business development. According to Gunasekaran et al. (2015), 17 specific SDGs aim to establish partnerships and cooperation on cross-sector as well as cross-country for sustainable development. The aim is to encourage organisations to align with the SDGs fostering collaborative planning, knowledge sharing and innovation among various stakeholders within a supply chain (Mehdikhani & Valmohammadi, 2019). To successfully advance such an agenda, the supply chain must be built on the foundation of inclusivity, sustainability and resilience. Based on the framework, the current study draws attention to industry, innovation and infrastructure (SDG09). The current study investigates how knowledge sharing can lead to sustainable supply chain management.

A previous study has shed light on the multifaceted factors that influence knowledge sharing across organisations, providing useful insights for fostering increased collaborations and innovation among various participants within the realm of the supply chain. One important factor is motivation (Bock et al., 2005; Wasko & Faraj, 2005). The researchers reveal that employees are inclined to share knowledge if they are intrinsically motivated to learn and improve. In addition, a study by Nahapiet and Ghoshal (1998) and Brown and Duguid (2001) emphasised that organisational culture plays a central role in knowledge sharing. The findings of the study suggested that knowledge sharing is more prevalent in groups with a strong sense of community and shared goals, emphasising the importance of a supportive work environment. Furthermore, the aspect of reward and recognition was illuminated by the research work of Kankanhalli et al. (2005) and Kwon and Suh (2005), who stated that acknowledging and appreciating employees' contributions serves as a vital motivator for knowledge sharing and insights. Effective communication is another critical factor highlighted by Hansen (1999) and Nonaka and Takeuchi (1995). They emphasised that successful knowledge sharing necessitates the conversion of tacit knowledge into explicit knowledge before it is shared with others. Likewise, in another study, a group of researchers postulated that opportunities for knowledge sharing are more likely to occur in businesses with an open communication and collaborative culture (Bartol & Srivastava, 2002; Cabrera et al., 2006; Witherspoon et al., 2013). While these approaches contribute to the dynamics of knowledge sharing in the supply environment, there is scope to do more empirical research on how employees' learning agility (ELA) can contribute to knowledge sharing behaviour (KSB) in the supply chain. In this context, learning agility refers to an employee's ability to learn new things quickly and adapt to change (De Meuse et al., 2011; Lombardo & Eichinger, 2000). The effectiveness of an organisation to respond rapidly to changing market conditions will predominantly depend on the capabilities of its employees. Hence, employees with learning agility are efficient, lean, customer-focused, quality-driven, proactive, and focused on adding value to their work. Their increased comfort with change and uncertainty makes them more receptive to sharing their expertise with others. Consequently, it has become an important phenomenon to investigate how ELA can also enhance KSB in the supply chain. As such, this study poses an important research question:

Can ELA impact their willingness to share knowledge?

We draw our focus on the theoretical lens of conservation of resource (COR) theory (Hobfoll, 1988), which provides a direction for explaining how KSB perpetuates at the workplace. As such, the present study introduces COR theory by identifying ELA as one of the drivers of KSB for two reasons: First, knowledge is a vital resource, and COR theory is the leading theory used to explore how employees manage resources (Hobfoll et al., 2018). Second, the COR theory is well established (Hobfoll et al., 2018). While applying this theoretical lens to KSB, this study will obtain an enlightening viewpoint by examining the crucial factors that influence knowledge sharing (Lee et al., 2018; Wu & Lee, 2016). According to Hobfoll (1988), employees invest their existing resources to enhance more resources. Since knowledge is a crucial resource, employees can learn from each other and thereby accumulate more knowledge. However, the flow of knowledge within supply chains is much more difficult (Mentzer et al., 2000), and little is known about the processes and determinants that drive individuals to actively participate in knowledge sharing. According to Sung and Kyung (2015), a lack of knowledge exchange has been found to be a failure factor in supply chain management. As such, this study reveals ELA as a driver for KSB in the supply chain. ELA has been hypothesised as the willingness and ability to learn from the past and acquire new ideas to achieve new results under difficult circumstances (De Meuse et al., 2011; Lombardo & Eichinger, 2000). Miles (2013) found that employees with high learning agility are more likely to adapt to market changes through their past experiences, improve their ability and skills to understand new things, and orchestrate the operations within the supply chain. As a result, partners in a supply chain can integrate their knowledge to identify market opportunities and perhaps gain a competitive edge (Gavirneni et al., 1996; Sambamurthy et al., 2003).

Besides assessing the relationship between ELA and employee KSB, this study aims to evaluate whether the relationship is moderated by psychological contract breaches (PCBs). Since psychological contracts are not part of formal commitments, there are mutual agreements to meet certain expectations, called 'unwritten expectations' (Schein, 1980, p. 22). Since these expectations are unwritten, breaches may occur; as a result, failure to fulfil commitments may have dire consequences for the relationship between ELA and KSB. Therefore, COR (Hobfoll, 1989) postulates that since losing resources weighs more than gain, an individual experiencing resource depletion will minimise resource loss by decreasing their effort for future display of resources, in this case, KSB. Furthermore, COR states that when an individual faces an adverse situation, such as a PCB in the organisation, their valued resources are threatened or are inadequate to handle certain adverse situations in the organisation (Grandey & Cropanzano, 1999; Harris et al., 2011; Hobfoll & Freedy, 1993; Hobfoll & Shirom, 2001). We anticipate that the moderating effect of PCB will adversely affect the association between ELA and KSB.

In conclusion, the findings of the current study revealed that as employees accumulate a wealth of resources through their experience, they can continue to actively engage in KSB. The study also suggested that KSB is an important way to transmit and acquire more knowledge. Furthermore, the study shows that PCB negatively affects the relationship between ELA and KSB. This suggests that the prevalence of PCBs may pose a serious obstacle to volunteer roles, resulting in social disengagement and a decreased likelihood of knowledge sharing. Finally, the study specifically calls policymakers' attention to industry, innovation, and infrastructure (SDG09), where immediate action is required to develop robust supply chain management through ELA. The conceptual framework is demonstrated in Fig. 1 for further elaboration.

THEORETICAL BACKGROUND AND HYPOTHESIS DEVELOPMENT

ELA and KSB

Supply chain management is a complex and ever-changing field. Organisations must be able to quickly adapt to changes in the market, technology and customer needs to remain competitive. One approach to accomplishing this is by placing more emphasis on ELA and KSB. As such, ELA is defined as 'the ability to move swiftly and smoothly; smartness' and 'the suitability to presume and produce outcomes rapidly; cognitive keenness' (Murphy, 2001). While knowledge sharing is regarded as a means to an end and sharing, such resources can enhance long-term sustainability, employee performance and organisational efficiencies (Cabrera & Cabrera, 2019; Cummings, 2004; Hansen, 2002; Mesmer-Magnus & DeChurch, 2009), and it is difficult to substitute (Nonaka & Takeuchi, 1995). Similarly, Ipe (2003) describes knowledge sharing as a process by which one person transforms knowledge into a form that can be comprehended, absorbed, and utilised by another person. Knowledge sharing is a discretionary behaviour, and the sharing of such knowledge will depend on the employee's ability to participate in the knowledge sharing process. Knowledge sharing plays a vital role in the realm of supply chain, with both knowledge sharing and ELA being essential in the quest to construct a more agile and responsive supply chain. In recent study by Cloutier et al. (2020) revealed that improvement in integrated supply chain management can be enhanced through real-time information sharing. Similarly, a study based on small scale logging in Amazon highlighted

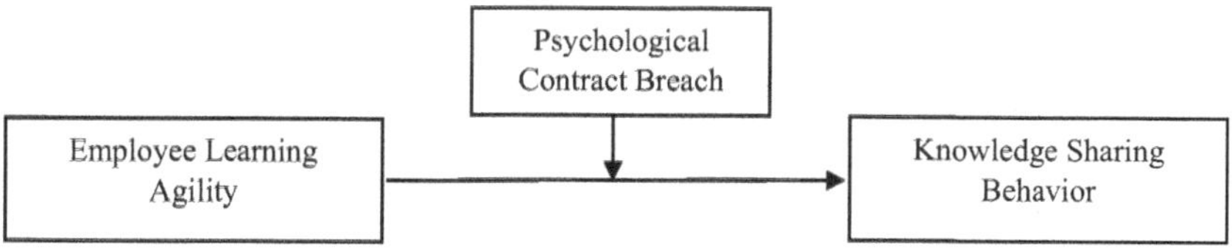

Fig. 1. Conceptual Framework.

bureaucracy as one of the factors causing time delay in management of supply chain (Elias et al., 2021). The researcher suggested that online portal could facilitate registration process effectively. Another group of scholars has highlighted that problems in supply chain management can be alleviated through a continuous flow of information between network actors (Huhns et al., 2002; Kumar, 2007). The findings of a recent study also highlighted that successful knowledge sharing improves collaboration and coordination creating sustainable supply chain performance (Mehdikhani & Valmohammadi, 2019; Pan et al., 2020; Whitehead et al., 2019). Therefore, we argue that networks with greater knowledge sharing processes will be able to 'out-innovate' rapidly, and this can be made possible through employees with greater learning agility. Employees who are receptive to learning are more likely to understand the value of knowledge sharing. They are more likely to interact and work well with others, which is critical for knowledge sharing. Nonaka and Takeuchi (1995) provided evidence that learning opportunities, whether inside or outside the company, give an employee a chance to accept, change and recombine their new information to create new information stock. Shih et al. (2011) also noted that employees with strong learning agility are more engaged in their jobs, have lower turnover intentions and are better able to adapt to changes through creative thinking (Dries & Pepermans, 2012; Tripathi & Dhir, 2022). Similarly, another group of scholars demonstrated that employees' willingness to learn from experience and the diffusion of knowledge is significantly linked to greater understanding and agreement, contributing towards the establishment of resilient supply chain management (De Meuse, 2017; Eisenberger et al., 2001; Lombardo & Eichinger, 2000; Nonaka & Takeuchi, 1995).

This study employs the COR theory (Hobfoll, 1989) to examine the relationship between ELA and KSB. According to COR, the knowledge sharing process is a good way for employees to accumulate knowledge by providing them with the opportunity to learn from each other. As such, knowledge sharing is not just sharing resources but also replenishing and gaining new insight (Hobfoll, 1988, 1989), this can ultimately lead to improvement in the management of the supply chain. ELA plays a crucial role in the dynamic and ever-changing realm of supply chain operations. Consequently, these employees demonstrate increased resourcefulness, which makes it easier for them to become highly involved in knowledge sharing. As such, employees with an abundance of resources and willingness to share are considered agile. Shared knowledge plays a crucial role in fostering the trust required for deeper collaboration between partners (Dyer & Nobeoka, 2000; Hobfoll et al., 2018). Likewise, Hobfoll et al. (2018) also highlighted that agile learners are better able to respond to disturbances, discover optimisation possibilities, and adapt to evolving market demands. This implies that robust interpersonal ties and trust among supply chain partners allow the transmission of important information and best practices. Furthermore, the COR theory further posits that individuals with a wealth of knowledge contribute to enhanced coordination and decision-making throughout the organisation by actively participating in knowledge sharing. Kumar et al. (2023) highlighted that employees with learning agility possess a proactive mindset which not only fosters active exchange of important information but also takes challenges that enable them to adjust effectively in rapidly changing environments. Consequently, implementing a distinctive employee experience and changing technology processes can improve adaptability, creativity, autonomy, strategy-based innovation, and the development of a resilient supply chain. This intangible value is seen in supply chain networks as the true basis for value creation (Allee, 2002) and enhancing the relationships within the networks in supply chain management. Based on this assertion, we propose the following:

H1. ELA will be positively associated with KSB.

The Moderating Role of PCB Between ELA and KSB

The PCB suggests that the working relationship between employee and employer revolves around implicit exchanges that exist beyond formal obligations (Rousseau, 1995). Given that the psychological contract exists outside the formal obligation, there is a mutual agreement to meet certain expectations, referred to as an 'unwritten set of expectations' (Schein, 1980, p. 22). Because these expectations are unwritten, breaches may occur, and as such, unmet obligations can have a detrimental impact on supply chain management. According to Welbourne and colleagues, when resource loss outweighs the gain, an agile employee under the threat of resource exhaustion will protect such resources against further depletion by reducing the investment of valuable resources on task-related activities and protecting the unused resources as a cope-up strategy (Welbourne et al., 2016). Increasing empirical evidence suggests that employees who effectively share knowledge from one entity to another are very productive and have high chances of survival (Baum & Ingram, 1998; Darr et al., 1995). Similarly, Machiondo (2012) also suggested that KSB can motivate individuals to effectively manage their workload and resources and enhance their networking within the supply chain; however, the prevalence of PCBs can become a critical barrier to voluntary roles, creating social disengagement and decreasing the likelihood of knowledge sharing.

At the heart of COR, individuals attempt to preserve, foster, retain, and expand resources in anticipation of future replenishment (Hobfoll, 1989). However, adverse workplace encounters can trigger psychological distress, causing resource depletion and subsequently affecting work-related outcomes. We propose that employees with strong learning agility are more likely to be aware of psychological contracts, and when such contracts are breached, these employees may allocate remaining resources for only mandatory tasks. Through the lens of COR theory, a PCB not only endangers the resources but also leads to an actual resource drain without replacement. Through the lens of the COR theory, a breach in the psychological contract not only jeopardises existing resources but also results in an actual loss of resources with no replenishment. Within the realm of PCB, the degree of discrepancies between promised obligations and what is perceived triggers individuals to behave reactively (Zhao et al., 2007). Such breaches of obligation will make employees frustrated and, more likely, too distant from the organisation (Lee et al., 2015). The feeling of being treated unfairly will ultimately make employees emotionally detached from the organisation, causing work disengagement (Colquitt et al., 2013). Agile employees constantly contribute with ideas, criticism, and fresh insights that can provide more innovative ideas for decision-making. However, if these employees perceive a breach of psychological contract, they may feel undervalued for their contribution and may become less inclined to share their valued resources towards the development of a resilient supply chain. In congruence, the findings of Kim et al. (2016) also stated that employees who fear resource depletion will engage less in KSB, which could have implications for supply chain management in terms of collaboration, knowledge sharing, and problem-solving, affecting its efficiency and effectiveness. Drawing from these interpretations, it is reasonable to conclude that having perceived PCB, highly agile employees may perceive knowledge sharing as risky behaviour, and to avoid further depletion of such valuable resources, they will shield themselves in a shell like a turtle. Therefore, we propose the following hypothesis:

H2. PCB will moderate the association between ELA and knowledge sharing; as such, PCB will weaken the association between ELA and KSB.

METHODOLOGY

Sample and Data Procedure

Scientific discoveries are guided by research paradigms, which provide the framework for scientific inquiry through underlying assumptions. Understanding paradigm-specific assumptions to ensure the quality of findings and identify gaps in generating sound evidence. This study explores the research paradigm of positivism. As such, positivism is consistent with the hypothetical deductive model of scientific studies which involves formulating hypothesis, designing experiment, and conducting rigorous testing of hypothesis to systematically evaluate and redefine scientific knowledge. The current study aligns with positivism in using quantitative approaches and emphasises large sample size for empirical findings. The study employs a quantitative to investigate the relationship between ELA and knowledge sharing in the supply chain. This approach allows the collection and analysis of numerical data, making it appropriate for testing hypotheses. To accomplish this, we collected the data through a random sampling of 418 individuals from the public service organisation, Fiji Island. A letter of explanation was attached to ensure that the survey data was collected voluntarily. The participants were requested to fill out and return the completed survey form in a closed envelope. The study reported no missing data. The present study included age, organisational experience, gender, and salary scale as a control variable as illustrated in Table 1. Gender was coded as a dummy variable (0 = male, 1 = female). Males made up 42.7% of the participants, while 57.3% were female.

Table 1. Control Variable.

Age	18–23 years 19.2%	23–28 years 32.7%	28–33 years 18.5%	33–38 years 6.1%	38 years and over 23.5%
Organisational experience	1–5 years 20.3%	5–10 years 39.6%	10–15 years 14.8%	15–20 years 3.4%	20 years and over 21.9%
	FJD	FJD	FJD	FJD	FJD
Salary scale	10,000 5.4%	10,000–20,000 10.2%	20,000–30,000 51.2%	300,00–40,000 20.1%	40,000 and over 13.1%

Measurements

All items on the survey were evaluated on a five-point Likert scale that ranged from 1 (strongly disagree) to 5 (strongly agree). ELA was measured using a seven-item scale proposed by Lombardo and Eichinger (2000). The sample items included 'team working is strongly encouraged in our department,' with a Cronbach's α of 0.92. KSB was measured through a six-item scale suggested by researcher Srivastava et al. (2006). The sample items included 'I shared factual knowledge (know-what) from work with my co-workers,' with a Cronbach's α of 0.89. PCB consists of five items adapted from Robinson and Wolfe Morrison (2000). The sample item included the 'I have not received everything promised to me in exchange for my contributions' coefficient α of 0.85.

Control Variables

We controlled a few variables that seem vital in resolving the limitations of research (Spector & Brannick, 2011). To eliminate any possible alternate annotations, our study also controlled the demographic variables (Bernerth & Aguinis, 2016; Spector & Brannick, 2011). Prior research highlighted that age, sex, and organisational experience are significant factors in determining generous behaviours in organisations (Barclay, 2010; Flynn et al., 2006). Furthermore, the above-mentioned demographic variables have also been included in prior research, as these variables were considered to have a spontaneous effect in explaining knowledge sharing. However, the effects were spurious, demonstrating positive and negative effects, and most of the time they did not show any effect on knowledge sharing (Kim & Yun, 2015; Lin, 2007; Srivastava et al., 2006). As such, our study also included age, sex, occupational experience, and salary scale as our demographic variables to check the disparity in the results without and with the inclusion of control variables (Becker, 2005; Spector & Brannick, 2011). The difference is tabulated next. The age was measured in years, while gender was measured as a dummy variable (0 = male, 1 = female). Occupational experience in a number of years; salary scale using the salary scale range (Fiji dollar). The results of descriptive statistics, inter-correlations, and reliability are illustrated in

Table 2. Descriptive Statistics and Correlations.

	Mean	SD	1	2	3	4	5	6
1. Age	2.02	0.96						
2. Gender	1.66	0.49	−0.068*					
3. Occupation	1.89	0.86	0.628**	−0.167**				
4. Salary	2.63	0.67	0.056	0.111**	0.121**			
5. ELA	3.79	0.94	0.024	−0.040	0.046	0.063		
6. K S	3.98	0.93	0.013	0.029	0.063	0.047	0.686**	
7. PCB	3.86	0.97	−0.001	−0.010	−0.027	0.009	−0.454**	−0.336**

Note: $*p < 0.05$, $**p < 0.01$, $***p < 0.001$.
Employee learning agility (ELA), knowledge sharing behaviour (KSB), psychological contract breach (PCB).

Table 2. The result was consistent with the proposed hypothesis: ELA is positively associated with KSB.

While PCB had a negative association between ELA and KSB. According to Tekleab and Taylor (2003), the control variable may confound significant interests such as age, gender, occupational experience, etc. Our analysis showed that none of the control variables had any effect on the ELA, KSB or PCB.

RESULTS

Before testing the proposed hypothesis, we analysed the construct validity, composite reliability (CR), and average variance construct (AVE) (Anderson & Gerbing, 1988). Table 4 shows that all items had a significant factor loading. While Table 5 shows the analysis of AVE, which extends from 0.60 to 0.78, exceeding the suggested level of 0.5, the composite reliability met the threshold of 0.70 (Fornell, 1981). In addition, the value of Cronbach's alpha also exceeded 0.7, indicating the excellent reliability of the study. Moreover, we performed several confirmatory factor analyses (CFA) to check the distinctiveness of the measured variable for this study. We used the Analysis of Moment Structures (AMOS) to ascertain chi-square (), the root means square error of approximation (RMSEA), the comparative fit index (CFI), and Tucker–Lewis's index (TLI) (Anderson & Gerbing, 1988). The best model for this study is illustrated in Table 3.

Table 3. The Model Fit.

x^2	df	RAMSEA	RMR	TLI	IFI	CFI
446.162	113	0.057	0.041	0.94	0.95	0.95

Table 4. Matrix of Loading and Cross-Loading.

	ELA	KS	PCB
ELA 1	0.704**	0.593**	−0.413**
ELA 2	0.735**	0.631**	−0.416**
ELA 3	0.747**	0.651**	−0.388**
ELA 4	0.725**	0.641**	−0.448**
ELA 5	0.707**	0.600**	−0.487**
ELA 6	0719**	0.609**	−0.454**
ELA 7	0.740**	0.607**	−0.348**
KS 1	0.614**	0.828**	−0.370**
KS 2	0.651**	0.874**	−0.331**
KS 3	0.642**	0.845**	−0.383**
KS 4	0.576**	0.804**	−0.233**
KS 5	0.552**	0.717**	−0.283**
KS 6	0.567**	0.717**	−0.327**
PCB 1	−0.400**	−0.309**	0.875**
PCB 2	−0.375**	−0.283**	0.892**
PCB 3	−0.364**	−0.295**	0.841**
PCB 4	−0.589**	−0.468**	0.709**

Note: $*p < 0.05$, $**p < 0.01$, $***p < 0.001$.
ELA = Employee learning agility, KS = Knowledge sharing behaviour, PCB = Psychological contract breach.

At times, common method bias (CMB) can be a critical risk of bias in organisational research. Normally, this occurs when data are collected at a single point; as such, this can be alleviated using several procedures and statistical tools (Podsakoff et al., 2012). With the procedure, we maintained respondents' anonymity, minimised evaluations and separated predictor variables from other variables. Through statistical remedies, several CFA were performed to exclude components of CMB. First, Bagozzi and Yi (1990) suggest that any correlation exceeding 0.9 will indicate the presence of CMB. The result of this study shows that all correlations within variables were only as high as 0.892. (Table 4). Second, using the common latent factor (CFL), we checked standardised regression weights for our conceptual model using CFL, and the difference was very minuscule (Table 5). Overall, our data analysis exhibits no threat of CMB. The proposed model was tested using conditional process analysis (Hayes, 2018).

H1 predicts that ELA will have a positive impact on knowledge sharing. The result in Table 6 shows knowledge sharing and the need for status ($\beta = 0.687, p < 0.001$), and *H1* is supported. *H2* predicts that PCB will moderate the connection between ELA and knowledge sharing (KSB). Table 6 shows a significant negative moderating interaction ($\beta = -0.106, p < 0.01$). *H2* is supported.

Based on the recommendation of Stone and Hollenbeck (1989), the analysis of moderating effects with two-way integration was carried out. Fig. 2 shows that employees with high learning agility engage more in knowledge sharing activities when PCB is low.

Table 5. Factor Loading With CFA.

Item	Mean	SD	Item-Total Correlation	Loading	Error	Cronbach's Alpha	Composite Reliability	AVE
ELA 1	3.71	0.83	0.374	0.752	0.036	0.92	0.91	0.78
ELA 2	3.82	0.75	0.445	0.849	0.038			
ELA 3	3.87	0.75	0.359	0.835	0.038			
ELA 4	3.75	0.80	0.360	0.855	0.040			
ELA 5	3.70	0.79	0.380	0.764	0.041			
ELA 6	3.68	0.81	0.341	0.872	0.042			
ELA 7	3.85	0.75	0.331	0.843	0.039			
KSB 1	3.86	0.84	0.350	0.801	0.036	0.89	0.90	0.68
KSB 2	3.96	0.79	0.460	0.885	0.033			
KSB 3	3.83	0.87	0.390	0.831	0.039			
KSB 4	3.07	0.73	0.392	0.775	0.036			
KSB 5	2.06	0.70	0.370	0.710	0.038			
KSB 6	3.00	0.71	0.400	0.714	0.036			
PCB 1	2.31	0.89	0.310	0.882	0.035	0.85	0.89	0.60
PCB 2	2.32	0.90	0.360	0.902	0.030			
PCB 3	2.29	0.92	0.320	0.745	0.033			
PCB 4	2.36	0.85	0.370	0.752	0.039			

ELA = Employee learning agility, KS = Knowledge sharing behaviour, PCB = Psychological contract breach.

Table 6. The Moderating Effect of Psychological Contract Breach (PCB).

	Knowledge Sharing Behaviour							
	Model 1		Model 2		Model 3		Model 4	
	SE	β	SE	β	SE	β	SE	β
Constant	0.117		0.122		0.130		0.131	
Age	0.028	−0.045	0.020	−0.016	0.014	−0.030	0.014	−0.030
Gender	0.043	0.037	0.031	0.065	0.022	0.011	0.022	0.012
Occupational experience	0.032	0.093	0.023	0.053	0.016	0.028	0.016	0.028
Salary scale	0.032	0.034	0.023	−0.009	0.017	0.004	0.017	0.004
Employee learning agility			0.024	0.687***	0.022	0.324***	0.022	0.321***
Moderators PCB					0.023	0.618	0.024	0.615
Interaction NS*PCB							0.38	−0.106 ***
R^2	0.008		0.476		0.737		0.742	
$\triangle R^2$			0.468***		0.261***		0.005***	

Dependent Variable: Knowledge sharing.
Note: $^{**}p < 0.01$, $^{***}p < 0.001$. Dummy variables: Gender (0 = male, 1 = female), age, occupational experience, salary scale.
ELA = Employee learning agility, KS = Knowledge sharing behaviour, PCB = Psychological contract breach.

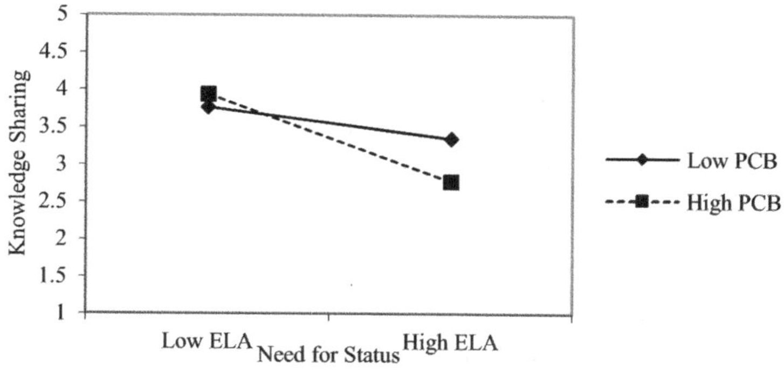

Fig. 2. The Moderating Role of Psychological Contract Breach.

DISCUSSION

This study examined how ELA drives an individual to share valuable resources, such as knowledge. The question arises: Why do individuals engage in such acts? According to Dixon (2012), the more an employee shares what they know (knowledge, experience, skills and ability), the more valuable they become. As a result, the current study's findings demonstrated that ELA positively influences KSB. Smith and Davidson (2014) highlighted that by 'sharing what we own, we secure our future'. Building upon the foundation laid by the researcher, our findings can be further concluded that learning agility as a competency can effectively and efficiently negate ambiguity and uncertainty through the dissemination of best practices, critical information, and problem-solving and fostering a culture of continuous improvement in today's business world. According to Swisher et al. (2013), agile employees strive for continuous improvement (Lombardo & Eichinger, 2000), are highly committed to their organisation (Shih et al., 2011), are goal-oriented and are curious to make connections between old and new information and strategies for solving complex problems. The notion of COR theory provides a clue that sharing accumulated knowledge enables employees to collaborate and connect with network actors within or outside the supply chain and simultaneously gain new insight to replenish the existing stock of knowledge. The theory further postulates that employees with resources are highly likely to invest (Hobfoll, 1988).

Furthermore, we moderated the relationship between ELA and KSB with PCB. In line with COR theory, our finding shows that PCB adversely impacts the correlation between ELA and KSB. Having experienced such, individuals may try to minimise the negative impacts by utilising time, effort, and energy to cushion the negative impact (Hobfoll, 1989). This suggests that due to adversities, the valuable resources that are much needed to enhance supply chain activity are at risk and may hinder employees from engaging in activities that may not provide a suitable return for the KSB.

Theoretical Implications

This is a unique study to investigate the link between ELA and KSB and how such behaviour can be affected by adversities such as PCBs. Knowledge sharing is a fundamental resource for enhancing the dissemination of critical information within the supply chain, thereby creating added value for customers (Chantrasa, 2005). It allows an employee to share desirable qualities that are very costly to acquire and strenuous to duplicate, as this is our new finding in the field of supply chain management. Therefore, we pioneered the study by adopting the conservation of theory (COR) in explaining the relationship between ELA and KSB. Additionally, we employed conservative resource theory (COR) to shed light on the subsequent effect of organisational challenges such as PCB. In line with the COR framework, this perplexing phenomenon indicates that employees with strong learning agility have greater potential and are more willing to tackle difficult tasks and challenge themselves (Yun et al., 2007). Furthermore, previous studies show that knowledge sharing is enhanced by external incentives such as earning a prestigious title, social motivation for group cooperation, and intentions and attitudes that can enhance individual contribution to the collective interest (Bolino, 1999; Grant & Mayer, 2009; Yun et al., 2007), yet our analysis indicates that instead of being merely driven by internal motivations, ELA can be a distinct internal driver for knowledge sharing, activating spontaneous exhibition of resources. Another challenge of applying COR theory to KSB is the paradoxical nature of shared knowledge. When less knowledge is disseminated, 'the value that it offers is greater by virtue of its exclusiveness' (McIver et al., 2013). However, sharing knowledge can be an excellent way to showcase a hidden quality acquired through the accumulation of past competencies. The current study also revealed that the link between ELA and KSB can be adversely affected by the perverseness of PCB. As such, employees are likely to hold back KSB until such a time when this behaviour can positively affect the group. According to Lin and Huang (2020), agile employees can identify changes, encourage innovations, and react quickly to changes (Lin & Huang, 2020). Based on our findings, we can conclude that ELA can be a boundary condition for the activation of the knowledge-centred era. This implies that individuals who are more capable of learning are also more willing to take on challenging tasks and find solutions to the most difficult tasks, which only occurs when PCB is low. Although prior literature has used COR theory to understand the consequences of PCB (Hur et al., 2015; Zhou et al., 2015), a study using PCB as a moderator has been lacking for some time. Based on COR theory, our findings reveal that the depletion of valuable resources disconnects the link between ELA and KSB, unpacking the 'black box' as to how the presence of such challenges can undermine one's competencies. Our results demonstrated compelling insinuations with both theoretical and managerial implications. Finally, considering knowledge sharing as a valuable resource, COR theory can be a useful framework to explain why and when an individual may share knowledge.

Practical Implications

The sharing of knowledge is an essential function of any business network, and as a result, the research specifically calls policymakers' attention to industry, innovation and infrastructure (SDG09), where immediate action is required to develop robust supply chain management through ELA in the following ways: First, create a culture of learning and sharing. This implies that organisations need to motivate employees to share their knowledge and expertise as well as be open to new experiences. This can be accomplished by offering chances for training and growth as well as by fostering an environment in which people feel comfortable sharing their ideas. Employees who are learning agile are more likely to share their knowledge with others because they feel comfortable with change and uncertainty (Gandhi et al., 2020). Second, reward KSB. Employees are more inclined to share their knowledge when they are compensated for doing so. This can be accomplished through formal rewards like bonuses or promotions as well as informal benefits like recognition and appreciation. According to Kumar et al. (2020), employees who were rewarded for sharing their knowledge were more engaged in their work and felt valued by their employers. The survey also discovered that these employees were less likely to quit the organisation. Third, the current study also enlightens how PCBs can negatively affect the relationship between ELA and KSB. As a result, the organisation should ensure that during the process of employment, they actively fulfil the obligations and avoid any instances of PCB. In line with prior studies, failure to uphold obligations and the prevalence of unethical behaviour could impede an employee's ability to realise their goals (Duhart, 2001; Moore et al., 2012). Fourth, PCBs can lead to resource depletion and discourage KSB. Instead, the manager needs to provide more psychological support and uphold its promised obligations through regular communication. To some extent, this will restore the unexpected loss (Fredrickson & Branigan, 2005). Finally, in the absence of a PCB, we saw a significant positive association between ELA and KSB. This suggests that managers should provide an employee with a supportive environment that increases person-environment fit (Ostroff & Judge, 2007), as this may establish a more resilient supply chain that is better equipped to respond to change by creating an atmosphere in which employees feel comfortable learning and sharing.

Creating a Resilient Supply Chain

The interaction between ELA and knowledge sharing plays a central role in establishing a resilient supply chain. The vulnerability of the supply chain during the recent pandemic emphasises the importance of organisations harnessing the management of the supply chain to withstand any disruptions (Chauhan et al., 2022). The finding of our research suggests that employees who are learning agile learn and adapt quickly to changing market dynamics, unforeseen challenges, and technological disruptions, through the dissemination of critical information, problem-solving strategies, and best practices within the realm of supply chain operations. This will ensure that customers continue getting value from the products and services they require. Moreover, Carter and Rogers (2008) highlighted that risk related to the supply chain can be managed through contingency planning and the development of a more agile supply chain. Similarly, another group of researchers highlighted that reducing the bureaucracies with efficient process would stimulate best practices with supply chain management (Elias et al., 2021). Our findings revealed that agile employees are quick learners, who can tackle complex problems or find innovative solutions, which in turn enables them to swiftly adapt to unexpected challenges. This will enable organisations to maintain a competitive advantage and meet customers' expectations. Furthermore, Chauhan and colleagues also highlighted that lack of effective communication is one of the significant barriers to implementing sustainable supply chains (Chauhan et al., 2022). These deficiencies in the communication process result in substantial costs in supply chain management (Seuring, 2001; Vachon, 2007). Consistent with the findings of experts like Elias et al. (2021) for the need to create integrated action between supply chain networks, our finding suggests that employees with strong learning agility tend to exhibit a strong culture of knowledge sharing. This proactive behaviour of sharing critical information within integrated supply chain will help address challenges and maintain operational integrity in the face of uncertainty.

Limitations and Future Research Direction

Although our finding makes an important contribution to the existing literature, several limitations need to be addressed. First, based on cross-sectional data, our analysis did not account for casual interference. However, future research may examine the causality between variables with controlled experiments. Second, turning KSB into a sharing it forward culture Based on the assertion that self-centred individuals may be more concerned with their own needs and ambivalent about assisting others, they might interpret generosity as an instance of exploitation (Sommerfeld, 2008). Future studies can investigate the sharing-forward behaviour from the perspective of the first giver. In other words, individuals who share knowledge are likely to experience higher satisfaction and joy in helping others. Third, there is a need to appreciate and acknowledge KSB. According to Mikulincer et al. (2006), managers' praise was conceded to be one of the top motivators, surpassing financial and other non-cash incentives. Praising individuals not only encourages them but also enhances their effectiveness. According to While Deloitte report (2015), organisations that implement recognition practices achieve 12 times better business outcomes. Consequently, acknowledging and recognising knowledge sharing can cultivate a willingness to share more valuable insights. Future research could explore the dynamic of recognition and praising behaviour within the organisation, as this can open new avenues for generous behaviour. Finally, the generalisation of our study should be made with caution as the present sample is from the context of Fiji Island. According to the findings, females showed a low level of KSB compared to males due to cultural context. Ostentation sharing of knowledge is regarded as socially undesirable as modesty is respected as a virtue, and such norms tend to position females in a passive role (Hofstede, 1991). A survey in Western countries highlighted that KSB between males and females was not significantly distinct (Cabrera et al., 2006). Future studies may include sex and national culture in knowledge sharing to investigate the generalisability of SEM within diverse cultural settings. In summary, grounded in COR theory, our study offers a new direction on how learning from experiences could foster greater KSB. Because today's business world is much more complex and multifaceted, knowledge sharing will enable employees to build and diversify their own skill sets while at the same time engaging in continuous learning. The COR theory can be further explored by establishing a nomological network of variables linked to KSB in organisational settings.

CONCLUSION

In conclusion, this research significantly contributes to both theoretical and practical domains by examining the intricate linkages between ELA, KSB and the moderating effect of PCB within the context of supply chain management. The finding of this research suggests that learning agility positively influences KSB, positioning it as a competency that enhances an employee's value by mitigating ambiguity and uncertainty in the business landscape. Furthermore, the research extends its contribution by moderating the ELA-KSB relationship with PCB, revealing that adverse experiences can impede KSBs as employees may redirect time and energy to counteract negative impacts. The research also emphasises the pivotal role of the interaction between ELA and knowledge sharing in establishing a resilient supply chain, crucial for navigating disruptions, as highlighted by the recent pandemic. As quick learners, agile employees are problem-solvers, contributors of critical information within the supply chain, ensure operational integrity and meet customer expectations. The practical implications advocate for fostering a culture of continuous learning, addressing PCBs and recognising the value of knowledge sharing in building agile and resilient supply chains for sustained success in today's dynamic business environment.

REFERENCES

Akkermans, H., Bogerd, P., & Vos, B. (1999). Virtuous and vicious cycles on the road towards international supply chain management. *International Journal of Operations & Production Management*, *19*(5/6), 565–581.

Allee, V. (2002). A value network approach for measuring and modeling intangibles. In *Paper presented at the transparent enterprise conference*. www.vernaallee.com

Anderson, J. C., & Gerbing, D. W. (1988). Structural equation modeling in practice: A review and recommended two-step approach. *Psychological Bulletin*, *103*(3), 411–423. https://doi.org/10.1037/0033-2909.103.3.411

Bagozzi, R. P., & Yi, Y. (1990). Assessing method variance in multitrait-multimethod matrices: The case of self-reported affect and perceptions at work. *Journal of Applied Psychology*, *75*(5), 547–560. https://doi.org/10.1037/0021-9010.75.5.547

Barclay, P. (2010). Altruism as a courtship display: Some effects of third-party generosity on audience perceptions. *British Journal of Psychology*, *101*, 123–135. https://doi.org/10.1348/000712609X435733

Bartol, K. M., & Srivastava, A. (2002). Encouraging knowledge sharing: The role of organisational reward systems. *Journal of Leadership & Organisational Studies*, *9*, 64–76.

Baum, J., & Ingram, P. (1998). Survival-enhancing learning in the Manhattan Hotel Industry, 1898–1980. *Management Science*, *44*, 996–1016. https://doi.org/10.1287/mnsc.44.7.996

Becker, T. E. (2005). Potential problems in the statistical control of variables in organisational research: A qualitative analysis with recommendations. *Organisational Research Methods*, *8*, 274–289. https://doi.org/10.1177/1094428105278021

Bernerth, J. B., & Aguinis, H. (2016). A critical review and best-practice recommendations for control variable usage. *Personnel Psychology*, *69*, 229–283. https://doi.org/10.1111/peps.12103

Bock, G. W., Zmud, R. W., Kim, Y. G., & Lee, J. N. (2005). Behavioral intention formation in knowledge sharing: Roles of extrinsic motivators, social-psychological forces, and business climate. *MIS Quarterly*, *29*(1), 87–112.

Bolino, M. C. (1999). Citizenship and impression management: Good soldiers or good actors? *Academy of Management Review*, *24*, 82–98. https://doi.org/10.5465/AMR.1999.1580442

Brown, J. S., & Duguid, P. (2001). Knowledge and organization: A social-practice perspective. *Organization Science*, *12*, 40–57.

Cabrera, A., Collins, W. C., & Salgado, J. F. (2006). Determinants of individual engagement in knowledge sharing. *International Journal of Human Resource Management*, *17*, 245–264. https://doi.org/10.1080/09585190500404614

Cabrera, D., & Cabrera, L. (2019). What is systems thinking?: Learning, design, and technology. *An International Compendium of Theory, Research, Practice, and Policy*. https://doi.org/10.1007/978-3-319-17727-4_100-1

Carter, C. R., & Rogers, D. S. (2008). A framework of sustainable supply chain management: Moving toward new theory. *International Journal of Physical Distribution & Logistics Management*, *38*(5), 360–387. https://doi.org/10.1108/09600030810882816

Chakraborty, A., & Tan, K. (2013). An empirical analysis on Six Sigma implementation in service organizations. *International Journal of Lean Six Sigma*, *4*, 141–170. https://doi.org/10.1108/20401461311319338

Chantrasa, R. (2005, May). *Decision making approaches for information sharing in a supply chain*. Dissertation, Graduate School of Clemson University.

Chauhan, C., Kaur, P., Arrawatia, R., Ractham, P., & Dhir, A. (2022). Supply chain collaboration and sustainable development goals (SDGs). Teamwork makes achieving SDGs dream work. *Journal of Business Research*, *147*, 290–307. https://doi.org/10.1016/j.jbusres.2022.03.044

Cloutier, C., Oktaei, P., & Lehoux, N. (2020). Collaborative mechanisms for sustainability-oriented supply chain initiatives: State of the art, role assessment and research opportunities. *International Journal of Production Research*. https://doi.org/10.1080/00207543.2019.1660821

Colquitt, J. A., Scott, B. A., Rodell, J. B., Long, D. M., Zapata, C. P., Conlon, D. E., & Wesson, M. J. (2013). Justice at the millennium, a decade later: A meta-analytic test of social exchange and affect based perspectives. *Journal of Applied Psychology*, *98*(2), 199–236.

Cummings, J. N. (2004). Work groups, structural diversity, and knowledge sharing in a global organisation. *Management Science*, *50*, 352–364. https://doi.org/10.1287/mnsc.1030.0134

Damien, P. (2005). Supply chain management integration and implementation: A literature review. *Supply Chain Management: An International Journal*, *10*(4), 252–263.

Darr, E., Argote, L., & Epple, D. (1995). The acquisition, transfer and depreciation of knowledge in service organisations: Productivity in franchises. *Management Science*, *41*, 1750–1762.

Deloitte. (2015). *Mind the gap: The 2015 Deloitte millennial survey executive summary*.

DeMeuse, K. P. (2017). Learning agility: Its evolution as a psychological construct and its empirical relationship to leader success. *Consulting Psychology Journal: Practice and Research*, *69*(4), 267–295. https://doi.org/10.1037/cpb0000100

DeMeuse, K. P., Dai, G., Zewdie, S., Page, R. C., Clark, L., & Eichinger, R. W. (2011). Development and validation of a self-assessment of learning agility [Paper presentation]. In *The society for industrial and organisational psychology conference, Chicago, IL*.

Dixon, N. (2012). Neglected receiver of knowledge sharing. *Ivey Business Journal*. http://iveybusinessjournal.com/publication/neglected-receiver-of-knowledge-sharing/

Dries, N., & Pepermans, R. (2012). How to identify leadership potential: Development and testing of a consensus model. *Human Resource Management*, 51(3), 361–385. https://doi.org/10.1002/hrm.21473

Duhart, D. T. (2001), *Violence in the workplace, 1993–1999*. US Department of Justice, Office of Justice Programs.

Dyer, J., & Nobeoka, K. (2000). Creating and managing a high-performance knowledge sharing network: The Toyota case. *Strategic Management Journal, 21*, 345–367. https://doi.org/10.1002/(SICI)1097-0266(200003)21:3<345::AID-SMJ96>3.0.CO;2-N

Eisenberger, R., Armeli, S., Rexwinkel, B., Lynch, P. D., & Rhoades, L. (2001). Reciprocation of perceived organisational support. *Journal of Applied Psychology, 86*, 42–51. https://doi.org/10.1037//0021-9010.86.1.42

Elias, A., Donadelli, F., Paiva, E., & Araujo, P. (2021). Analysing the complexities of sustainable wood supply chain in the Amazon: A systems thinking approach. *International Journal of Logistics Management*. ahead-of-print. https://doi.org/10.1108/IJLM-07-2020-0276

Flynn, F. J., Reagans, R. E., Amanatullah, E. T., & Ames, D. R. (2006). Helping one's way to the top: Self-monitors achieve status by helping others and knowing who helps whom. *Journal of Personality and Social Psychology, 91*, 1123–1137. https://doi.org/10.1037/0022-3514.91.6.1123

Fornell, C. (1981). Structural equation models with unobservable variables and measurement error: Algebra and statistics. *Journal of Marketing Research, 18*(3), 382–388. https://doi.org/10.2307/3150980

Fredrickson, B. L., & Branigan, C. (2005). Positive emotions broaden the scope of attention and thought-action repertoires. *Cognition & Emotion, 19*(3), 313–332.

Gandhi, S., Srivastava, A. K., Ray, U., & Tripathi, P. P. (2020). Is the collapse of the respiratory center in the brain responsible for respiratory breakdown in COVID-19 patients? *ACS Chemical Neuroscience, 11*, 1379–1381.

Gavirneni, S., Kapuscinski, R., & Tayur, S. (1996). Value of information in capacitated supply chains. *Management Science, 45*. https://doi.org/10.1287/mnsc.45.1.16

Gold, S., Seuring, S., & Beske, P. (2010). Sustainable supply chain management and interorganizational resources: A literature review. *Corporate Social Responsibility and Environmental Management, 17*(4), 230–245.

Gong, Y., Kim, T. Y., Zhu, J., & Lee, D. R. (2013). A multilevel model of team goal orientation, information exchange, and creativity. *Academy of Management Journal, 56*, 827–851. https://doi.org/10.5465/amj.2011.0177

Grandey, A. A., & Cropanzano, R. (1999). The conservation of resources model applied to work-family conflict and strain. *Journal of Vocational Behavior, 54*, 350–370.

Grant, A. M., & Mayer, D. M. (2009). Good soldiers and good actors: Prosocial and impression management motives as interactive predictors of affiliative citizenship behaviors. *Journal of Applied Psychology, 94*, 900–912. https://doi.org/10.1037/a0013770

Gunasekaran, A., Subramanian, N., & Rahman, S. (2015). Green supply chain collaboration and incentives: Current trends and future directions. *Transportation Research Part E: Logistics & Transportation Review, 74*, 1–10. https://doi.org/10.1016/j.tre.2015.01.002

Hansen, M. T. (1999). The search-transfer problem: The role of weak ties in sharing knowledge across business subunits. *Administrative Science Quarterly, 44*(1), 82–111.

Hansen, M. T. (2002). Knowledge networks: Effective knowledge sharing in multiunit companies. *Organisation Science, 13*(3), 232–248.

Harris, K. J., Harvey, P., & Kacmar, K. M. (2011). Abusive supervisory reactions to coworker relationship conflict. *The Leadership Quarterly, 22*, 1010–1023. https://doi.org/10.1016/j.leaqua.2011.07.0 20

Hayes, A. F. (2018). *Introduction to mediation, moderation and conditional process analysis, a regression-based approach*. Guilford Press.

Hobfoll, S. E. (1989). Conservation of resources: A new attempt at conceptualizing stress. *American Psychologist, 44*, 513–524.

Hobfoll, S. E. (1988). *The ecology of stress*. Hemisphere Publishing Corp.

Hobfoll, S. E., & Freedy, J. (1993). Conservation of resources: A general stress theory applied to burnout. In W. B. Schaufeli, C. Maslach, & T. Marek (Eds.), *Professional burnout: Recent developments in theory and research* (pp. 115–133). Taylor & Francis.

Hobfoll, S. E., Halbesleben, J., Neveu, J.-P., & Westman, M. (2018). Conservation of resources in the organizational context: The reality of resources and their consequences. *Annual Review of Organizational Psychology and Organizational Behavior*, *5*, 103–128. https://doi.org/10.1146/annurev-orgpsych-032117-104640

Hobfoll, S. E., & Shirom, A. (2001). Conservation of resources theory: Applications to stress and management in the workplace. In R. T. Golembiewski (Ed.), *Handbook of organisational behavior* (2nd ed., pp. 57–80). Marcel Dekker, Inc.

Hofstede, G. (1991). *Cultures and organisations: Software of the mind.* McGraw-Hill. https://doi.org/10.1021/acschemneuro.0c00217

Huhns, M., Stephens, L., & Ivezic, N. (2002). *Automating supply-chain management* (pp. 1017–1024). https://doi.org/10.1145/545056.545061

Hur, W. M., Kim, B. S., & Park, S. J. (2015). The relationship between coworker incivility, emotional exhaustion, and organisational outcomes: The mediating role of emotional exhaustion. *Human Factors and Ergonomics in Manufacturing and Service Industries*, *25*(6), 701–712.

Ipe, M. (2003). Knowledge sharing in organisations: A conceptual framework. *Human Resource Development Review*, *2*, 337–359. https://doi.org/10.1177/1534484303257985

Kankanhalli, A., Tan, B., & Wei, K.-K. (2005). Understanding seeking from electronic knowledge repositories: An empirical study: Special topic section on knowledge management in Asia. *Journal of the American Society for Information Science and Technology*, *56*, 1156–1166. https://doi.org/10.1002/asi.20219

Kaufman, R. (1997). Nobody wins until the consumer says, 'I'll take it. *Apparel industry Magazine*, *58*(3), 14–16.

Kim, S. L., Lee, S., & Yun, S. (2016). Abusive supervision, knowledge sharing, and individual factors: A conservation-of-resources perspective. *Journal of Managerial Psychology*, *31*(6), 1106–1120. https://doi.org/10.1108/JMP-05-2015-0169

Kim, S. L., & Yun, S. (2015). The effect of coworker knowledge sharing on performance and its boundary conditions: An interactional perspective. *Journal of Applied Psychology*, *100*, 575–582. https://doi.org/10.1037/a0037834

Kogut, B., & Zander, U. (1992). Knowledge of the firm, combinative capabilities, and the replication of technology. *Organisation Science*, *3*, 383–397. https://doi.org/10.1287/orsc.3.3.383

Kumar, S. (2007). *Connective technologies in the supply chain.* Auerbach Publication.

Kumar, S., Kang, S., & Kishore, R. (2020). Examining workplace incivility as an antecedent of knowledge hiding behavior. *Journal of Southwest Jiaotong University*, *55*. https://doi.org/10.35741/issn.0258-2724.55.5.27

Kumar, S., Narayan, S., Sharma, K., Kaur, R., & Sen, R. (2023). Creating sustainable high-performance human resource practice through employees learning agility. The transition adaptive approach. *ABAC Journal*, *43*. https://doi.org/10.59865/abacj.2023.40

Kwon, I. W. G., & Suh, T. (2005). Trust, commitment and relationships in supply chain management: A path analysis. *Supply Chain Management: An International Journal*, *10*(1), 26–33.

Lee, Y. H., Chelladurai, P., & Kim, Y. (2015). Emotional labor in sports coaching: Development of a model. *International Journal of Sports Science Coach*, *10*, 561–575.

Lee, S., Kim, S. L., & Yun, S. A. (2018). Moderated mediation model of the relationship between abusive supervision and knowledge sharing. *The Leadership Quarterly*, *29*, 403–413.

Li, W., Pomegbe, W. W. K., Dogbe, C. S. K., & Novixoxo, J. D. (2019). Employees' customer orientation and customer satisfaction in the public utility sector: The mediating role of service quality. *African Journal of Economic and Management Studies*, *10*(4), 408–423. https://doi.org/10.1108/AJEMS-10-2018-0314

Lin, H.-F. (2007). Effects of extrinsic and intrinsic motivation on employee knowledge sharing intentions. *Journal of Information Science*, *33*, 135–149. https://doi.org/10.1177/0165551506068174

Lin, C.-Y., & Huang, C.-K. (2020). Employee turnover intentions and job performance from a planned change: The effects of an organisational learning culture and job satisfaction. *International Journal of Manpower*, *42*, 409–423. https://doi.org/10.1108/IJM-08-2018-0281

Lombardo, M. M., & Eichinger, R. W. (2000). High potential as high learners. *Human Resources Management*, *39*(4), 32.

Machiondo, L. A. (2012). *What were they thinking? A meaning-making model of workplace incivility from the target's perspective*. Ph.D., thesis, University of Michigan.

McIver, D., Lengnick-Hall, C. A., Lengnick-Hall, M. L., & Ramachandran, I. (2013). Understanding work and knowledge management from a knowledge-in-practice perspective. *Academy of Management Review*, *38*, 597–620. https://doi.org/10.5465/amr.2011.0266

Mehdikhani, R., & Valmohammadi, C. (2019). Strategic collaboration and sustainable supply chain management: The mediating role of internal and external knowledge sharing. *Journal of Enterprise Information Management*. https://doi.org/10.1108/JEIM-07-2018-0166

Mentzer, J., Min, S., & Zacharia, Z. (2000). The nature of interfirm partnering in supply chain management. *Journal of Retailing*, *76*, 549–568. https://doi.org/10.1016/S0022-4359(00)00040-3

Mesmer-Magnus, J. R., & DeChurch, L. A. (2009). Information sharing and team performance: A meta-analysis. *Journal of Applied Psychology*, *94*, 535–546.

Mikulincer, M., Shaver, P. R., & Slav, K. (2006). Attachment, mental representations of others, and gratitude and forgiveness in romantic relationships. In M. Mikulincer & G. S. Goodman (Eds.), *Dynamics of romantic love: Attachment, caregiving, and sex* (pp. 190–215). Guilford Press.

Miles, A. (2013). Agile learning: Living with the speed of change. *Development and Learning in Organisations*, *27*(2), 20–22. https://doi.org/10.1108/14777281311302058

Moore, C., Detert, J. R., Trevino, L., Baker, V. L., & Mayer, D. M. (2012). Why employees do bad things: Moral disengagement and unethical organisational behavior. *Personnel Psychology*, *65*(1), 1–48. https://doi.org/10.1111/j.1744-6570.2011. 01237.x

Murphy, M. L. (2001). The American heritage dictionary of the English language. *Dictionaries: Journal of the Dictionary Society of North America*, *22*(1), 1–54.

Nahapiet, J., & Ghoshal, S. (1998). Social capital, intellectual capital and the organizational advantage, academy of management. *The Academy of Management Review*, *3*, 242–266. http://staffweb.hkbu.edu.hk/vwschow/lectures/ism3620/rp01.pdf

Nonaka, I., & Takeuchi, H. (1995). *The knowledge-creating company: How Japanese companies create the dynamics of innovation*. Oxford University Press.

Ostroff, C. L., & Judge, T. (2007). *Perspectives on organisational fit*. Psychology Press.

Pan, X., Pan, X., Song, M., & Guo, R. (2020). The influence of green supply chain management on manufacturing enterprise performance: Moderating effect of collaborative communication. *Production Planning & Control*. https://doi.org/10.1080/09537287.2019.1631457

Podsakoff, P. M., MacKenzie, S. B., & Podsakoff, N. P. (2012). Sources of method bias in social science research and recommendations on how to control it. *Annual Review of Psychology*, *63*(1), 539–569. https://doi.org/10.1146/annurev-psych-120710-100452

Robinson, S. L., & Wolfe Morrison, E. (2000). The development of psychological contract breach and violation: A longitudinal study. *Journal of Organisational Behavior*, *21*(5), 525–546. https://doi.org/10.1002/1099-1379(200008)21:53.0.CO;2-T

Rousseau, D. M. (1995). *Psychological contracts in organisations. Understanding written and unwritten agreements*. Sage.

Sambamurthy, V., Bharadwaj, A., & Grover, V. (2003). Shaping agility through digital options: Reconceptualizing the role of information technology in contemporary firms. *MIS Quarterly*, *27*, 237–263. https://doi.org/10.2307/30036530

Schein, E. H. (1980). *Organisational psychology*. Prentice Hall.

Schiuma, G., Carlucci, D., & Lerro, A. (2012). Managing knowledge processes for value creation. *Vine*, *42*, 4–14. https://doi.org/10.1108/03055721211207815

Seuring, S. (2001). Green supply chain costing – Joint cost management in the polyester linings supply chain. *Greener Management International*, *33*, 71–80.

Shih, S. P., Jiang, J. J., Klein, G., & Wang, E. (2011). Learning demand and job autonomy of IT personnel: Impact on turnover intention. *Computers in Human Behavior*, *27*(6), 2301–2307.

Smith, C., & Davidson, H. (2014). *The paradox of generosity: Giving we receive, grasping we lose.* Oxford University Press. https://doi.org/10.1093/acprof:oso/9780199394906.001.0001

Sommerfeld, E. (2008). *The subjective experience of generosity.* Ariel University Centre. http://portal.idc.ac.il/en/symposium/herzliyasymposium/documents/dcsommerfeld. pdf

Spector, P. E., & Brannick, M. T. (2011). Methodological urban legends: The misuse of statistical control variables. *Organisational Research Methods, 14*, 287–305. https://doi.org/10.1177/1094428110369842

Srivastava, A., Bartol, K. M., & Locke, E. A. (2006). Empowering leadership in management teams: Effects on knowledge sharing, efficacy, and performance. *Academy of Management Journal, 49*, 1239–1251. https://doi.org/10.5465/AMJ.2006.23478718

Stone, E. F., & Hollenbeck, J. R. (1989). Clarifying some controversial issues surrounding statistical procedures for detecting moderator variables: Empirical evidence and related matters. *Journal of Applied Psychology, 74*(1), 3–10.

Sung, Y. R., & Kyung, K. K. (2015). The impact of knowledge complementarities on supply chain performance through knowledge exchange. *Expert Systems With Applications, 42*(6), 3029–3030.

Swisher, V. V., Hallenbeck, G. S., Jr, Orr, E. J., Eichinger, R. W., Lombardo, M. M., & Capretta, C. C. (2013). *FYI for learning agility: A must-have resource for high potential development.* Korn Ferry.

Tekleab, A. G., & Taylor, M. S. (2003). Aren't there two parties in an employment relationship? Antecedents and consequences of organisation-employee agreement on contract obligations and violations. *Journal of Organisational Behavior, 24*(5), 585–608. https://doi.org/10.1002/job.204

Tripathi, A., & Dhir, S. (2022). HRD interventions, learning agility and organisational innovation: A PLS-SEM modelling approach. *International Journal of Organisational Analysis.* ahead-of-print. https://doi.org/10.1108/IJOA-12-2021-3064

Vachon, S. (2007). Green supply chain practices and the selection of environmental technologies. *International Journal of Production Research, 45*(18), 4357–4379.

Wang, S., & Noe, R. A. (2010). Knowledge sharing: A review and directions for future research. *Human Resource Management Review, 20*, 115–131. https://doi.org/10.1016/j.hrmr.2009.10.001

Wasko, M. M., & Faraj, S. (2005). Why should I share? Examining social capital and knowledge contribution in electronic networks of practice. *MIS Quarterly, 29*, 35–57.

Welbourne, J. L., Gangadharan, A., & Esparza, C. A. (2016). Coping style and gender effects on attitudinal responses to incivility. *Journal of Managerial Psychology, 31*(3), 720–738. https://doi.org/10.1108/JMP-11-2014-0340

Whitehead, K., Zacharia, Z., & Prater, E. (2019). Investigating the role of knowledge transfer in supply chain collaboration. *International Journal of Logistics Management.* https://doi.org/10.1108/IJLM-07-2017-0184

Witherspoon, C. L., Bergner, J., Cockrell, C., & Stone, D. N. (2013). Antecedents of organisational knowledge sharing: A meta-analysis and critique. *Journal of Knowledge Management, 17*(2), 250–277.

Wu, W. L., & Lee, Y. C. (2016). Do employees share knowledge when encountering abusive supervision? *Journal of Management Psychology, 31*, 154–168.

Yun, S., Takeuchi, R., & Liu, W. (2007). Employee self-enhancement motives and job performance behaviors: Investigating the moderating effects of employee role ambiguity and managerial perceptions of employee commitment. *Journal of Applied Psychology, 92*(3), 745–756. https://doi.org/10.1037/0021-9010.92.3.745

Zeraati, H., Rajabion, L., Molavi, H., & Navimipour, N. J. (2020). A model for examining the effect of knowledge sharing and new IT-based technologies on the success of the supply chain management systems. *Kybernetes, 49*(2), 229–251.

Zhao, H., Wayne, S. J., Glibkowski, B. C., & Bravo, J. (2007). The impact of psychological contract breach on work-related outcomes. *A meta-analysis. Personnel Psychology, 60*, 647–680.

Zhou, Z. E., Yan, Y., Che, X. X., & Meier, L. L. (2015). Effect of workplace incivility on end-of-work negative affect: Examining individual and organisational moderators in a daily diary study. *Journal of Occupational Health Psychology, 20*(1), 117–130. https://doi.org/10.1037/a0038167

AVENUES FOR SYSTEMS THINKING TOWARDS EXPLORING THE ETHICS OF SUSTAINABILITY WITHIN SUPPLY CHAINS

Jonathon Mackay

University of Wollongong, Australia

ABSTRACT

This paper explores sustainability within supply chain management and its link towards resilience through the lens of ethics. The wicked problem of sustainability impacts supply chains and society at large, and the ability of supply chains to remain viable in the future is based on the sustainability of business practices. The paper argues that a substantive proportion of sustainability mechanisms (such as the Triple Bottom Line approach and codes of conducts) can be viewed within the ethical paradigm of deontology, *whereby the morality of an action is based on adherence to rules. However, there are numerous critiques of such approaches and their success in creating more sustainable practices. Therefore, the paper proposes there is a need for systems thinking approaches to be incorporated into the exploration of the link between ethics, sustainability and supply chain resilience. Using two examples of social sustainability issues in Australia – modern slavery legislation and horticultural[1] worker exploitation – the paper demonstrates the utility of various systems thinking methodologies to explore the complexity of these issues. The paper sets out a conceptual call to arms for researchers and practitioners to apply a holistic lens towards how the morality of actions is shaped and influences supply chain sustainability practices.*

Keywords: Sustainability; ethics; supply chain resilience; systems thinking; morality

Sustainable and Resilient Supply Chain
Advances in Environmental Accounting & Management, Volume 12, 115–139

Published under exclusive licence by Emerald Publishing Limited
ISSN: 1479-3598/doi:10.1108/S1479-359820240000012011

INTRODUCTION

Sustainability has emerged as a core component of businesses and their wider supply chains over the past few decades. Famous cases such as Nike's use of sweatshops in the 1990s and the *Deepwater Horizon* Oil Spill in 2010 have all served as a reminder of the reputational and financial need for companies to act both in the interests of themselves and external stakeholders. This shift has led to the emergence of business sustainability as well as wider *supply chain* sustainability (Beamon, 2005), recognising that businesses are part of a wider supply network that also includes the communities that they operate in. Popular frameworks – such as the Triple Bottom Line (TBL) approach (Elkington, 1997, 2018) – serve as tools for companies to evaluate and use their traditional financial metrics of performance alongside environmental and social impact. However, there is debate about the success of the TBL and other sustainability mechanisms, and this paper undertakes a conceptual analysis of these issues. Ethics – the normative rules and behaviours that help delineate if an action is 'right' or 'wrong' (Clegg et al., 2021) – is often based upon three distinct categories: deontological (or rules-based), utilitarian (or consequentialist) and virtue ethics, of which the first dominates most ethical decision-making processes (Draščeк et al., 2021).

A concurrent area of study relevant to this paper is supply chain resilience and its emergent links towards sustainability. The idea of resilience – the ability for a system to maintain structure and return to acceptable performance after a disruption (Haimes, 2009; Walker et al., 2004) – is regarded as a critical component of understanding risk within supply chains (Katsaliaki et al., 2022). It has been well established in the literature that risks towards supply chain resilience can emerge from 'outside' the supply chain (Christopher & Peck, 2004; Katsaliaki et al., 2022), and recent research has proposed a link between sustainability initiatives and resilience (Shishodia et al., 2023).

Despite the emergence of sustainability and supply chain resilience as two popular areas both in terms of research and practitioner implications, there appears to be a lack of critical analysis of ethical frameworks within supply chain actors and the role that ethics plays in influencing sustainability mechanisms. This paper argues that there is a greater need for academics and practitioners to explore the role of ethics within supply chain sustainability through a *systems thinking approach*. This approach – whereby complex behaviours are viewed through the intersection of various parts (Elias, 2022; Jackson, 2019; Kast & Rosenzweig, 1972) – allows for a variety of methodologies to be adopted that can explore the wicked nature of sustainability through a holistic lens. The paper uses the example of two contemporary issues within sustainability in Australia: modern slavery reporting legislation and horticultural worker exploitation to demonstrate the utility of various systems methodologies. The paper is conceptual in nature, which is an important step within theory building (Burton-Jones et al., 2015), and is also referred to as *theory approximation* (Weick, 1995). By establishing a conceptual argument towards understanding the link between ethics, sustainability frameworks and supply chain resilience, the paper sets an agenda for future empirical research.

The paper aims to explore the following questions:

- What are the ethical frameworks that underpin supply chain sustainability practices?
- What are the conceptual links between poor sustainability practices and supply chain resilience?
- How does a systems thinking approach offer new insights into exploring the ethics of sustainability?

Through answering these questions, the paper aims to serve as a 'call to arms' for a greater use of systems thinking tools within the SSCM discipline, building upon emergent research in this space. The paper is set out as follows. The next section undertakes a literature review looking at three main sections. The first section explores the concept of sustainability and its relevance towards supply chains, as well as its link towards supply chain risk and resilience. The second section aims to unpack the processes the lead to sustainability practices by looking at popular mechanisms that are employed by organisations to meet sustainability objectives. The third part of the literature review looks at the ethical underpinnings of these mechanisms and explores the critiques of these approaches. Following this critique, the paper explores how systems thinking and methodologies within this paradigm can be used to explore these issues, using two examples (namely Australia's Modern Slavery Act, and worker exploitation within Australia's horticultural sector) and sets up the agenda for future research projects.

LITERATURE REVIEW

Supply Chain Sustainability

A seminal definition by Carroll (1991) argues that corporations are sustainable if they achieve four kinds of social responsibility; economic, legal, ethical and philanthropic. The idea that an organisation needs to consider environmental quality and social justice alongside 'traditional' economic prosperity has emerged within contemporary discussions around business sustainability (Miemczyk & Luzzini, 2019). Broadly defined as the ability to meet the needs of the present without compromising the ability of future generations (World Commission on Environment and Development, 1987), the idea has often been operationalised within businesses and supply chains as a balance between economic, environmental and social considerations (Negri et al., 2021; Saeed & Kersten, 2019). The overarching idea is that sustainability allows organisations to link traditional business objectives around profitability with external stakeholder considerations (Ahi & Searcy, 2013).

The area of sustainability is not confined to single businesses, but rather centres around the relationships (both direct and indirect) that businesses will have. All businesses are part of a wider supply chain, which consists of three or more nodes involved in upstream and downstream flows (Mentzer et al., 2001). The incorporation of sustainability initiatives into supply chain management has led to the emergence of the field of sustainable supply chain management, or SSCM (Rebs et al., 2019; Seuring & Müller, 2008). This has often led to a demarcation between environmental – or *green* – supply chain management (Ahi & Searcy, 2013; Biswas et al., 2018) and the exploitation of workers within supply chains and wider societal impacts of supply chain operations (Emmelhainz & Adams, 1999; Stevenson, 2022; Stevenson & Cole, 2018). A core concept within SSCM is the *traceability* of goods (Garcia-Torres et al., 2019) which explores the location and origin of goods within a supply chain (Cousins et al., 2019). Traceability has often been espoused as a mechanism to lead towards greater supply chain sustainability (Agyabeng-Mensah et al., 2021; Garcia-Torres et al., 2019). However, there is often a paradoxical relationship with technology, sustainability and traceability (e.g. the energy consumption within Blockchain technology as discussed by Biswas et al., 2023). Furthermore as discussed by Cousins et al. (2019), greater traceability may have little-to-no mediating effect on environmental sustainability due to a wider lens of issues being uncovered through more effective transparency.

Supply Chain Risk and Resilience

Another subset of this academic area of supply chain management is supply chain risk which explores how to manage disruptions to continuity of service within supply chains (Mackay et al., 2020). Within supply chain risks, there is a triadic interaction between individuals, disruptions and the systems involved (Mackay et al., 2023; Scheibe & Blackhurst, 2017) which demonstrates the need for a holistic approach towards risk management strategies (Mackay et al., 2023). Risks towards supply chain can arise from a variety of sources (Heckmann et al., 2015), inclusive of both human and natural origins such as climate change (Katsaliaki et al., 2022). Accordingly, sustainability initiatives can be viewed as exploring the future risks to supply chains from social and environmentally sources (Giannakis & Papadopoulos, 2016).

Supply chain risk can often be delineated based on the interaction between the probability of an event, its magnitude and the complexity of system states (Haimes, 2009, 2011; Kaplan & Garrick, 1981; Sheffi, 2005) as well as the practitioner perceptions of these parameters (Mackay et al., 2019). These system states often include areas such as vulnerability, resilience and robustness (Haimes, 1998; Kamalahmadi & Parast, 2016; Mackay et al., 2020, 2023). Resilience is a state of a system that refers to its ability to withstand disruptions and return to acceptable performance parameters (Walker et al., 2004), and is influenced by overall supply chain risk (Katsaliaki et al., 2022; Mackay et al., 2020). Understanding the role of resilience within supply chain risk has been explored thoroughly within the literature (Negri et al., 2021; Shishodia et al., 2023; Wieland &

Durach, 2021), with emergent research demonstrating the link between resilience and sustainability (Elias et al., 2021; Shishodia et al., 2023). Wieland and Durach (2021) argue that the idea of socio-ecological resilience – governed by open connectedness and adaptability – offers a differing perspective than the traditional engineering-driven perspectives on resilience; therefore, resilience expands away from being isolated to one system (e.g. a single organisation or supply chain). This has led to the proposal of a rethink away from the engineering-based focuses of resilience towards the concepts of *persistence, adaption* and *transformation* (Wieland et al., 2023).

SUSTAINABILITY MECHANISMS

The next section of the literature review will explore several sustainability mechanisms within supply chain management.

The TBL Approach

> Is it possible, for example, to evolve new types of corporation which are less inclined to operate as economic, social and ecological predators? Elkington (1997, p. x).

The above quote from the 1997 book *Cannibals with Forks: The Triple Bottom Line of 21st Century Business* (Elkington, 1997) introduced many academics and practitioners to the concept of the TBL, which argues that social and environmental goals need to be included alongside 'traditional' financial goals of an organisation (Negri et al., 2021). This has led to a surge in popularity of this approach as it has become almost second nature in many discussions around sustainability (Miemczyk & Luzzini, 2019). The popularity can be attributed to treating it as a framework that can be applied or measured within a given context (Hollos et al., 2012) as it is often seen as an accounting mechanism to supplement traditional financial managements (Ahi & Searcy, 2013; Norman & MacDonald, 2004). At times this is overtly mentioned, such as Norman and MacDonald (2004, p. 243) stating that:

> The apparent novelty of the [TBL] lies in its supporters' contention that the overall fulfilment of obligations to communities, employees, customers and suppliers...should be measured, calculated, audited and reported.

Within supply chains, the TBL has become a popular tool to measure sustainability (Saeed & Kersten, 2019), with papers incorporating aspects of TBL into areas such as channel coordination (Biswas et al., 2018), Industry 4.0 implementation (Birkel & Müller, 2021), blockchain technology (Saberi et al., 2019), procurement (Marshall et al., 2019; Walker et al., 2012) and performance measurement (Neri et al., 2021). It is common to see the TBL incorporated into published reports by companies: such as quantitative tools outlined in sustainability reports to address environment (e.g. Telstra, 2022) and social (e.g. Intel, 2022) concerns (Topp-Becker & Ellis, 2017). Another example is 34 quantitative metrics proposed by the World Economic Forum (2020) designed to communicate value creation for business and supply chains, including (pp. 8–9):

- Greenhouse gas emissions (for both business and their supply chains).
- Water consumption and withdrawal in water-stressed areas (measures including megalitres of water withdrawn/consumed).
- Risk for incidents of child, forced or compulsory labour.

Codes of Conduct and Legislative Tools

Beamon (2005, p. 221) discusses ethical supply as following 'an ethical code' that individuals and business subscribe to. A basic example of these are codes of conduct; which can include governing individual workplace behaviours (Adam & Rachman-Moore, 2004) but also those of suppliers within a supply chain (Pedersen & Andersen, 2006). Codes of conducts within supply chains are often designed to require adherence to particular norms such as worker protections (Egels-Zandén & Lindholm, 2015; Jiang, 2009).

Other examples of this approach include specific standards such as ISO26000 or Fairtrade (Miemczyk & Luzzini, 2019) as well as mechanisms such as the Global Reporting Initiative and Dow Jones Sustainability Indexes (Elkington, 2018).

Legislative approaches have emerged as tools for enshrining particular sustainability mechanisms into law: these include various instruments to mitigate modern slavery (such as those found in Commonwealth of Australia, 2018; NSW, 2018; State of California, 2010; UK, 2015, mineral sourcing (Dalla Via & Perego, 2018) and the enforcement of environmental laws (such as the National Greenhouse and Energy Reporting Act outlined in Commonwealth of Australia, 2007).

ETHICAL BASIS OF SUSTAINABILITY MECHANISMS

The next section aims to explore the ethics underpinning the various sustainability frameworks that have been discussed. Normative ethics broadly aims to explore how supply chains – and the businesses and individuals within them – should act through rule or value-based approaches (Clegg et al., 2021). Commonly normative ethics are split into three categories: deontological, consequentialism (namely utilitarianism) and virtue (Chakrabarty & Erin Bass, 2015; Draščcek et al., 2021; Van Staveren, 2007; Whetstone, 2001). As discussed in Draščcek et al. (2021), deontology is the most popular theory to use in empirical studies on ethical decision-making.

Deontology

Discussions around deontology within business ethics has been a longstanding academic tradition (e.g. Brady, 1999; L'etang, 1992; Van Staveren, 2007).

Deontology is an ethical approach whereby the rightness or wrongness of an action is based on specific principles rather than the outcomes or consequences (Van Staveren, 2007). In other words, conformance to duty as expressed through laws and norms determines the morality of an action (Brady, 1999). The basis of this approach towards ethics is the idea of a *categorial imperative* as discussed by the German philosophy Immanuel Kant. The whole basis of the application of Kantian philosophy is centred on the idea of universal and objective laws as a *categorical imperative*:

> Act only according to that maxim by which you can at the same time will that it should become a universal law. Kant (1785/1990, p. 38)

It is a core foundation of the categorical imperative (and thus wider deontological ethics) that the moral rightness of an action is whether it is enacted as part of a duty. The categorical nature of an action means that it is unconditional (Sandel, 2009), as Kant (1785/1990, pp. 16–17) outlines:

> Duty is the necessity to do an action from respect for law. . .Thus the moral worth of an action does not lie in the effect which is expected from it or in any principle of action which has to borrow its motive from this perceived effect.

Within businesses and supply chains, the most common form of deontological ethics are codes of conduct as discussed earlier (Emmelhainz & Adams, 1999; Roberts, 2003). These include supplier codes of conduct (Ahmed et al., 2022), workplace behaviour codes of conduct (Adam & Rachman-Moore, 2004) and legislative codes of conduct (Dalla Via & Perego, 2018) as discussed above.

Consequentialism

Often contrasted to deontological ethics is consequentialist ethics, whereby an action is moral based on its consequences rather than its adherence to a categorical imperative. The most common type of consequentialist framework is *utilitarianism*, whereby an action is good if it maximises 'happiness' for the most number of people (Sandel, 2009). Espoused in the works by the English philosophy Jeremy Bentham (Bentham, 1823; Kahneman et al., 1997), the basic premise of this philosophical doctrine comes down to a base comparison between *pleasure* or *pain* (Sandel, 2009). Simply put, if the outcomes of an action benefits the most amount of people, then this makes an action morally justifiable. Consequentialist approaches based on the idea of utilitarianism are often popular to use within discussions of business ethics (Burnes & By, 2012). The idea of serving as many needs as possible is often expressed through contemporary business ideas such as the United Nation's Sustainability Development Goals or SDGs (United Nations, 2021) which has been attributed to an uptick in research and interest looking at sustainability (Chopra et al., 2021). Notwithstanding its popularity, the subjective concepts often used within this ethical framework such as 'happiness' and 'utility' make utilitarianism a less-than-popular contemporary approach (Norman & MacDonald, 2004), which may explain the dominance of deontological approaches within business ethics.

Virtue Ethics

Virtue ethics centres on the individual and personal morality (Whetstone, 2001) and the continuous development towards a more virtuous state (Jordan & Kristjánsson, 2017). Within this ethical framework, both deontological and utilitarian perspectives can be adopted with the underlying premise on an individual having a 'praiseworthy character trait' (Audi, 2012, p. 273). Virtue ethics has received a degree of attention within the supply chain literature (Drake & Schlachter, 2008), often with a focus on relationship-building and trust between supply chain partners (Dubey et al., 2017).

Although virtue ethics does not have the same degree of popularity as deontological/consequentialist ethical theories (Drašček et al., 2021), it offers a unique insight into individual decision-making due to its focus on personality morality and motivation (Whetstone, 2001). As discussed by Chakrabarty and Erin Bass (2015), virtue ethics can extend towards sustainability through the development of values and behaviours at both the individual and institutional level. Virtue ethics could be seen as the ethical basis for sustainability initiatives such as standard accreditation (discussed in Miemczyk & Luzzini, 2019) and the UN SDGs (United Nations, 2021).

CRITICISMS OF SUSTAINABILITY MECHANISMS

The next section explores several criticisms of the mechanism discussed earlier. The conceptual argument underpinning many of these criticisms is that many mechanisms do not take into account the idea of sustainability being a *wicked problem* (Alexander et al., 2022). Proposed by Rittel and Webber (1973), wicked problems can be regarded as 'large-scale social problems' (Reinecke & Ansari, 2016, p. 300) that often have conflicting voices and perspectives (Head, 2018).

First, the critiques surrounding TBL are often based upon empirical application of this framework. A common criticism of the TBL is that it is seldom adopted by organisations that instead prioritise their financial concerns (Montabon et al., 2016). Montabon et al. (2016, p. 6) argues that quite often organisations are able to use the TBL to offset blame for not pursuing sustainability practises:

> For instance, firms in a supply chain can argue that it is not their fault that customers do not buy more sustainable products. Thus, it is not surprising that firms choose to emphasize the economic nature of the TBL over the other two aspects as there are no institutions that can ensure that all three aspects of the TBL are given equal treatment and thus supply chains can shift blame to customer.

Another argument is made by Elkington (2018, p. 5), that there is a fundamental misinterpretation of the TBL approach:

> Critically, too, TBL's stated goal from the outset was system change – pushing toward the transformation of capitalism. It was never supposed to be just an accounting system.

Elkington (2018, p. 4) further argues that the contemporary prevalence of the TBL as a trade-off between different accountancy measures is a fundamental misinterpretation:

> It was supposed to provoke deeper thinking about capitalism and its future, but many early adopters understood the concept as a balancing act, adopting a trade-off mentality.

Despite the departure from its original aims, the TBL is often regarded as an accounting framework that exists alongside traditional financial metrics (Biswas et al., 2018; Norman & MacDonald, 2004). This in itself has become problematic, as organisations have framed sustainability as what Montabon et al. (2016) refer to as an *instrumental logic*, whereby focus is on how supply chains can benefit from sustainability.

Another shortfall of many sustainable mechanisms within supply chains can be argued as the over-reliance on deontological approaches. There is an assumption made within many articles about the adoption of universal morality, for example, Ha-Brookshire (2017, p. 235):

> The moral responsibility theory of sustainable supply chain illustrates that, in order for the entire supply chain to be sustainable...the members of the entire supply chain must view sustainability as a perfect duty.

Another issue that can emerge is the issue with application. The development of legal frameworks – whether they be codes of conduct or even government legislation (e.g. the British Modern Slavery Act and the Australian Modern Slavery Act) – themselves contradict Kant's own perspective on individual law formulation (L'etang, 1992). As argued by L'etang (1992, p. 743):

> If they [codes of ethics] are imposed by management and communicated top-down they may infringe the autonomy of employees. If, however, the codes are arrived at through discussion then they may represent the general will of the organisation.

Within the business literature, phrases such as 'moral' or 'immoral' are often left undefined (e.g. Dempsey, 2015; Velasquez, 2003). For example, Ha-Brookshire (2017) state that the definition of sustainability used is based upon the TBL approach; however, there is no delineation of what these environmental and social considerations are. This is an important delineation to make given that the three components of the TBL are often paradoxical (Walker et al., 2020).

Furthermore, there are questions about the success of approaches such as codes of conduct (Emmelhainz & Adams, 1999; Roberts, 2003). Egels-Zandén and Lindholm (2015) identify a paradox between the perception of the success of codes and the actual improvements. Within the various forms of legislation that necessitates supply chains to 'act' in a particular way (namely to remove 'slavery' within their supply chains), there are also critiques. Vijeyarasa (2019, 2020) outlines a series of these issues, including the lack of inclusion of key submissions into the legislation (such as the lack of substantial consequences for organisations failing to report). This follows similar critiques with other jurisdictions, such as lack of compliance to the UK's Modern Slavery Act (Voss et al., 2019), and a paper by Ma et al. (2016) who found that less than half of retail and manufacturing companies within California's apparel industry complied with California's supply chain slavery legislation. This feeds into an ongoing debate about the ability of such legislative tools to create legitimate organisational change (New & Hsin, 2021).

Greenwashing and Moralwashing

Another problem with the assumptions of universal moral behaviour is the proliferation of unethical behaviour. Although ethical behaviour has become part of the lexicon of contemporary businesses, unethical behaviours have not been eliminated. For example, as discussed by ILO (2022); Kara (2017) there are higher numbers of individuals who are classified as being under the conditions of slavery than at any other point in history. A possible explanation for the abundance of unethical behaviour is the proliferation of 'washing' behaviours, whereby ethical actions are either undertaken for ulterior motives (such as public/consumer relations), or an organisation actively covers up unethical actions. These behaviours often sit paradoxically with virtue ethics.

The most common of these is an idea referred to as *greenwashing*, whereby a company will outwardly claim that they are meeting specific targets associated with environmental sustainability, but in actual fact, these are a cover for non-sustainable activities. As discussed in Delmas and Burbano (2011, p. 66), greenwashing is the 'act of misleading consumers regarding the environmental practises of a company or the environmental benefits of a product or service'. Although popularised by examples such as misleading energy usage mechanisms (Delmas & Burbano, 2011), it can be argued that greenwashing takes many different characteristics (de Freitas Netto et al., 2020). These many characteristics demonstrate that a simple rules-based framework to sustainability will continuously be subject to these types of issues.

However, there is an emergent area around the idea of *moralwashing*. There are two observable ideas around this:

(1) purposeful moralwashing
(2) moral disengagement

The first of these – purposeful moralwashing – is the 'social' equivalent of the greenwashing idea. Also referred to as *ethics-washing,* the concept broadly refers to appearances of ethical behaviour that are ultimately self-serving (Bietti, 2021). For this paper, a more specific definition to the social components espoused by the TBL would be scenarios when companies purposely act in a way to mislead their credentials around social issues. These may occur in situations where companies act in a certain way to distract from other issues, such as advocating for various social causes while ignoring documented intra-firm social issues. In situations where companies advocate their own virtue ethics, a moralwashing approach would exist if their actions countered the stated ethical positions. As discussed in L'etang (1992, p. 738):

> The pretension to a false morality is wrong even if it achieves good ends because its ignoble intention is self-promotion rather than the moral improvement of self and the development of good will for its own sake.

The second of these, moral disengagement, occurs when an individual or company acts in a way that violates their morals without feeling guilt or responsibility of their actions (Eriksson & Svensson, 2016). Within this approach, Bandura (1999) proposes four categories: cognitive reconstruction of the conduct, minimise agentic role, the consequences of action and the devaluation of the victims. The third of these – minimise agentic role – is evidenced within various deontological and utilitarian sustainability approaches. For example, supplier code of conduct approaches can be viewed as a form of diffusion of responsibilities (as defined in Bandura, 1999) as responsibility for ethical actions are passed onto external agents. However, adapting this concept from the individual to the supply chain is debatable, as discussed by Eriksson and Svensson (2016).

Gaps and the Need for Further Conceptualisation

The paper thus far has discussed that although sustainability mechanisms can be linked to supply chain resilience through a reduction of risk, there are several issues with application. The underlying issue within many of the discussed frameworks is the tacit universal assumptions of ethics that can arise. The paper thus far has instead argued that the dominance of deontological and utilitarian ethics within many sustainability mechanisms serves as an explanation of the shortfalls discussed in the previous section. However, from the current literature, there is a gap linking the morality of sustainability decisions (i.e. the ethical basis) with supply chain risk and resilience. To explore the measures to address this gap, it is proposed that future research projects can utilise the paradigm of systems thinking. The next part of the paper will discuss the role that systems thinking can have in addressing these shortfalls.

THE ROLE OF SYSTEMS THINKING IN SUSTAINABLE SUPPLY CHAIN MANAGEMENT: A DISCUSSION BASED ON TWO EXPLORATORY CASES

In dealing with the inherent paradoxes that can be associated with applying ethics within supply chains, the paper proposes that systems thinking offers a conceptual tool towards exploring the variance among ethics and sustainability. This section will discuss the role that systems thinking can play within sustainability SCM and resilience and look at two main examples within Australia: the Modern Slavery Act (2018) and horticultural worker exploitation. This section will first discuss the paradigm of *systems thinking* before discussing several popular methodologies associated with systems thinking. From here, an overview of the exploratory cases will be provided before a discussion of the value of systems thinking towards addressing the ethical components of these problems.

Systems Thinking

The concepts of systems thinking can be traced to antiquity (Jackson, 2019); however, contemporary discussions are often linked back to the concept of general system theory (GST) proposed in the early 20th century (von Bertalanffy, 1950, 1972). Designed as a counterpoint towards the dominance of reductionism, whereby the mathematic-logical laws within the physical sciences were regarded as the forefront of knowledge (von Bertalanffy, 1950), GST argues instead for an exploration of holistic interactions within a system. Within this, a system is broadly any entity that has a number of interconnected parts (Kast & Rosenzweig, 1972), and systems thinking argues that focusing on small, isolated parts risks missing the interconnections and interrelationships that can emerge from looking at the whole (Werhane, 2002). The adaptation of systems thinking towards supply chains is not new (Defee et al., 2010; Nilsson & Gammelgaard, 2012), and indeed the originally stated aims of the TBL as a holistic critical analysis tool can be viewed as an operationalisation of systems theory (Elkington, 2018). In addition to the foundational ideas of GST, there have been substantial theoretical variations discussed within the literature, including complex adaptive systems, or CAS (Levin, 2003) and complexity theory (Anderson, 1999; Schneider & Somers, 2006). As discussed by Nilsson and Gammelgaard (2012, p. 778), the latter paradigms offer a shift away from what can be viewed as 'mechanical beliefs inherent in the SA [systems approach] applied'. When dealing with inherent complex problems such as sustainability (Matthews et al., 2016), these theoretical approaches allow for the complexities to be unpacked in a more thorough way than the basic GST approaches (Nilsson & Gammelgaard, 2012).

Applied Systems Thinking and Methodologies

Systems thinking has been a popular approach for the use within sustainability discussions (Elias, 2022; Rebs et al., 2019; Williams et al., 2017). As a paradigmatic tool, systems thinking has a rich history of methodological applications (Jackson, 2019). Often, these are delineated into two separate 'camps': *hard* systems thinking which is often based on quantitative and technical application and *soft* systems thinking with a focus on identification of problems and conflicting worldviews (Forrester, 1994; Jackson, 2019). Within supply chain management research, system dynamics (SD) – which aims to explore the causal relationship between variables through model development (Forrester, 1994; Jackson, 2019) – is one of the most popular systems thinking methodologies (Wilden et al., 2022). SD is commonly delineated into several tools including causal loop diagrams, simulation modelling and the identification of system archetypes (Forrester, 1994; Senge, 2006). A core part of SD is often the development of feedback models such as causal loop diagrams (Elias et al., 2021) and simulation models (Forrester, 1994; Pruyt, 2013).

Conversely, other methodologies aim to embrace the inherent paradoxes that exist within many social systems. Soft systems methodology (SSM) uses tools such as rich pictures (which serves as a creative mechanism to create a representation of the problem system) and root definitions (a statement of what the system is) to unpack the predominant norms, values and behaviours within a social system (Checkland & Poulter, 2020; Checkland & Winter, 2006; Jackson, 2019). A commonly used tool within SSM is the CATWOE mnemonic (adapted from Jackson, 2019, p. 424):

C = "customers" – the beneficiaries/victims of a given transformation process within a system.
A = "actors" – those who would undertake the transformation process/intervention within the system.
T = "transformation" – the conversion of inputs to outputs in the system.
W = "world view" – the world view that makes this transformation meaningful.
O = "owners" – those who could stop the transformation.
E = "environmental constraints" – elements outside the system that are taken as given.

Although applying SSM towards SCM is not as popular as SD, there are still examples of this approach being used within supply chains (e.g. Mello et al., 2017) and within sustainability projects (e.g. Nguyen et al., 2019; Paucar-Caceres et al., 2022). Additionally, critical systems heuristics, or CSH (Ulrich, 1987), offers a pathway of undertaking reflection as a means of applying systems thinking (Tavella, 2023). Based on the concept of using a series of 12 questions to identify normative assumptions (Jackson, 2019; Ulrich, 1987), the approach has been utilised within several academic works on sustainability (e.g. Tavella, 2023; Ulrich & Reynolds, 2020).

Overview of the Exploratory Cases

The next section will discuss these exploratory cases and how different systems thinking methodologies can be applied towards unpacking the complexity around ethics, sustainability and resilience.

Albeit with varying definitions (Crane, 2013; Gutierrez-Huerter O et al., 2021), the phrase modern slavery broadly refers to the most extreme forms of labour exploitation (Caruana et al., 2021). Australia's Modern Slavery Act (2018) was introduced to the Australian parliament as a mechanism for companies to report their risks of slavery within their supply chain operations. This has followed similar legislative instruments introduced in other jurisdictions, such as in the US State of California (2010) and the United Kingdom (UK, 2015).

Australia's Modern Slavery Act requires companies of a certain size (revenue of >$100m AUD) to provide an annual report within a publicly available register identifier the risks of modern slavery within entities that are either owned or directly controlled by the company. There is also the ability for volunteer contributions to the register; as of 2023, there were 5,120 mandatory statements and 696 volunteer statements available on the register (Department of Home Affairs, 2023). As identified earlier within the paper, these types of frameworks to address sustainability concerns (akin to codes of conduct) can be viewed as falling under the deontological ethical label.

The criticisms of these approaches as discussed earlier can be evidenced within this case. For example, a noncompliance issue with the reports discussed in the annual report by the Australian Government (2022) is a lack of description of how companies assess the effectiveness of actions to measure/report modern slavery. This critique has been expressed across several of the jurisdictional approaches towards addressing modern supply (Gutierrez-Huerter O et al., 2021; Vijeyarasa, 2019). Furthermore, due to an inherent limitation in the legislation that focuses on 'describing the risks of modern slavery in the operations and supply chains of reporting entities and *entities owned or controlled* by those entities' (Commonwealth of Australia, 2018, p. 10, bold emphasis by author), there is arguably a risk of companies developing modern slavery reports which outsource responsibility to opaque supply chain structures.

Secondly, within the horticultural sector in Australia, there has been substantial reporting on labour exploitation (Cavanough & Wherrett, 2020; Fair Work Ombudsman, 2018; Sydney Morning Herald, 2016), including payment below national standards (ABC News, 2021a) and other forms of 'wage theft' (Farm Online, 2021). One large supermarket identified this sector as being at high risk within their modern slavery report (ABC News, 2020). The risk factors have often been attributed to the reliance on transient migrant labour (Howe et al., 2020) and offers an interesting example to explore the variance amongst ethical frameworks and applications across many agents in these systems. For example, within Australia's horticultural system, there is often a complex interplay between cultural and political factors, including:

- The dismissal of labour issues being systemic and instead blamed on localised components (Fair Work Ombudsman, 2018; Migrant Workers' Taskforce, 2019; Sydney Morning Herald, 2016).
- Price pressures caused by supermarkets (Howe et al., 2019) with have led to vulnerable payment schemes such as piece-rates where payment is based on payment-by-piece rather than a minimum wage (The Guardian, 2021).

Within this case, there is a substantive link between the risk of slavery and the power dynamics between actors in the system. Due to the reliance on migrant labour (including both legal and illegal sources), there are unique power dynamics at play (e.g. visa restrictions that limit the ability for workers to find additional employment) which can result in workers finding themselves in slavery-like conditions (ABC News, 2021c). Furthermore, the subversive nature of these sources of labour had led to other criminal behaviour including sexual harassment/assault (Howe et al., 2021). The flow-on effect of the reliance foreign workers transcends from the supply chain to communities, such as increased racism and stigmatisation faced by the children of foreign horticultural workers (Nishitani & Lee, 2023). Furthermore, other scholars looking at modern slavery have discussed the role of power and agency of the exploited individuals whose slavery-like circumstances may still be a preferable alternative (Kara, 2017).

The area for further exploration within this research area is unpacking the role that different ethical frameworks play in either supporting or inhibiting SC resilience (through sustainability) in this case. As outlined above, it is commonplace for sustainability issues to be dismissed due to the actions of localised SC components, therefore supporting the use of deontological frameworks (e.g. legislative) as the mechanism to reduce sustainability risks. However, the systemic factors such as power and even supply chain efficiency can be viewed as contributing to overall risk of worker exploitation despite legislative tools being introduced (such as the introduction of minimum pay rates discussed in ABC News, 2021b; and the Modern Slavery Act as per Commonwealth of Australia, 2018).

Avenues for Systems Thinking

To demonstrate the utility of systems thinking, two methodologies (which serve as future research and practitioner avenues) will be discussed. Within the case of modern slavery reports, tools within SD can be applied as a mechanism to explore the overarching risk of slavery within a supply chain. In particular, particular system archetypes – such as the 'fixes that fail' whereby an intervention ends up creating unintended consequences (Senge, 2006) – can be utilised to unpack the potential consequences of the strict deontological, legislative approach. For example, Fig. 1 illustrates a basic causal loop diagram outlining the concerns discussed in Australian Government (2022) and Vijeyarasa (2019)

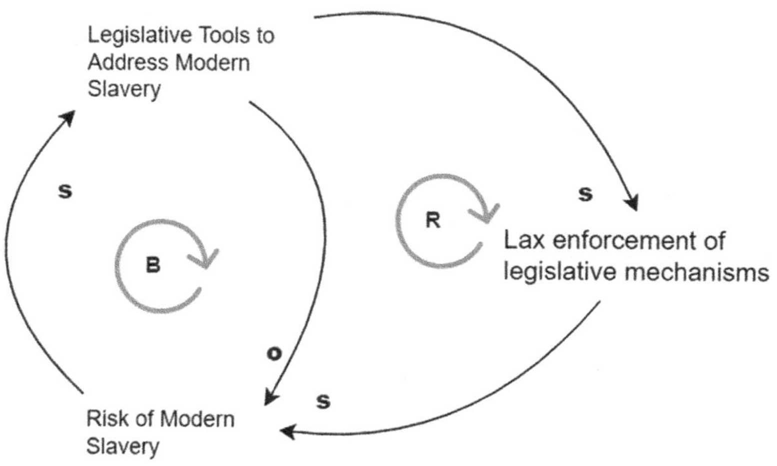

Fig. 1. Conceptual Causal Loop Diagram on Modern Slavery Legislation.

around the lack of mandatory reporting and the lax impacts of non-compliance (based on the 'unintended consequences' system archetype as discussed in Senge, 2006).

Although not captured in Fig. 1, the exploration of feedback within supply chains can further unpack the proposed causal link between variance within ethical frameworks and supply chain resilience. This would allow practitioners and researchers alike to further extrapolate the causality between variables associated with ethics, sustainability and supply chain resilience.

However, a shortfall of a methodology such as SD is that it will not capture the rich variance among actors in a system compared to other systems approach, therefore will be limited when attempting to unpack the complexity of ethical frameworks. Although useful, these attempts may reinforce deontological approaches such as supplier codes of conduct which may allow diffusion of responsibility to take place.

Therefore, a 'soft' systems approach would allow for different types of attitudes, norms and behaviours to be uncovered which would allow for the link between ethical variance and supply chain resilience to be more readily unpacked. For example, the method of SSM (Checkland & Poulter, 2020; Checkland & Winter, 2006) explicitly aims to explore the cultural and political factors that influence a problem by looking at the role, norms and values of the actors within a given system.

This approach would further allow for the normative judgements associated with sustainability to be critiqued (e.g. the ideas of critical heuristics discussed by Ulrich, 1987). In particular, in-depth analyses of power within organisations (and therefore supply chains) allow for a richer understanding of the links between power and bodies (Clegg et al., 2006; Foucault, 1980).

For example, the concepts of boundary judgements (Jackson, 2019; Ulrich, 1987) help understand what voices or worldviews are included or excluded within particular interventions. This can be seen within some interventions such as media stories of worker exploitation (ABC News, 2021c; The Guardian, 2020, 2021) that incorporate a variety of conflicting worldviews such as workers, business owners, unions and the government.

To demonstrate the conceptual utility of SSM towards unpacking the variance among ethical frameworks and sustainability within the horticultural supply chain, consider the following root definition based on the CATWOE analysis using the hypothetical example of a process to reduce horticultural worker exploitation through greater enforcement of laws and worker education. This example has been derived from the case discussed.

Root definition: A government, union, farmer and worker-run system to reduce the risk of wage exploitation on farms for seasonal fruit-pickers through the greater enforcement of laws and training of worker's industrial knowledge acknowledging the need for farms to be cost-effective.

As can be derived from Table 1, various actors will have their own intentions for the system (such as the different perspectives from unions and farmer groups). While the work of the Fair Work Commission (FWC) can be viewed through a deontological lens, virtue ethics can also be arguably demonstrated in the

Table 1. Conceptual CATWOE Associated With a Hypothetical Transformation Process to Reduce Worker Exploitation.

Component	Examples
C = "customers"	Seasonal fruit-pickers and farm employers
A = "actors"	The Australia Fair Work Commission (FWC), relevant unions, farmers, other workers who wish to improve their colleagues' industrial knowledge
T = "transformation"	Greater enforcement of laws + training of industrial knowledge
W = "world view"	A belief that greater adherence to laws will reduce exploitation (e.g. a deontological approach)
O = "owners"	Same as the actors
E = "environmental constraints"	Downward pressure from supermarkets and other supply chain actors to reduce costs and increase supply chain efficiency

example of workers who wish to educate other workers. An interesting avenue for the above case is the future potentiality of looking at the dominant worldviews within these analyses: therefore, the role of boundary judgements within critical system heuristics (Ulrich & Reynolds, 2020) can serve as a mechanism to unpack which voices are being centralised within any intervention.

It is also important to consider that these methodologies are not intended to be mutually exclusive. Another approach would be to utilise multiple methods and methodologies within systems thinking. Proposed as *multi-methodology* (Mingers, 2006) or *critical systems practice* (Jackson, 2019), these approaches have been proposed as tools for dealing with wicked problems (Jackson, 2023). The value of this is that it would allow for system tools for exploring the links between ethical frameworks and resilience (e.g. linking worker exploitation to food supply chain shortages through causal link diagrams) to be incorporated alongside other system methods (e.g. an analysis of power and norms within SSM). Any rules-based framework will naturally have boundaries – akin to any system possessing boundaries (Kast & Rosenzweig, 1972) – however, the argument can be made that using deontological frameworks as discrete measurement tools prevents the ability for system-wide criticism to be made, warranting the need for systems thinking approaches.

CONCLUSION

The purpose of this paper has been to provoke thinking and to set future research agendas that explore the complexities of sustainability through a holistic lens by arguing that there is a greater need for more critical and adventurous thinking within the supply chain sustainability literature. Quite often within the supply chain literature, several philosophical assumptions are made; therefore, there is a need for research to challenge and encourage deeper thinking on these areas. The purpose of this paper has been to explore the intersection between supply chain resilience, sustainability and ethics by looking at how decision-making around sustainability is often centred on deontological ethics. As discussed, this approach has its key benefits; however, it is often a misinterpretation of the overall message espoused by the TBL approach. By adopting new theoretical frameworks – in this case systems thinking – researchers and practitioners alike can explore novel ways of trying to address the wicked problem of sustainability within an increasing globalised and linked capitalist economy. Furthermore, the increased risk to supply chain resilience brought by environmental and social sources necessitates a critical approach towards understanding the complexities of sustainability.

Practitioner and Research Implications

Notwithstanding the conceptual nature of the paper, there are several implications for practise and research. In terms of practitioner implications, the paper argues that many of the current approaches towards grappling with sustainability issues within supply chains – in particular modern slavery – run the risk of being oversimplified to the point of redundancy through the over-reliance on measurement tools. Therefore, the paper serves as a tool to assist practitioners to develop a more critical and comprehensive understanding of the complexities (through systems thinking) associated with moving towards a TBL approach as part of any strategic focus on sustainability. For example, utilising the above systems methodologies towards projects exploring the variance in ethics within actors in given system will provide a great holistic appreciation of role of ethics within sustainability.

Another practical approach is the use of tools such as SD to explore where sustainability risks can arise from. For example, using this approach as an identifier of risks of modern slavery and how particular initiatives can have flow-on feedback effects through a system. This in turn can help practitioners determine appropriate interventions within a system to reduce the risk of modern slavery and explore how different ethical frameworks may be the normative worldviews within a given system. An additional avenue for practitioners is to use the tools set out within SSM and CSH through a multi-methodological approach to unpack the dominating worldviews within sustainability and supply chain resilience projects.

In terms of research implications, the paper sets forth a future research agenda to apply the above systems thinking methodologies – such as SD and SSM – towards looking at the complexity of ethical frameworks and sustainability. A brief overview of how these two methodologies can be used for future research projects has been discussed earlier within the paper. As a goal of the paper has been to unpack how unethical behaviour can manifest itself within systems, future research endeavours can utilise this discussion through a systems thinking lens to explore the factors that lead to variance in the different ethical frameworks and resultant unethical behaviours.

Combined with the practitioner implications, the paper's overall goal has been to propose a critique of how we view sustainability and some of its inherent paradoxes through the lens of ethics. Systems thinking approaches demonstrate the utility of exploring the wicked problem of sustainability from a more holistic lens to ensure that research and practise alike are best equipped to deal with this issue. A more critical approach towards sustainability and supply chain risk is essential towards building resilience and ensuring that business viability does not come at the detriment of the societies and environments that they operate in.

NOTE

1. The paper acknowledges that many sources oscillate between describing these systems as 'agricultural' and 'horticultural'. As the paper focuses on exploitation among fruit-picking workers, for the purposes of consistency, the phrase 'horticultural' is used.

REFERENCES

ABC News. (2020). Australian berry and citrus farms most at risk of having slave-like working conditions, Woolworths modern slavery report finds. https://www.abc.net.au/news/2020-11-26/berries-grapes-modern-slavery-coles-woolworths/12918122. Accessed on 3 November 2023.

ABC News. (2021a). Fair work rules every farm worker on every farm entitled to take home a minimum rate of pay. https://www.abc.net.au/news/rural/2021-11-04/fair-work-rules-every-farm-worker-entitled-minimum-rate-of-pay/100592806. Accessed on 15 August 2022.

ABC News. (2021b). Fruit picker minimum wage fight taken to Fair Work Commission. https://www.abc.net.au/news/2021-07-14/push-for-minimum-wage-assurance-for-fruit-pickers/100291380. Accessed on 10 August 2022.

ABC News. (2021c). Inside horticulture's 'dark underbelly': The unseen workers propping up the farm industry. https://www.abc.net.au/news/2021-12-14/australias-farm-industry-seasonal-workers-exploited-labour-short/100687182. Accessed on 10 August 2022.

Adam, A. M., & Rachman-Moore, D. (2004). The methods used to implement an ethical code of conduct and employee attitudes. *Journal of Business Ethics*, *54*(3), 225–244.

Agyabeng-Mensah, Y., Afum, E., Acquah, I. S. K., Dacosta, E., Baah, C., & Ahenkorah, E. (2021). The role of green logistics management practices, supply chain traceability and logistics ecocentricity in sustainability performance. *International Journal of Logistics Management*, *32*(2), 538–566.

Ahi, P., & Searcy, C. (2013). A comparative literature analysis of definitions for green and sustainable supply chain management. *Journal of Cleaner Production*, *52*, 329–341. https://doi.org/10.1016/j.jclepro.2013.02.018

Ahmed, S., Chapple, L., Christ, K., & Osborne, S. (2022). Modern slavery risk disclosures in business operations and supply chains. In *Environmental sustainability and agenda 2030: Efforts, progress and prospects* (pp. 67–104). Emerald Publishing Limited.

Alexander, A., Walker, H., & Delabre, I. (2022). A decision theory perspective on wicked problems, SDGs and stakeholders: The case of deforestation. *Journal of Business Ethics*, *180*(4), 975–995. https://doi.org/10.1007/s10551-022-05198-8

Anderson, P. (1999). Perspective: Complexity theory and organization science. *Organization Science*, *10*(3), 216–232.

Audi, R. (2012). Virtue ethics as a resource in business. *Business Ethics Quarterly*, *22*(2), 273–291.

Australian Government. (2022). Implementing the Modern Slavery Act 2018: The Australian Government's Annual Report 1 January 2021–31 December 2021. https://modernslaveryregister.gov.au/resources/Modern_Slavery_Act_Annual_Report_2021.pdf

Bandura, A. (1999). Moral disengagement in the perpetration of inhumanities. *Personality and Social Psychology Review*, *3*(3), 193–209.

Beamon, B. M. (2005). Environmental and sustainability ethics in supply chain management. *Science and Engineering Ethics*, *11*(2), 221–234.

Bentham, J. (1823). *An introduction to the principles of morals and legislation (Chapters I–V)*. Wiley Online Library.

Bietti, E. (2021). From ethics washing to ethics bashing: A moral philosophy view on tech ethics. *Journal of Social Computing, 2*(3), 266–283.

Birkel, H., & Müller, J. M. (2021). Potentials of industry 4.0 for supply chain management within the triple bottom line of sustainability – A systematic literature review. *Journal of Cleaner Production, 289*, 125612.

Biswas, D., Jalali, H., Ansaripoor, A. H., & De Giovanni, P. (2023). Traceability vs. sustainability in supply chains: The implications of blockchain. *European Journal of Operational Research, 305*(1), 128–147.

Biswas, I., Raj, A., & Srivastava, S. K. (2018). Supply chain channel coordination with triple bottom line approach. *Transportation Research Part E: Logistics and Transportation Review, 115*, 213–226. https://doi.org/10.1016/j.tre.2018.05.007

Brady, F. N. (1999). A systematic approach to teaching ethics in business. *Journal of Business Ethics, 19*(3), 309–318.

Burnes, B., & By, R. T. (2012). Leadership and change: The case for greater ethical clarity. *Journal of Business Ethics, 108*, 239–252.

Burton-Jones, A., McLean, E. R., & Monod, E. (2015). Theoretical perspectives in IS research: From variance and process to conceptual latitude and conceptual fit. *European Journal of Information Systems, 24*(6), 664–679.

Carroll, A. B. (1991). The pyramid of corporate social responsibility: Toward the moral management of organizational stakeholders. *Business Horizons, 34*(4), 39–48.

Caruana, R., Crane, A., Gold, S., & LeBaron, G. (2021). Modern slavery in business: The sad and sorry state of a non-field. *Business & Society, 60*(2), 251–287.

Cavanough, E., & Wherrett, C. (2020). Blue Harvest: Wage theft & other labour infringements in the NSW Mid-North Coast's 2019/20 Berry Harvest. https://mckellinstitute.org.au/wp-content/uploads/2022/02/McKell-Institute-Blue-Harvest-Final.pdf

Chakrabarty, S., & Erin Bass, A. (2015). Comparing virtue, consequentialist, and deontological ethics-based corporate social responsibility: Mitigating microfinance risk in institutional voids. *Journal of Business Ethics, 126*, 487–512.

Checkland, P., & Poulter, J. (2020). Soft systems methodology. In *Systems approaches to making change: A practical guide* (pp. 201–253). Springer.

Checkland, P., & Winter, M. (2006). Process and content: Two ways of using SSM. *Journal of the Operational Research Society, 57*(12), 1435–1441.

Chopra, M., Saini, N., Kumar, S., Varma, A., Mangla, S. K., & Lim, W. M. (2021). Past, present, and future of knowledge management for business sustainability. *Journal of Cleaner Production, 328*, 129592.

Christopher, M., & Peck, H. (2004). Building the resilient supply chain. *International Journal of Logistics Management, 15*(2), 1–14.

Clegg, S. R., Courpasson, D., & Phillips, N. (2006). *Power and organizations*. Sage.

Clegg, S. R., Pitsis, T. S., & Mount, M. (2021). *Managing and organizations: An introduction to theory and practice*. Sage.

Commonwealth of Australia. (2018). *Modern Slavery Act 2018*. Australia. https://www.legislation.gov.au/C2018A00153/asmade

Cousins, P. D., Lawson, B., Petersen, K. J., & Fugate, B. (2019). Investigating green supply chain management practices and performance: The moderating roles of supply chain ecocentricity and traceability [Green supply chain management]. *International Journal of Operations & Production Management, 39*(5), 767–786. https://doi.org/10.1108/IJOPM-11-2018-0676

Crane, A. (2013). Modern slavery as a management practice: Exploring the conditions and capabilities for human exploitation. *Academy of Management Review, 38*(1), 49–69.

Dalla Via, N., & Perego, P. (2018). Determinants of conflict minerals disclosure under the Dodd–Frank Act. *Business Strategy and the Environment, 27*(6), 773–788. https://doi.org/10.1002/bse.2030

de Freitas Netto, S. V., Sobral, M. F. F., Ribeiro, A. R. B., & Soares, G. R. d. L. (2020). Concepts and forms of greenwashing: A systematic review. *Environmental Sciences Europe, 32*(1), 1–12.

Defee, C. C., Williams, B., Randall, W. S., & Thomas, R. (2010). An inventory of theory in logistics and SCM research. *International Journal of Logistics Management, 21*(3), 404–489. https://doi.org/10.1108/09574091011089817

Delmas, M. A., & Burbano, V. C. (2011). The drivers of greenwashing. *California Management Review, 54*(1), 64–87. https://doi.org/10.1525/cmr.2011.54.1.64

Dempsey, J. (2015). Moral responsibility, shared values, and corporate culture. *Business Ethics Quarterly, 25*(3), 319–340.

Department of Home Affairs. (2023). *Modern slavey register*. https://modernslaveryregister.gov.au/statements/. Accessed on 10 July 2023.

Drake, M. J., & Schlachter, J. T. (2008). A virtue-ethics analysis of supply chain collaboration. *Journal of Business Ethics, 82*, 851–864.

Draščěk, M., Rejc Buhovac, A., & Mesner Andolšek, D. (2021). Moral pragmatism as a bridge between duty, utility, and virtue in managers' ethical Decision-Making. *Journal of Business Ethics, 172*, 803–819.

Dubey, R., Gunasekaran, A., Childe, S. J., Papadopoulos, T., & Wamba, S. F. (2017). World class sustainable supply chain management: Critical review and further research directions. *International Journal of Logistics Management, 28*(2), 332–362.

Egels-Zandén, N., & Lindholm, H. (2015). Do codes of conduct improve worker rights in supply chains? A study of fair wear foundation. *Journal of Cleaner Production, 107*, 31–40.

Elias, A. A. (2022). Multi-stakeholder participation for achieving sustainable development goals: A systems thinking approach. In *Environmental sustainability and agenda 2030: Efforts, progress and prospects* (pp. 45–65). Emerald Publishing Limited.

Elias, A. A., Donadelli, F., Paiva, E. L., & Bacic Araujo, P. P. (2021). Analysing the complexities of sustainable wood supply chain in the Amazon: A systems thinking approach. *International Journal of Logistics Management, 32*(4), 1481–1505.

Elkington, J. (1997). *Cannibals with forks: The triple bottom line of 21st century*. Capstone.

Elkington, J. (2018). 25 years ago I coined the phrase 'triple bottom line.' Here's why it's time to rethink it. *Harvard Business Review, 25*, 2–5.

Emmelhainz, M. A., & Adams, R. J. (1999). The apparel industry response to 'sweatshop' concerns: A review and analysis of codes of conduct. *Journal of Supply Chain Management, 35*(2), 51–57.

Eriksson, D., & Svensson, G. (2016). The process of responsibility, decoupling point, and disengagement of moral and social responsibility in supply chains: Empirical findings and prescriptive thoughts. *Journal of Business Ethics, 134*(2), 281–298.

Fair Work Ombudsman. (2018). Harvest trail inquiry. https://www.fairwork.gov.au/about-us/compliance-and-enforcement/inquiries/harvest-trail-inquiry

Farm Online. (2021). Rampant' wage theft reported in fruit picking jobs, survey suggests. https://www.farmonline.com.au/story/7297294/fruit-pickers-victims-of-rampant-wage-theft-on-farms-survey/. Accessed on 3 May 2023.

Forrester, J. W. (1994). System dynamics, systems thinking, and soft OR. *System Dynamics Review, 10*(2-3), 245–256.

Foucault, M. (1980). *Power/knowledge: Selected interviews and other writings 1972–1977*. Pantheon.

Garcia-Torres, S., Albareda, L., Rey-Garcia, M., & Seuring, S. (2019). Traceability for sustainability – Literature review and conceptual framework. *Supply Chain Management: An International Journal, 24*(1), 85–106.

Giannakis, M., & Papadopoulos, T. (2016). Supply chain sustainability: A risk management approach. *International Journal of Production Economics, 171*, 455–470.

Gutierrez-Huerter O, G., Gold, S., & Trautrims, A. (2021). Change in rhetoric but not in action? Framing of the ethical issue of modern slavery in a UK sector at high risk of labor exploitation. *Journal of Business Ethics*. https://doi.org/10.1007/s10551-021-05013-w

Ha-Brookshire, J. (2017). Toward moral responsibility theories of corporate sustainability and sustainable supply chain. *Journal of Business Ethics, 145*(2), 227–237.

Haimes, Y. Y. (1998). Reducing vulnerability of water supply systems to attack. *Journal of Infrastructure Systems, 4*(4), 164–177. https://doi.org/10.1061/(ASCE)1076-0342(1998)4:4(164

Haimes, Y. Y. (2009). On the complex definition of risk: A systems-based approach. *Risk Analysis, 29*(12), 1647–1654.

Haimes, Y. Y. (2011). On the complex quantification of risk: Systems-based perspective on terrorism. *Risk Analysis*, *31*(8), 1175–1186. https://doi.org/10.1111/j.1539-6924.2011.01603.x

Head, B. W. (2018). Forty years of wicked problems literature: Forging closer links to policy studies. *Policy and Society*, *38*(2), 180–197. https://doi.org/10.1080/14494035.2018.1488797

Heckmann, I., Comes, T., & Nickel, S. (2015). A critical review on supply chain risk – Definition, measure and modeling. *Omega*, *52*, 119–132.

Hollos, D., Blome, C., & Foerstl, K. (2012). Does sustainable supplier co-operation affect performance? Examining implications for the triple bottom line. *International Journal of Production Research*, *50*(11), 2968–2986.

Howe, J., Clibborn, S., Reilly, A., van den Broek, D., & Wright, C. F. (2019). *Towards a durable future: Tackling labour challenges in the Australian horticulture industry*.

Howe, J., Reilly, A., Clibborn, S., van den Broek, D., & Wright, C. F. (2020). Slicing and dicing work in the Australian horticulture industry: Labour market segmentation within the temporary migrant workforce. *Federal Law Review*, *48*(2), 247–271.

Howe, J., Shi, E., & Clibborn, S. (2021). *Fruit picking in fear: An examination of sexual harassment on Australian farms* (Vol. 45, pp. 1140). Melbourne University Law Review.

ILO. (2022). Global estimates of modern slavery: Forced labour and forced marriage. https://www.ilo.org/wcmsp5/groups/public/ed_norm/ipec/documents/publication/wcms_854733.pdf

Intel. (2022). 2021–2022 corporate responsibility report. https://csrreportbuilder.intel.com/pdfbuilder/pdfs/CSR-2021-22-Full-Report.pdf

Jackson, M. C. (2019). *Critical systems thinking and the management of complexity*. John Wiley & Sons.

Jackson, M. C. (2023). Critical systems practice 4: Check – Evaluating and reflecting on a multimethodological intervention. *Systems Research and Behavioral Science*, *40*(4), 617–632.

Jiang, B. (2009). Implementing supplier codes of conduct in global supply chains: Process explanations from theoretic and empirical perspectives. *Journal of Business Ethics*, *85*, 77–92.

Jordan, K., & Kristjánsson, K. (2017). Sustainability, virtue ethics, and the virtue of harmony with nature. *Environmental Education Research*, *23*(9), 1205–1229.

Kahneman, D., Wakker, P. P., & Sarin, R. (1997). Back to Bentham? Explorations of experienced utility. *Quarterly Journal of Economics*, 375–405.

Kamalahmadi, M., & Parast, M. M. (2016). A review of the literature on the principles of enterprise and supply chain resilience: Major findings and directions for future research. *International Journal of Production Economics*, *171*(1), 116–133.

Kant, I. (1785/1990). *Foundations of the metaphysics of morals* (2nd ed., L. W. Beck Trans.). Macmillan.

Kaplan, S., & Garrick, B. J. (1981). On the quantitative definition of risk. *Risk Analysis*, *1*(1), 11–27. http://ezproxy.uow.edu.au/login?url=http://search.ebscohost.com/login.aspx?direct=true&db=edb&AN=90752536&site=eds-live

Kara, S. (2017). *Modern slavery: A global perspective*. Columbia University Press.

Kast, F. E., & Rosenzweig, J. E. (1972). General systems theory: Applications for organization and management. *Academy of Management Journal*, *15*(4), 447–465.

Katsaliaki, K., Galetsi, P., & Kumar, S. (2022). Supply chain disruptions and resilience: A major review and future research agenda. *Annals of Operations Research*, *319*(1), 965–1002. https://doi.org/10.1007/s10479-020-03912-1

L'etang, J. (1992). A Kantian approach to codes of ethics. *Journal of Business Ethics*, *11*(10), 737–744.

Levin, S. (2003). Complex adaptive systems: Exploring the known, the unknown and the unknowable. *Bulletin of the American Mathematical Society*, *40*(1), 3–19.

Ma, Y. J., Lee, H. H., & Goerlitz, K. (2016). Transparency of global apparel supply chains: Quantitative analysis of corporate disclosures. *Corporate Social Responsibility and Environmental Management*, *23*(5), 308–318.

Mackay, J., Munoz, A., & Pepper, M. (2019). A disaster typology towards informing humanitarian relief supply chain design. *Journal of Humanitarian Logistics and Supply Chain Management*, *9*(1), 22–46. https://doi.org/10.1108/JHLSCM-06-2018-0049

Mackay, J., Munoz, A., & Pepper, M. (2020). Conceptualising redundancy and flexibility towards supply chain robustness and resilience. *Journal of Risk Research*, *23*(12), 1–21.

Mackay, J., Pepper, M., & Munoz, A. (2023). Disruptions, systems and individual agents – Exploring the intersections. *Systems Research and Behavioral Science*, *40*(1), 43–60.

Marshall, D., McCarthy, L., Claudy, M., & McGrath, P. (2019). Piggy in the middle: How direct customer power affects first-tier suppliers' adoption of socially responsible procurement practices and performance. *Journal of Business Ethics*, *154*(4), 1081–1102. https://doi.org/10.1007/s10551-016-3387-0

Matthews, L., Power, D., Touboulic, A., & Marques, L. (2016). Building bridges: Toward alternative theory of sustainable supply chain management. *Journal of Supply Chain Management*, *52*(1), 82–94.

Mello, M. H., Gosling, J., Naim, M. M., Strandhagen, J. O., & Brett, P. O. (2017). Improving coordination in an engineer-to-order supply chain using a soft systems approach. *Production Planning & Control*, *28*(2), 89–107.

Mentzer, J. T., DeWitt, W., Keebler, J. S., Min, S., Nix, N. W., Smith, C. D., & Zacharia, Z. G. (2001). Defining supply chain management. *Journal of Business Logistics*, *22*(2), 1–25.

Miemczyk, J., & Luzzini, D. (2019). Achieving triple bottom line sustainability in supply chains. *International Journal of Operations & Production Management*, *39*(2), 238–259. https://doi.org/10.1108/IJOPM-06-2017-0334

Migrant Workers' Taskforce. (2019). Report of the migrant workers' Taskforce. https://www.ag.gov.au/sites/default/files/2020-03/mwt_final_report.pdf

Mingers, J. (2006). A critique of statistical modelling in management science from a critical realist perspective: Its role within multimethodology. *Journal of the Operational Research Society*, *57*(2), 202–219. https://doi.org/10.1057/palgrave.jors.2601980

Modern Slavery Act 2018 No 30. (2018).

Montabon, F., Pagell, M., & Wu, Z. (2016). Making sustainability sustainable. *Journal of Supply Chain Management*, *52*(2), 11–27.

National Greenhouse. (2007). Energy Reporting Act. https://www.legislation.gov.au/Details/C2022C00258

Negri, M., Cagno, E., Colicchia, C., & Sarkis, J. (2021). Integrating sustainability and resilience in the supply chain: A systematic literature review and a research agenda. *Business Strategy and the Environment*, *30*(7), 2858–2886.

Neri, A., Cagno, E., Lepri, M., & Trianni, A. (2021). A triple bottom line balanced set of key performance indicators to measure the sustainability performance of industrial supply chains. *Sustainable Production and Consumption*, *26*, 648–691.

New, S., & Hsin, L. (2021). *Deconstructing modern slavery statements: A detailed analysis of arcadia group and babcock international*. SSRN 3768495.

Nguyen, T. T., Scognamillo, D. G., & Comer, C. E. (2019). Revealing community perceptions for ecological restoration using a soft system methodology. *Systemic Practice and Action Research*, *32*, 429–442.

Nilsson, F., & Gammelgaard, B. (2012). Moving beyond the systems approach in SCM and logistics research. *International Journal of Physical Distribution & Logistics Management*, *42*(8/9), 764–783.

Nishitani, M., & Lee, H. (2023). Fruit picking and farmwork as racialised stigma: The children of pacific migrant workers in rural Australia. *Journal of Intercultural Studies*, 1–17.

Norman, W., & MacDonald, C. (2004). Getting to the bottom of triple bottom line. *Business Ethics Quarterly*, 243–262.

Paucar-Caceres, A., Cavalcanti-Bandos, M. F., Quispe-Prieto, S. C., Huerta-Tantalean, L. N., & Werner-Masters, K. (2022). Using soft systems methodology to align community projects with sustainability development in higher education stakeholders' networks in a Brazilian university. *Systems Research and Behavioral Science*, *39*(4), 750–764.

Pedersen, E. R., & Andersen, M. (2006). Safeguarding corporate social responsibility (CSR) in global supply chains: How codes of conduct are managed in buyer-supplier relationships. *Journal of Public Affairs: An International Journal*, *6*(3–4), 228–240.

Pruyt, E. (2013). *Small system dynamics models for big issues: Triple jump towards real-world complexity*. TU Delft Library.

Rebs, T., Brandenburg, M., & Seuring, S. (2019). System dynamics modeling for sustainable supply chain management: A literature review and systems thinking approach. *Journal of Cleaner Production*, *208*, 1265–1280.

Reinecke, J., & Ansari, S. (2016). Taming wicked problems: The role of framing in the construction of corporate social responsibility. *Journal of Management Studies*, *53*(3), 299–329.

Rittel, H. W., & Webber, M. M. (1973). Dilemmas in a general theory of planning. *Policy Sciences*, *4*(2), 155–169.

Roberts, S. (2003). Supply chain specific? Understanding the patchy success of ethical sourcing initiatives. *Journal of Business Ethics*, *44*(2), 159–170.

Saberi, S., Kouhizadeh, M., Sarkis, J., & Shen, L. (2019). Blockchain technology and its relationships to sustainable supply chain management. *International Journal of Production Research*, *57*(7), 2117–2135.

Saeed, M. A., & Kersten, W. (2019). Drivers of sustainable supply chain management: Identification and classification. *Sustainability*, *11*(4), 1137.

Sandel, M. J. (2009). *Justice*. Farrar, Straus and Giroux.

Scheibe, K. P., & Blackhurst, J. (2017). Supply chain disruption propagation: A systemic risk and normal accident theory perspective. *International Journal of Production Research*, *56*(1–2), 43–59.

Schneider, M., & Somers, M. (2006). Organizations as complex adative systems: Implications of complexity theory for leadership research. *The Leadership Quarterly*, *17*(4), 351–365. http://ac.els-cdn.com/S1048984306000373/1-s2.0-S1048984306000373-main.pdf?_tid=e5e1452e-39c6-11e6-b22f-00000aab0f6c&acdnat=1466743890_c7226a87cbc21bc56215a044de637396

Senge, P. M. (2006). *The fifth discipline: The art and practice of the learning organisation*. Doubleday.

Seuring, S., & Müller, M. (2008). From a literature review to a conceptual framework for sustainable supply chain management. *Journal of Cleaner Production*, *16*(15), 1699–1710.

Sheffi, Y. (2005). *The resilient enterprise: Overcoming vulnerability for competitive advantage*. MIT Press.

Shishodia, A., Sharma, R., Rajesh, R., & Munim, Z. H. (2023). Supply chain resilience: A review, conceptual framework and future research. *International Journal of Logistics Management*, *34*(4), 879–908.

State of California. (2010). *California transparency in supply chains act of 2010*. United States. https://leginfo.legislature.ca.gov/faces/billTextClient.xhtml?bill_id5200920100SB657

Stevenson, M. (2022). Hidden in plain sight: The bystander effect and the mobilisation of modern slavery whistleblowing [article]. *Supply Chain Management*, *27*(1), 128–139. https://doi.org/10.1108/SCM-08-2020-0373

Stevenson, M., & Cole, R. (2018). Modern slavery in supply chains: A secondary data analysis of detection, remediation and disclosure. *Supply Chain Management: An International Journal*, *23*(2), 81–99.

Sydney Morning Herald. (2016). Fruits of their labour: Investigation into exploitation of migrant fruit picking workers in Australia. https://www.smh.com.au/interactive/2016/fruit-picking-investigation/

Tavella, E. (2023). 'And what did you do about my emotions during Covid-19?' Making sense of negative emotions at work through institutional logics and Critical Systems Heuristics. *Systems Research and Behavioral Science*, *40*(6), 836–852.

Telstra. (2022). Bigger picture: 2022 sustainability report. https://exchange.telstra.com.au/wp-content/uploads/2022/08/Telstra-Bigger-Picture-2022-Sustainability-Report.pdf

The Guardian. (2021). 'I was desperate': The fight to get Australia's fruit pickers a fair wage. https://www.theguardian.com/australia-news/2021/jul/18/i-was-desperate-the-fight-to-get-australias-fruit-pickers-a-fair-wage. Accessed on 12 October 2022.

The Guardian. (2020). The fruit pickers: Inside Australia's seasonal worker program – A photo essay. https://www.theguardian.com/australia-news/2020/oct/18/the-fruit-pickers-inside-australias-seasonal-worker-program-a-photo-essay. Accessed on 12 October 2022.

Topp-Becker, J., & Ellis, J. D. (2017). The role of sustainability reporting in the agri-food supply chain. *Journal of Agriculture and Environmental Sciences*, *6*(1), 17–29.

United Kingdom. (2015). *Modern Slavery Act 2015*. United Kingdom. https://www.legislation.gov.uk/ukpga/2015/30/contents/enacted

Ulrich, W. (1987). Critical heuristics of social systems design. *European Journal of Operational Research*, *31*(3), 276–283.

Ulrich, W., & Reynolds, M. (2020). Critical systems heuristics: The idea and practice of boundary critique. In *Systems approaches to making change: A practical guide* (pp. 255–306).

United Nations. (2021). *Sustainable development goals*. https://www.un.org/sustainabledevelopment/sustainable-development-goals/. Accessed on 2 June 2021.

Van Staveren, I. (2007). Beyond utilitarianism and deontology: Ethics in economics. *Review of Political Economy*, *19*(1), 21–35.

Velasquez, M. (2003). Debunking corporate moral responsibility. *Business Ethics Quarterly*, 531–562.

Vijeyarasa, R. (2019). A missed opportunity: How Australia failed to make its Modern Slavery Act a global example of good practice. *Adelaide Law Review*, *40*, 857.

Vijeyarasa, R. (2020). Women, work and global supply chains: The gender-blind nature of Australia's modern slavery regulatory regime. *Australian Journal of Human Rights*, *26*(1), 74–92.

von Bertalanffy, L. (1950). An outline of general system theory. *The British Journal for the Philosophy of Science*, *1*(2), 134–165.

von Bertalanffy, L. (1972). The history and status of general systems theory. *Academy of Management Journal*, *15*(4), 407–426.

Voss, H., Davis, M., Sumner, M., Waite, L., Ras, I. A., Singhal, D., & Jog, D. (2019). International supply chains: Compliance and engagement with the Modern Slavery Act. *Journal of the British Academy*, *7*(s1), 61–76. https://doi.org/10.5871/jba/007s1.061

Walker, B., Holling, C. S., Carpenter, S. R., & Kinzig, A. (2004). Resilience, adaptability and transformability in social-ecological systems. http://www.ecologyandsociety.org/vol9/iss2/art5/

Walker, H., Miemczyk, J., Johnsen, T., & Spencer, R. (2012). *Sustainable procurement: Past, present and future* (Vol. 18, pp. 201–206). Elsevier.

Walker, K., Yu, X., & Zhang, Z. (2020). All for one or all for three: Empirical evidence of paradox theory in the triple-bottom-line. *Journal of Cleaner Production*, *275*, 122881.

Weick, K. E. (1995). What theory is not, theorizing is. *Administrative Science Quarterly*, *40*(3), 385–390. https://doi.org/10.2307/2393789

Werhane, P. H. (2002). Moral imagination and systems thinking. *Journal of Business Ethics*, *38*(1), 33–42.

Whetstone, J. T. (2001). How virtue fits within business ethics. *Journal of Business Ethics*, *33*, 101–114.

Wieland, A., & Durach, C. F. (2021). *Two perspectives on supply chain resilience* (Vol. 42, pp. 315–322). Wiley Online Library.

Wieland, A., Stevenson, M., Melnyk, S. A., Davoudi, S., & Schultz, L. (2023). Thinking differently about supply chain resilience: What we can learn from social-ecological systems thinking. *International Journal of Operations & Production Management*, *43*(1), 1–21.

Wilden, D., Hopkins, J., & Sadler, I. (2022). The prevalence of systems thinking in supply chain management: A systematic literature review. *Systemic Practice and Action Research*, *35*(4), 491–526.

Williams, A., Kennedy, S., Philipp, F., & Whiteman, G. (2017). Systems thinking: A review of sustainability management research. *Journal of Cleaner Production*, *148*, 866–881.

World Commission on Environment and Development. (1987). Our common future. http://www.un-documents.net/our-common-future.pdf

World Economic Forum. (2020). Measuring stakeholder capitalism towards common metrics and consistent reporting of sustainable value creation. https://www3.weforum.org/docs/WEF_IBC_Measuring_Stakeholder_Capitalism_Report_2020.pdf

ASSESSING THE SUSTAINABILITY AND RESILIENCE OF URBAN TRANSIT: THE CASE OF KOCHI WATER METRO

George Joseph[a] and Arun A. Elias[a,b]

[a]*Rajagiri Business School, India*
[b]*Victoria University of Wellington, New Zealand*

ABSTRACT

The study aims to critically evaluate the Kochi Water Metro as a model for sustainable urban transportation and extract valuable lessons for policymakers and cities seeking similar initiatives. The study employs a qualitative data-driven approach, utilising a longitudinal case study design, open-ended interview questions, direct observations and qualitative content analysis. The Kochi Water Metro has emerged as a transformative urban mobility initiative, enhancing connectivity while simultaneously reducing congestion on roads. The project's sustainable practices have minimised its carbon footprint, contributing to environmental sustainability. Economic benefits have accrued through increased tourism, employment opportunities and improved local livelihoods. The project's adaptability to local conditions and changing needs further underscores its sustainability. Limited data from the project's early years necessitate further longitudinal analysis. The focus on benefits may overlook potential challenges, warranting broader investigation. Reliance on qualitative data may restrict generalisability. The Kochi Water Metro serves as a beacon for sustainable and equitable transportation solutions. It serves as a blueprint for policymakers, providing practical lessons in project implementation, especially its integration with existing modes enhances overall urban mobility. Policymakers should consider replicating elements such as electric boats and integrated networks, while emphasising environmental sustainability, accessibility and community engagement. The comprehensive evaluation provides valuable insights into the project's tangible impacts and

Sustainable and Resilient Supply Chain
Advances in Environmental Accounting & Management, Volume 12, 141–157

ISSN: 1479-3598/doi:10.1108/S1479-359820240000012012

replicable elements. The innovative approach blends sustainable practices, operational resilience and community engagement, serving as a model for cities seeking sustainable, equitable and efficient transportation solutions.

Keywords: Kochi Water Metro; sustainable urban transport; electric hybrid boats; renewable energy; operational challenges; community impact

INTRODUCTION

Kochi, historically known as a significant port city and a hub in the global trade network, has played a pivotal role in trade due to its strategic location along the Arabian Sea (Menon, 2010). Yet, the city is not immune to the adverse impacts of climate change, as recent extreme weather events have clearly demonstrated. The severe floods experienced by Kerala in 2018 and 2019 have intensified the search for innovative and resilient urban solutions to these emerging challenges (Kumar & Bindu, 2022).

The Kochi Water Metro project emerges in response to these challenges, representing a significant investment in urban infrastructure aimed at integrating sustainability and resilience into the city's public transportation system. The project is particularly timely as Kochi, like many rapidly urbanising areas, is confronting the limitations of traditional transport systems and their environmental implications (Thekkeyil et al., 2023). Kerala's vulnerability to climate change, exemplified by unpredictable monsoon patterns and flooding, necessitates a re-examination of urban mobility and disaster preparedness (Sudheer et al., 2023).

In this vein, the Kochi Water Metro represents an innovative approach to urban transport. The adoption of eco-friendly boats powered by hybrid sources illustrates a shift towards reduced carbon emissions and a departure from traditional diesel-powered vessels, setting a new standard for sustainable urban transit (Raftis et al., 2023). By leveraging natural waterways, the project aims to enhance the efficiency of public transport while offering an alternative to congested roadways and contributing to disaster readiness (Singh et al., 2021). The Water Metro system ensures the continuous flow of commerce and daily life by reliably transporting goods and people, independent of road networks that are often disrupted by climate events. Its resilience offers a crucial alternative, although it's important to note that waterways too can be impacted by climate change (Bosher & Chmutina, 2017). Furthermore, the project's alignment with the United Nations' Sustainable Development Goals – particularly Goals 11 (Sustainable Cities and Communities) and 13 (Climate Action) – underscores its commitment to sustainable development and urban connectivity (UNDP, 2023).

As the world contends with urbanisation and climate change, the Kochi Water Metro presents an opportunity to study how sustainable innovation in urban transit systems can address these global challenges. Celebrated as the first water-based public transport of its kind in South Asia, the project seeks to enhance urban mobility while simultaneously tackling environmental and infrastructural concerns (Kochi Water Metro, 2023). The current study aims to provide an objective examination of the Kochi Water Metro as a case in sustainable urban transportation, potentially offering valuable insights for broader applications. It will scrutinise the system's role as an environmentally sustainable alternative, a resilient infrastructure against climate-related challenges, a contributor to social equity by connecting disparate communities and a possible stimulant for economic activity through local commerce and tourism. Additionally, the study will look at operational efficiencies that could serve as lessons for other urban centres seeking to implement sustainable mobility solutions.

Against this backdrop, this research seeks to comprehensively evaluate the Kochi Water Metro's role in sustainable mass transit, its capability to inform similar projects in different regions and the specific elements that contribute to its resilience and sustainability within an urban setting.

LITERATURE REVIEW

The integration of sustainable transportation models into urban planning, epitomised by projects like the Kochi Water Metro, necessitates an in-depth analysis to understand their impacts on operations management, supply chain dynamics and climate change resilience.

Strategic Role of Public Transit in Urban Supply Chains

The extant literature has consistently underlined the importance of public transit systems, asserting that they are pivotal for the strategic development of supply chains, broader urban economic landscape and its role in achieving Sustainable Development Goals (Elias, 2022). Indeed, such systems significantly affect employee mobility, business connectivity and the fluidity of e-commerce, particularly in the context of burgeoning urbanisation (Nash & Johnson, 2019).

The sustainable supply chain management literature has acknowledged the critical role of green logistics (Paskannaya & Shaban, 2019) and environmentally responsible transport networks as vital components in the progression towards sustainable urban development. Within this context, the Kochi Water Metro initiative stands out as an exemplar of sustainable transport integration within an urban supply chain (Eldien et al., 2020). It operates on the principles of reducing carbon footprint and promoting energy-efficient practices, aligning with the broader goals of sustainability. Furthermore, this literature emphasises the importance of stakeholder engagement and the socio-economic benefits (Kannabiran, 2009) of sustainable supply chain practices. The Kochi Water Metro addresses this by improving accessibility and connectivity (Velaga et al., 2012) for local communities, which potentially stimulates economic activity and inclusivity, particularly for those in remote island regions. By integrating with the existing transport network and providing last-mile connectivity (Kanuri et al., 2019), it enhances the overall efficiency of the urban supply chain, demonstrating the tangible benefits of investing in sustainable infrastructure. The project's challenges and operational hurdles provide a realistic perspective on the implementation of sustainable transport initiatives, highlighting the need for resilience and adaptability in planning and execution (Aslam et al., 2020). These contributions to the sustainable supply chain management literature underscore the potential for innovative transport solutions to support sustainable urban development goals. The sustainable supply chain management literature (e.g. Elias et al., 2021) has also acknowledged the role of public transport in making supply chain sustainably resilient (Izadikhah et al., 2021). The unique geographic composition of Kochi, with its extensive waterways and islands, presents a compelling case for examining the Water Metro's revolutionary effects on the local supply chain and logistics sectors (Kuriakose & Philip, 2021). The Kochi Water Metro project utilises the unique geography of Kochi's waterways to enhance public transportation and connectivity. Water Metro is expected to commute 34,000 passengers daily in the first phase decongesting the roads, reducing the carbon footprints of the city of Kochi. A reduction of 44,000 tons of CO_2 emission per annum is expected when it is fully operational, and achieving its green energy targets, contributing to the ambitious targets of the country to become carbon neutral. It addresses congestion and pollution challenges by integrating with other transport modes and promoting sustainable transportation. This project is notable for its eco-friendly approach, employing electric boats and aiming for reduced CO_2 emissions. It also focuses on inclusivity and accessibility, improving the socio-economic status of island residents and boosting tourism (Elets eGov, 2023).

Researchers have underscored the intrinsic difficulties inherent in road-based networks across similar terrains, including congestion and susceptibility to climate disruptions (Rajasekar et al., 2018). Moreover, the transition to green-powered eco-friendly transport modes is hailed not merely for operational advantages but for the alignment with broader sustainability objectives (Pietrzak & Pietrzak, 2020).

Urban Resilience and Climate Adaptation

Urban resilience literature accentuates the need for adaptable infrastructure in response to escalating climate change threats, such as those faced by Kochi – frequent flooding and other environmental adversities (Driessen et al., 2018). The Water Metro's strategic design principles appear to be in synergy with academic advocacy for environmentally adaptable transportation solutions (Zhou et al., 2019). A critical element of this discussion revolves around sustainability. Conventional, fossil fuel-dependent transit systems are significant environmental antagonists due to their greenhouse gas (GHG) emissions (Miller et al., 2016). Hence, the shift towards hybrid electric-powered vessels is a crucial step towards mitigating the environmental impact of transportation (Pietrzak & Pietrzak, 2020).

The socio-economic ramifications of the Water Metro are equally significant. Research indicates that such infrastructural enhancements can invigorate local economies, catalyse tourism and underpin social inclusivity (Lucas & Musso, 2014). The Kochi Water Metro offers an affordable and accessible transportation option. A single ride costs 30 rupees, with various passes available ranging from

180 to 1,500 rupees for more frequent travellers. These options include weekly and monthly passes. The Kochi One Card, which can also be used for the Kochi Metro, is accepted for the Water Metro. The boats are designed to be accessible for individuals with disabilities, ensuring inclusivity in public transportation (Nativeplanet, 2023).

Improved access can spur local industries, abbreviate supply chains and introduce cost benefits (Allen & Farber, 2020). Climate change's inexorable impact on urban settings, particularly in coastal zones like Kochi, underscores the vulnerability of cities to sea-level rise, severe weather events and flooding – all of which exert substantial strain on transportation networks (Arsenio et al., 2016; Sobrino & Monzon, 2013; Tauringana & Moses, 2023). Given transportation's significant contribution to global emissions, sustainable alternatives are not only operationally superior but also pivotal for reducing urban pollution and carbon emissions (Hrelja et al., 2015; Mashayekh et al., 2012). Integrating public transportation systems with renewable energy sources, such as solar or wind power, significantly reduces ecological footprints in cities. This approach lessens reliance on fossil fuels, thereby reducing GHG emissions and air pollution. Renewable energy is sustainable and cleaner, contributing to a healthier urban environment. Additionally, it can lead to energy independence and stability in energy costs for public transportation systems, further promoting their efficiency and sustainability. This integration is a step towards more environmentally friendly and resilient urban infrastructure (Schiller & Kenworthy, 2017).

Transportation Resilience in the Face of Unpredictability

With the unpredictability of climate change–induced events and various crises such as pandemics and geopolitical instability, urban centres are pressed to bolster the resilience of their infrastructures, particularly public transportation systems (Heino et al., 2019). Resilience is characterised by robustness, rapid recovery and adaptability to ensure continuous urban mobility (Coaffee et al., 2018). Mass transit solutions, thus, have gained favour as they outperform the car-dependent models that predominate in densely populated urban areas, alleviating congestion, pollution and reducing travel times (Narayanaswami, 2017; Vullapu et al., 2023). Water-based transit offers a distinctive approach, especially apt for cities with extensive waterways. The Kochi Water Metro is poised to redefine urban supply chains, enhance regional connectivity and provide a resilient and sustainable transportation alternative less susceptible to climate-induced challenges (Levy et al., 2017; Pietrzak & Pietrzak, 2020). In times of infrastructure failure due to natural disasters, waterways can ensure the continuity of transportation where land-based options falter (Schiessel Harvey, 2021).

Gaps in Sustainable Transportation Research

There is a substantial chasm in empirical research concerning the actual efficacy of these sustainable interventions, particularly in their ability to support the attainment of global sustainability goals (Hailemariam et al., 2019). Moreover, the societal impacts of integrating such novel transit systems into the urban matrix require thorough investigation. How do these advancements affect socio-economic inequalities and the living standards of the populace? Prolonged studies are necessitated to chronicle the evolutionary impact on urban economic patterns, employment prospects and civic involvement post the introduction of these sustainable transport avenues. The dynamic shift in urban supply chain mechanisms and the economic fluctuations attributable to the operationalisation of these systems call for an empirical elucidation (Sun et al., 2019). This conspicuous research void presents an opportunity for in-depth studies that coalesce practical insights from the implementation of the Kochi Water Metro with the prevailing theoretical discourse. For stakeholders ranging from policymakers and urban planners to operations managers, such research could serve as a crucial instrument for evaluating and enhancing the efficacy of sustainable urban transportation networks, thereby contributing to an optimised amalgamation of social, economic and environmental well-being (Young et al., 2019).

RESEARCH METHODOLOGY

To investigate the multifaceted aspects of the Kochi Water Metro, our research methodology was grounded in pragmatism, leveraging qualitative data to derive meaningful and practical insights. This approach is supported by the belief that social realities can be observed objectively and assessed through methodological measures (Park et al., 2020). The study was designed as a longitudinal case study, enabling an in-depth exploration of this unique urban transit intervention within its real-life context over an extended period. This design aligns with established qualitative research methods that offer a nuanced understanding of complex phenomena through detailed contextual analysis (Rashid et al., 2019).

Data Collection

As suggested by Whitehead (2005), our research approach for this case study involved the gathering of primary data through a combination of semi-structured interviews and direct observations. Respondents (See Table 1) were identified using a purposive sampling strategy, targeting individuals with direct experience or knowledge relevant to the Kochi Water Metro. This included selecting participants across various demographics and roles to ensure a comprehensive understanding of the system's impact. To account for potential biases, we employed triangulation, comparing data from different sources – interviews, observations and existing literature – to validate the findings and provide a balanced representation of the Water Metro's effectiveness and its wider implications. As recommended by Xiahou et al. (2022), the research incorporated interviews with a broad array of stakeholders, including city planners, Kochi Water Metro officials, local business owners, commuters and residents, thereby

Table 1. Respondent Profile.

No.	Stakeholder Group	Specific Stakeholder	Interviewee Numbers
1	Local Community and Residents	Business Owner	1
2	Academia and Education Sector	Student	1
3	Local Community and Residents	Homemaker	1
4	Advocacy and Activism	Sustainability Enthusiast	1
5	Media and Information Sector	Journalist	1
6	Professional Experts and Service Providers	Architect	1
7	Advocacy and Activism	Environmental Activist	1
8	Academia and Education Sector	College Student	2
9	Academia and Education Sector	School Teacher	1
10	Local Community and Residents	Resident, Vypeen Island	1
11	Local Community and Residents	Daily Commuter	1
12	Economic and Financial Sector	Economist	1
13	Advocacy and Activism	Person with Disabilities	1
14	International Traveller	Tourist	1
15	Local Community and Residents	Local Entrepreneur	1
16	Local Community and Residents	Women's Self-help Group Member	1
17	Professional Experts and Service Providers	Local Self Government Engineer	1
18	Professional Experts and Service Providers	Project Manager	1
19	Local Community and Resident	Daily Commuter	1
20	Professional Experts and Service Providers	Chartered Accountant	1
21	Professional Experts and Service Providers	IT employee	1
22	Academia and Education Sector	Faculty of B School	1
23	Professional Experts and Service Providers	Kochi Corporation Staff	1
24	Professional Experts and Service Providers	KWM staff	1
25	Professional Experts and Service Providers	Project Personnel	1

ensuring a multifaceted perspective on the system's effectiveness and its broader impact.

Interview questions were crafted to be open-ended, allowing respondents the flexibility to express their views and experiences (Jiménez & Orozco, 2021). This approach provided rich, nuanced data that reflected the complexity of individuals' interactions with and perceptions of the Water Metro project. Direct observations complemented the interviews, offering tangible evidence of the Water Metro's operations and its integration into the urban landscape. Observational data included user interactions, operational workflows and the physicality of the infrastructure. Secondary data were culled from a variety of sources to support and contextualise findings from primary data (Sileyew, 2019). Peer-reviewed research articles provided academic perspectives on sustainable urban transit and its implications, while government publications supplied official statistics and policy insights. As Van Krieken and Sanders (2021) suggested, news reports and media articles were examined to understand the public narrative and reception of the Water Metro project.

DATA ANALYSIS

Data analysis was conducted through qualitative content analysis, emphasising the discernment of patterns, themes, and insights that emerged from the dataset. Transcripts from interviews were systematically coded to organise the data thematically, thus enhancing the reliability and validity of the study. The longitudinal aspect allowed for observing changes over time, providing a dynamic perspective on the project's development and its socio-economic impacts. Thematic analysis was particularly useful in constructing a comprehensive picture of the Water Metro's operational efficiency, socio-economic impact and contribution to sustainable urban development. This method enabled the identification of recurring themes that were indicative of broader trends and implications, which were essential for drawing informed conclusions from the case study.

RESULTS

Case: Kochi Water Metro: Towards Sustainable Urban Transport

The visionary Kochi Water Metro project is a transformative venture into the realm of urban public transport, introducing a pioneering approach that integrates an advanced water-based transit system with the existing urban transport network. This initiative promises to elevate standards for future urban development globally through its innovative and sustainable design. Kochi's Water Metro distinguishes itself with its deployment of 78 battery-operated electric hybrid boats across 16 routes, constituting a robust fleet that challenges traditional transport norms by emphasising energy efficiency and environmental responsibility (Jacob, 2023).

> I never thought I would be able to comfortably use public transport until the Water Metro came along... —Person with Disabilities

Central to the Water Metro's mission is the reduction of chronic traffic congestion within Kochi. The introduction of a convenient water-based transport alternative will help disperse the heavy vehicle accumulation on roads, thus expediting traffic flow and curtailing commute durations. In turn, this alleviation of congestion is projected to diminish stress for commuters and decrease vehicular air pollution significantly (Asian Infrastructure Investment Bank, 2023). The project also prioritises enhancing access to key economic and commercial hubs for urban and island residents alike, aiming to narrow the existing accessibility divide. Such improvements in connectivity are expected to spark further employment, commerce and social engagement, contributing substantially to regional prosperity (Marcus, 2023).

> Our collaboration with KMRL on the Canal Rejuvenation Project and now the Water Metro highlights the excellent scope for international partnerships... —IT employee

Fleet and Technology

The Kochi Water Metro's fleet, comprising electric hybrid boats, stands as the initiative's beating heart, revolutionising waterborne public transport. The fleet is envisaged to serve as a benchmark for renewable energy application in public conveyance, promoting reduced urban carbon footprints and showcasing a viable model for clean energy utilisation in transit systems. These boats, accommodating about 100 commuters each, are outfitted with state-of-the-art technologies – specifically, lithium-ion batteries that boast rapid recharging capabilities and high energy density, making them optimal for the intended short-haul operations. The boats' quiet electric motors not only represent a leap in eco-friendliness but also contribute to a more serene city soundscape (Nagaraj, 2023). Passengers' travel experience is taken care of by interiors designed for comfort, featuring air conditioning, ergonomic seating and sophisticated real-time navigation systems to keep them apprised of travel updates. Safety provisions are meticulously integrated into the boats, with life jackets, fire suppression systems and high-tech navigational aids as standard fittings to guarantee secure passage.

Terminal Network

Complementing the fleet is a series of 38 terminals that are more than mere points of embarkation and disembarkation; they are envisioned as community hubs with amenities. These terminals are crucial pivots in the project's infrastructure, strategically positioned to mesh with existing bus stops and forthcoming metro stations, thus fostering a harmonious intermodal transport ecosystem (The Times of India, 2023). Designed for expeditious boat docking and featuring sophisticated ticketing apparatus, they will minimise wait times and amplify service regularity. Real-time vessel tracking will also be available, enhancing journey planning for commuters.

Sustainability Initiatives

Sustainability is woven into the fabric of the Water Metro's blueprint. By steering clear of fossil fuels in favour of renewable energy sources for propulsion, the project significantly cuts carbon emissions and sets a precedent for public transportation policies worldwide. The Kochi Water Metro project significantly contributes to sustainability by adopting renewable energy sources for its operations, which sets a notable example for public transportation policies globally. The project has laid out plans to achieve complete energy self-sufficiency by 2024 through the implementation of rooftop solar installations at all Water Metro terminals across the city. This initiative is part of Kochi Water Metro Limited's (KWML's) strategy to meet its energy demands, which are estimated to be around eight megawatts, through various government-supported solar projects. Additionally, a dedicated solar plant is planned in the Alappuzha district specifically to cater to the energy needs of Water Metro boats. These efforts align with the project's commitment to using electric propulsion for the boats, anticipated to reduce GHG emissions by at least 16,500 tonnes annually. Furthermore, Kochi Metro Rail Limited (KMRL) already sources more than 50% of its energy requirements from solar power, and the Water Metro is expected to follow this path to energy independence and sustainability (Subhashini, 2022). The innovative boat designs take aquatic ecosystem preservation into account by precluding direct waste discharge into the water, thereby mitigating water pollution – a significant concern for a venture heavily reliant on the city's waterways (The Hindu, 2023). The project's overarching renewable energy mandate extends to the terminals as well, which are planned to incorporate solar panel installations for self-sustaining operations and rainwater harvesting systems for water conservation.

> The project has not only made commuting easier but also provided employment opportunities for women like me... —Women's Self-help Group Member

Financial Overview

The financial contours of the Water Metro are as ambitious as its ecological and infrastructural objectives, with the investment pegged at around 100 million USD. A distinctive combination of local and international financial support structures the project's funding, with a sizeable investment from the German KFW bank, an institution with a storied history of supporting sustainable urban growth and renewable energy undertakings. This influx of international capital not only lends credence to the project's sustainability ethos but also signifies a collective global investment in the future of eco-conscious urban transit (Kochi Water Metro, 2023).

> Good to see the report, however, there is room for a more judicious use of public funds. While the project stands out on promotional materials, the substantial expenses it has amassed point to a need for greater efficiency in the allocation of resources, ensuring that the project's value extends beyond aesthetic appeal and into practical, cost-effective execution. Chartered Accountant

Operational Challenges

The venture's path is not devoid of obstacles; the complex waterways of Kochi present a labyrinth of operational challenges. These include erratic climatic conditions and potential navigational conflicts with traditional fishing vessels, necessitating sophisticated navigational systems, extensive pilot training and rigorous safety measures. Community concerns, particularly from local fishers apprehensive about their economic future, are being addressed through dialogue and collaborative planning (News18, 2023). Technical limitations, such as the durability of electric components in saline conditions and the logistics of battery charging, are under constant review for innovative solutions. Moreover, the project's scale entails navigating a complex web of regulatory approvals, necessitating a careful balancing of development goals with environmental and legal considerations.

Impact

The economic implications of the Kochi Water Metro project are far-reaching. By fostering improved access to various parts of the city, the project is poised to stimulate local economies, particularly in the less accessible areas. Small businesses and tourism are expected to experience a boost as the water metro enhances mobility and opens up new markets.

> Thanks to the Water Metro, footfall has increased in the islands... —Local Entrepreneur

This economic ripple effect can lead to the creation of jobs not only within the transport system but also in ancillary services and sectors, contributing to a more dynamic local economy. Environmental gains are also a cornerstone of the project's impact, with a significant reduction in GHG emissions at the forefront (Kuriakose & Philip, 2021). The shift from road to water transport is anticipated to lower the burden on road infrastructure, leading to a decline in maintenance emissions and costs. Furthermore, the project contributes to the conservation of urban water bodies by raising awareness about the importance of clean waterways, fostering a culture of environmental stewardship among residents and stakeholders.

> The Water Metro has done an excellent job in Safety and Cleanliness. It's not just about fast or clean transport; it's also inclusive. The boats are air-conditioned and can be accessed by people with disabilities, which is a step forward in making public transport truly public. Project Personnel

On the social front, the Water Metro serves as a catalyst for inclusivity, enabling more equitable access to transportation across economic classes. By integrating ticketing systems with other forms of public transport, the project ensures affordability and ease of use, thereby promoting higher public transport usage rates. It also provides a safer and more pleasant commuting experience, which is particularly beneficial for women, the elderly and people with disabilities. The enhancement of water transport can also lead to a cultural renaissance by reconnecting residents with the city's maritime heritage and fostering a renewed sense of community around the waterways that have historically been central to Kochi's identity (The Times of India, 2023).

DISCUSSION

The success of Kochi Water Metro resonates both in academic and practical realms. Academically, it contributes to existing theories on sustainability, urban planning and social welfare. Practically, it provides a working model for policymakers, urban planners and business strategists. However, it's crucial to address the project's limitations and operational gaps, such as safety concerns, efficient utilisation of public money and the limited geographical reach. Future research and practical work should aim at optimising these aspects to make water-based public transport more robust, inclusive and effective.

CONCLUSIONS

In responding to the research objectives, this study has illuminated how the Kochi Water Metro project aligns with the concepts of sustainability and resilience, presenting it as a pioneering case in urban water transportation. However, while the study has yielded a detailed case study and conducted a SWOT analysis (See Table 2), it acknowledges that the real measure of success lies in the project's tangible impacts. The Water Metro's steadfast emphasis on sustainable practices, its operational resilience amid a myriad of challenges and its inclusive approach to social impact set it apart, marking its significance on a global scale. The project exemplifies an urban development strategy that synergises technological advancements with fiscal prudence and communal welfare. As urban centres worldwide navigate the complex demands of growth, environmental stewardship and equitable development, the case of Kochi offers a model of what an integrated, resilient and sustainable urban transit solution can look like, suggesting a path forward that balances innovation with the imperative of sustainability.

This study has identified several theoretical implications, among which is the affirmation of the Kochi Water Metro's success as an empirical substantiation of sustainable urban transportation theories. By incorporating crucial features such as energy-efficient vessels and alleviating traffic congestion, the project serves as a tangible instance that not only corroborates but also enriches scholarly debates concerning the sustainability of urban transport systems, as discussed by Wey and Huang (2018). The project supports theories advocating for integrated urban development. It's not merely a transportation project but also a catalyst for urban revitalisation, supporting retail, housing and more (Yigitcanlar & Teriman, 2015). The Water Metro's impact on local employment and accessibility provides a case study for theories on social capital and community building. The project's influence on social and emotional aspects like pride, reassurance and lifestyle changes provides material for in-depth academic inquiry (Portes & Landolt, 2000). The project's innovative funding mechanisms could inform theories related to Public Private Partnership (PPP) models in infrastructure development. With international collaborations, this stands as a unique model for global cooperation in public transport systems (Siemiatycki, 2009).

Table 2. SWOT Analysis.

Strengths	Weaknesses
1. *Sustainable Transport*: The project emphasises the use of environmentally friendly modes of transportation, like electric boats.	1. *High Initial Costs*: Setting up the infrastructure like jetties, boats and terminals will require significant capital expenditure.
2. *Tourist Attraction*: The picturesque routes and unique travel experience can serve as a tourist attraction, thereby increasing tourism revenue for the city.	2. *Operational Complexity*: Managing a water-based transport system comes with its own set of challenges such as weather conditions, safety, and maintenance.
3. *Reduced Traffic Congestion*: By providing an alternative to road transportation, the water metro helps in reducing traffic congestion on Kochi's roads.	3. *Limited Coverage*: Being water-based, it can't serve all areas of the city, and integration with other forms of transport is crucial for its effectiveness.
4. *Efficient Use of Natural Resources*: Utilises the existing water bodies for commuting, thus efficiently using natural resources.	4. *Regulatory Hurdles*: Various permits and clearances are required, which may slow down the project.
5. *Job Creation*: The project is likely to create several job opportunities ranging from construction to operation and maintenance.	5. *Safety Concerns*: Water transport can pose certain safety risks such as capsizing, especially during rough weather.
6. *Integrated Transportation*: Planned to be seamlessly integrated with other modes of public transport like metro, buses, and auto-rickshaws.	
7. *Scalability*: The design allows for future expansion and the addition of more routes and boats as needed.	
Opportunities	**Threats**
1. *Urban Development*: The areas surrounding the jetties could see development opportunities like retail, restaurants, and housing.	1. *Environmental Concerns*: There is potential for environmental degradation if not properly managed, such as water pollution and disturbance to aquatic life.
2. *Clean Energy*: The project opens doors for innovation in clean energy for water-based transport.	2. *Public Adoption*: Success is highly dependent on how quickly and widely the public adopts this new mode of transportation.
3. *Collaboration*: Opportunities for international partnerships can help in funding and operational capabilities.	3. *Weather Dependent*: Operations could be severely affected by extreme weather conditions.
4. *Tourism Packages*: Special tourism packages can be created around the water metro, attracting more tourists along with daily commuters.	4. *Competition*: Alternative means of transport like road-based public transport or private cabs may offer stiff competition.
5. *Ferry Services*: Future expansion could also include cargo or specialised ferry services for even more revenue.	5. *Economic Fluctuations*: Economic downturns could result in lower usage and revenue, affecting the sustainability of the project.

Source: Authors' own work.

The practical implications include the potential for the Water Metro's diverse advantages to inspire additional cities to pursue comparable initiatives in sustainable transportation. Kochi's example could serve as a blueprint for policymakers aiming to establish analogous water-based public transport systems in geographically amenable regions, as suggested by Cheemakurthy (2017). The integration with other modes of transport, for instance, provides practical lessons for future urban mobility solutions (Mouratidis, 2021). For business owners and entrepreneurs, the increased footfall and development around the metro jetties offer new economic opportunities. The lessons could be invaluable for business strategists looking to capitalise on infrastructure projects (Singh, 2020). The project, despite its delays and challenges, provides insights into effective governance and project management, particularly in dealing with public funds and regulatory hurdles. This can serve as a practical guide for future public projects (Akomea-Frimpong et al., 2021).

However, we acknowledge the limitations of this study relating to the data period, which is restricted to the early years of the project, omitting insights from prolonged operational and maintenance phases. Furthermore, the study is primarily oriented towards highlighting benefits, which may result in an incomplete portrayal of potential issues, including the enduring financial sustainability, the evolution and technological advancement of the electric fleet and the socio-economic repercussions for the fishing community, as indicated by Pinz et al. (2021).

The scope for further research is clearly delineated by the need to bridge the gaps presented in this study. Prospective investigations should focus on longitudinal analyses to gauge the enduring operational efficiency and fiscal viability of the Water Metro project. A thorough assessment of the socio-economic effects on indigenous populations, predominantly the fishing communities, is essential to fully understand the broader impacts of the initiative. It would be equally advantageous to explore how the Kochi model could be adapted and replicated in varied geographic settings, determining the prerequisites and modifications needed for the success of comparable endeavours globally, as per insights from Loorbach et al. (2020). The project's resilience in the face of challenges – technological, navigational and societal – has not only solidified its operational viability but has also offered valuable lessons for urban planning initiatives worldwide.

REFERENCES

Akomea-Frimpong, I., Jin, X., & Osei-Kyei, R. (2021). A holistic review of research studies on financial risk management in public–private partnership projects. *Engineering Construction and Architectural Management*, *28*(9), 2549–2569.

Allen, J., & Farber, S. (2020). Planning transport for social inclusion: An accessibility-activity participation approach. *Transportation Research Part D: Transport and Environment*, *78*, 102212.

Arsenio, E., Martens, K., & Di Ciommo, F. (2016). Sustainable urban mobility plans: Bridging climate change and equity targets? *Research in Transportation Economics*, *55*, 30–39.

Asian Infrastructure Investment Bank. (2023, November 10). India: Kochi Metro Rail Project – Phase II. https://www.aiib.org/en/projects/details/2023/proposed/India-Kochi-Metro-Rail-Project-Phase-II.html

Aslam, H., Khan, A. Q., Rashid, K., & Rehman, S. U. (2020). Achieving supply chain resilience: The role of supply chain ambidexterity and supply chain agility. *Journal of Manufacturing Technology Management*, *31*(6), 1185–1204.

Bosher, L., & Chmutina, K. (2017). *Disaster risk reduction for the built environment*. John Wiley & Sons.

Cheemakurthy, H. (2017). *Urban waterborne public transport systems: An overview of existing operations in world cities*.

Coaffee, J., Therrien, M. C., Chelleri, L., Henstra, D., Aldrich, D. P., Mitchell, C. L., ... & Participants. (2018). Urban resilience implementation: A policy challenge and research agenda for the 21st century. *Journal of Contingencies and Crisis Management*, *26*(3), 403–410.

Driessen, P. P., Hegger, D. L., Kundzewicz, Z. W., Van Rijswick, H. F., Crabbé, A., Larrue, C., & Wiering, M. (2018). Governance strategies for improving flood resilience in the face of climate change. *Water*, *10*(11), 1595.

Eldien, H. H., Gazzeh, K., & Hammad, E. (2020). Urban characterization by the green supply chain management concept: A review. *International Journal of Supply Chain Management*, *9*(4), 962–971.

Elets, eGov. (2023, April 4). Kochi Water Metro: An incredible success story of transformation in transport sector. https://egov.eletsonline.com/2023/04/kochi-water-metro-an-incredible-success-story-of-transformation-in-transport-sector/

Elias, A. A. (2022). Multi-stakeholder participation for achieving sustainable development goals: A systems thinking approach. In V. Tauringana & O. Moses (Eds.), *Environmental sustainability and agenda 2030. Advances in environmental accounting & management* (Vol. 10, pp. 45–65). Emerald Publishing Limited. https://doi.org/10.1108/S1479-359820220000010003

Elias, A. A., Donadelli, F., Paiva, E. L., & Bacic Araujo, P. P. (2021). Analysing the complexities of sustainable wood supply chain in the Amazon: A systems thinking approach. *The International Journal of Logistics Management*, *32*(4), 1481–1505.

Hailemariam, M., Bustos, T., Montgomery, B., Barajas, R., Evans, L. B., & Drahota, A. (2019). Evidence-based intervention sustainability strategies: A systematic review. *Implementation Science*, *14*(1), 1–12.

Heino, O., Kalalahti, J., & Jukarainen, P. (2019). Rethinking resilience in a context: How to address severe disruptions. *Resilient Water Services and Systems: The Foundation of Well-Being*, *69*.

Hrelja, R., Hjerpe, M., & Storbjörk, S. (2015). Creating transformative force? The role of spatial planning in climate change transitions towards sustainable transportation. *Journal of Environmental Policy & Planning*, *17*(5), 617–635.

Izadikhah, M., Azadi, M., Toloo, M., & Hussain, F. K. (2021). Sustainably resilient supply chains evaluation in public transport: A fuzzy chance-constrained two-stage DEA approach. *Applied Soft Computing*, *113*, 107879.

Jacob, J. (2023, October 27). Kochi water metro. *Geospatial World*. https://www.geospatialworld.net/prime/business-and-industry-trends/kochi-water-metro/

Jiménez, T. R., & Orozco, M. (2021). Prompts, not questions: Four techniques for crafting better interview protocols. *Qualitative Sociology*, *44*, 507–528.

Kannabiran, G. (2009). Sustainable stakeholder engagement through innovative supply chain strategy: An exploratory study of an Indian organization. *Asian Business & Management*, *8*, 205–223.

Kanuri, C., Venkat, K., Maiti, S., & Mulukutla, P. (2019). Leveraging innovation for last-mile connectivity to mass transit. *Transportation Research Procedia*, *41*, 655–669.

Kochi Water Metro. (2023). About Kochi water metro. https://watermetro.co.in/about

Kumar, K., & Bindu, C. A. (2022). Resilience master plan as the pathway to actualize sustainable development goals–a case of Kozhikode, Kerala, India. *Progress in Disaster Science*, *14*, 100226.

Kuriakose, P. N., & Philip, S. (2021). City profile: Kochi, city region-Planning measures to make Kochi smart and creative. *Cities*, *118*, 103307.

Levy, C., Allen, A., Broto, V. C., & Westman, L. (2017). Unlocking urban trajectories: Planning for environmentally just transitions in Asia. In *Sustainable cities in Asia* (pp. 7–22). Routledge.

Loorbach, D., Wittmayer, J., Avelino, F., von Wirth, T., & Frantzeskaki, N. (2020). Transformative innovation and translocal diffusion. *Environmental Innovation and Societal Transitions*, *35*, 251–260.

Lucas, K., & Musso, A. (2014). Policies for social inclusion in transportation: An introduction to the special issue. *Case Studies on Transport Policy*, *2*(2), 37–40.

Marcus, L. (2023, April 26). *Kochi, Kerala: Indian city reveals fleet of 'water metro' ferries*. CNN. https://edition.cnn.com/travel/article/kochi-india-water-metro-intl-hnk/index.html

Mashayekh, Y., Jaramillo, P., Samaras, C., Hendrickson, C. T., Blackhurst, M., MacLean, H. L., & Matthews, H. S. (2012). Potentials for sustainable transportation in cities to alleviate climate change impacts. *Environmental Science & Technology*, *46*(5), 2529–2537.

Menon, A. S. (2010). *Legacy of Kerala*. DC Books.

Miller, P., de Barros, A. G., Kattan, L., & Wirasinghe, S. C. (2016). Analyzing the sustainability performance of public transit. *Transportation Research Part D: Transport and Environment*, *44*, 177–198.

Mouratidis, K. (2021). Urban planning and quality of life: A review of pathways linking the built environment to subjective well-being. *Cities*, *115*, 103229.

Nagaraj, R. (2023, November 2). Took a ride on Kochi's water metro: Experience & report. *Team-BHP*. https://www.team-bhp.com/news/took-ride-kochis-water-metro-experience-report

Narayanaswami, S. (2017). Urban transportation: Innovations in infrastructure planning and development. *The International Journal of Logistics Management*, *28*(1), 150–171.

Nash, C., & Johnson, D. (2019). Public transport. In *A research agenda for transport policy* (pp. 51–59). Edward Elgar Publishing.

Nativeplanet. (2023, April 26). India's first water metro launched in Kochi, Kerala, know features, routes, ticket prices, timings. https://www.nativeplanet.com/travel-news/2023/04/26/indias-first-water-metro-launched-in-kochi-kerala-know-features-routes-ticket-prices-timings-033523.html

News18. (2023, September 27). Kochi's water metro goes the distance in less than 6 months; eco-friendly boats serve 10 lakh passengers. https://www.news18.com/india/kochis-water-metro-goes-the-distance-in-less-than-6-months-eco-friendly-boats-serve-10-lakh-passengers-8629168.html

Pietrzak, K., & Pietrzak, O. (2020). Environmental effects of electromobility in a sustainable urban public transport. *Sustainability*, *12*(3), 1052. https://doi.org/10.3390/su12031052

Park, Y. S., Konge, L., & Artino Jr, A. R. (2020). The positivism paradigm of research. *Academic Medicine*, *95*(5), 690–694.

Paskannaya, T., & Shaban, G. (2019). *Innovations in green logistics in smart cities: USA and EU experience*.

Pinz, A., Roudyani, N., & Thaler, J. (2021). Public-private partnerships as instruments to achieve sustainability-related objectives: The state of the art and a research agenda. *Sustainable Public Management*, 3–24.

Portes, A., & Landolt, P. (2000). Social capital: Promise and pitfalls of its role in development. *Journal of Latin American Studies*, *32*(2), 529–547.

Raftis, C. C., Vanelslander, T., & van Hassel, E. (2023). A global analysis of emissions, decarbonization, and alternative fuels in inland navigation – A systematic literature review. *Sustainability*, *15*(19), 14173. https://doi.org/10.3390/su151914173

Rajasekar, U., Chakraborty, S., & Bhat, G. (2018). Climate resilient smart cities: Opportunities for innovative solutions in India. *Climate Change in Cities: Innovations in Multi-Level Governance*, 203–227.

Rashid, Y., Rashid, A., Warraich, M. A., Sabir, S. S., & Waseem, A. (2019). Case study method: A step-by-step guide for business researchers. *International Journal of Qualitative Methods*, *18*. https://doi.org/10.1177/1609406919862424

Schiessel Harvey, N. (2021). The multiple values of urban waterways. In *The Palgrave handbook of climate resilient societies* (pp. 1–27). Springer International Publishing.

Schiller, P. L., & Kenworthy, J. (2017). *An introduction to sustainable transportation: Policy, planning and implementation*. Routledge.

Siemiatycki, M. (2009). Delivering transportation infrastructure through public-private partnerships: Planning concerns. *Journal of the American Planning Association*, *76*(1), 43–58.

Sileyew, K. J. (2019). Research design and methodology. *Cyberspace*, 1–12.

Singh, M. (2020). India's shift from mass transit to MaaS transit: Insights from Kochi. *Transportation Research Part A: Policy and Practice*, *131*, 219–227.

Singh, P., Amekudzi-Kennedy, A., Woodall, B., & Joshi, S. (2021). Lessons from case studies of flood resilience: Institutions and built systems. *Transportation Research Interdisciplinary Perspectives*, *9*.

Sobrino, N., & Monzon, A. (2013). Management of urban mobility to control climate change in cities in Spain. *Transportation Research Record, 2375*(1), 55–61.

Subhashini, V. B. (2022, November 16). Kochi metro, water metro to run entirely on solar power by 2024. *Swarajya*. https://swarajyamag.com/infrastructure/kochi-metro-kochi-water-metro-to-run-entirely-on-solar-power-by-2024

Sudheer, K. P., Thomas, J., Jainet, P. J., Nizar, S., Beegum, S., Sebastian, D. E., Jesna, & Pai, D. S. (2023). From science to policy – Toward an approach linking extreme rainfall events to climate resilience and policy development: A case study from Kerala, India. In K. S. Kasiviswanathan, B. Soundharajan, S. Patidar, J. He, & C. S. P. Ojha (Eds.), *Developments in environmental science* (Vol. 14, pp. 143–172). Elsevier. ISBN 9780443186400.

Sun, H., Wan, Y., Zhang, L., & Zhou, Z. (2019). Evolutionary game of the green investment in a two-echelon supply chain under a government subsidy mechanism. *Journal of Cleaner Production, 235*, 1315–1326.

Tauringana, V., & Moses, O. (2023). Greenhouse gas reporting and management in top emitting countries and companies. In V. Tauringana & O. Moses (Eds.), *Green house gas emissions reporting and management in global top emitting countries and companies. Advances in environmental accounting & management* (Vol. 11, pp. 1–9). Emerald Publishing Limited. https://doi.org/10.1108/S1479-359820230000011001

The Hindu. (2023, April 27). Explained: How the Kochi Water Metro will improve Islanders' socio-economic status, boost tourism. https://www.thehindu.com/news/national/kerala/explained-how-the-kochi-water-metro-will-improve-islanders-socio-economic-status-boost-tourism/article66785278.ece

The Times of India. (2023, October 17). Kochi Water Metro total ridership crosses 10L mark. https://timesofindia.indiatimes.com/city/kochi/kochi-water-metro-total-ridership-crosses-10l-mark/articleshow/104483872.cms

Thekkeyil, A., George, A., Abdurazak, F., Kuriakose, G., Nameer, P. O., Abhilash, P. C., & Joseph, S. (2023). Land use change in rapidly developing economies – A case study on land use intensification and land fallowing in Kochi, Kerala, India. *Environmental Monitoring and Assessment, 195*, 1089.

UNDP. (2023). *Sustainable development goals*. United Nations Development https://www.undp.org/sustainable-development-goals

Van Krieken, K., & Sanders, J. (2021). What is narrative journalism? A systematic review and an empirical agenda. *Journalism, 22*(6), 1393–1412.

Velaga, N. R., Beecroft, M., Nelson, J. D., Corsar, D., & Edwards, P. (2012). Transport poverty meets the digital divide: Accessibility and connectivity in rural communities. *Journal of Transport Geography, 21*, 102–112.

Vullapu, S. S., Jain, J., & Tarafdar, A. K. (2023). Streamlining freight transport through planning interventions in Vijayawada City. In *Urban commons, future smart cities and sustainability* (pp. 847–885). Springer International Publishing.

Wey, W. M., & Huang, J. Y. (2018). Urban sustainable transportation planning strategies for livable city's quality of life. *Habitat International, 82*, 9–27.

Whitehead, T. (2005). Secondary data analysis, fieldwork, observation/participant observation, and informal and semi-structured interviewing.

Xiahou, X., Tang, L., Yuan, J., Zuo, J., & Li, Q. (2022). Exploring social impacts of urban rail transit PPP projects: Towards dynamic social change from the stakeholder perspective. *Environmental Impact Assessment Review, 93*, 106700.

Yigitcanlar, T., & Teriman, S. (2015). Rethinking sustainable urban development: Towards an integrated planning and development process. *International Journal of Environmental Science and Technology, 12*, 341–352.

Young, D., Woods, W., & Reeves, M. (2019). *Optimize for both social and business value*. Boston Consulting Group-Henderson Institute.

Zhou, Y., Wang, J., & Yang, H. (2019). Resilience of transportation systems: Concepts and comprehensive review. *IEEE Transactions on Intelligent Transportation Systems, 20*(12), 4262–4276.

Printed and bound by CPI Group (UK) Ltd, Croydon, CR0 4YY

13/09/2026

14961063-0008